MW01534484

The St. Joseph

Rivers of Michigan Series

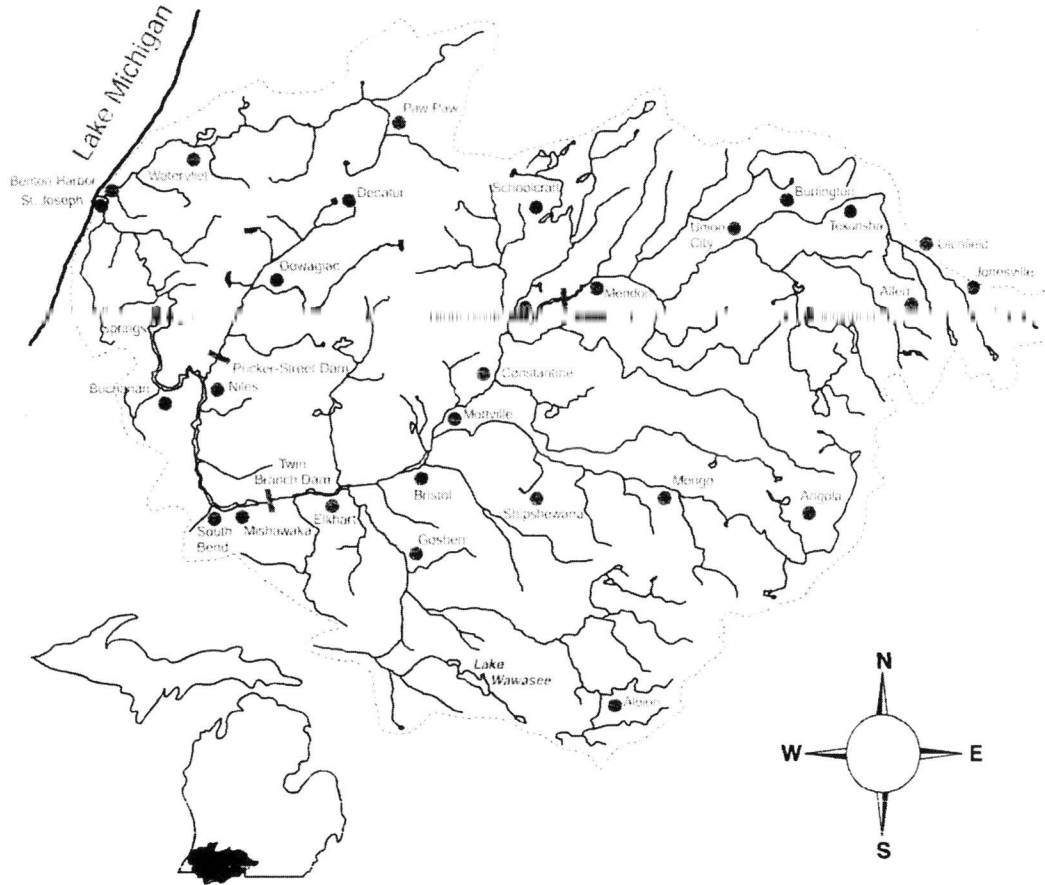

By Kit Lane

Pavilion Press

P. O. Box 250
Douglas, Michigan 49406

Copyright 2010

By Pavilon Press

All Rights Reserved

International Standard Book Number
978-1-877703-05-8

Front Cover: (Top) *The dam on the St. Joseph River at Three Rivers from a postcard published about 1910. Just upstream from the dam is the Wood Street Bridge.*

(Bottom) *The excursion steamer **Tourist** turning around in front of the old Southern Michigan Railway Company bridge at Berrien Springs in the 1920s. The electric railroad ceased operation in 1934 and the spans were later removed, but the piers still stand in the north end of Lake Chapin..*

Back Cover: *Pedestrians streaming over the old State Street Bridge at St. Joseph from a 1909 postcard.*

Table of Contents

A detail from Delisle's 1703 Carte du Canada ou de la Nouvelle France. Rivers flowing into southern Lac de Illinois (Lake Michigan) are the Grande (Grand), the Marameg (Kalamazoo), the Noire (Black) and the southernmost is unnamed, but it is noted that it is the home of the Miamis natives. The fork not far from its mouth is probably the Paw Paw River, which enters the St. Joseph less than a mile from the mouth. Another possible construction would make the upper fork of the southernmost river the St. Joseph with the dark spot indicating the site of Fort St. Joseph, near the dotted line which shows a cross peninsula trail. The lower fork would then be the Pigeon River.

The River

John T. Blois in the 1838 *Gazetteer of the State of Michigan* wrote:

> St. Joseph river of Lake Michigan, takes its rise in the north-eastern part of the county of Hillsdale, and flowing north-west through Hillsdale, south-west through Calhoun, Branch, St. Joseph and Cass counties, into the State of Indiana, thence west through Elkhart and St. Joseph counties in that State; thence passing north-west into and through the county of Berrien in the State of Michigan, discharges its waters into Lake Michigan. In length and volume of water, it will rank as the second in the Peninsula. Its course is very serpentine and irregular, and it has been estimated by some to be 250 miles in length, following its many deviations; but from the source to the lake, in a direct line, it would not exceed 120. It is navigable for keel boats, to Lockport, 130 miles. The breadth, near its mouth, is one fourth of a mile and its depth from 9 to 14 feet. At the mouth is a good harbor, which, when the pier is finished, will be sufficiently capacious for any assigned number of vessels, and to answer the purposes which a lake port in future may required. . . The St. Joseph river is a beautiful stream of gradual descent and equable current. It is not often known to rise at its mouth more than 18 inches even in times of the highest freshets, although far above it rises from four to six feet.[1]

Glaciers Shape a River

Glaciers covered the area which was later Michigan, advancing and retreating several times until about 11,000 years ago which marks the most recent retreat of the glacier and the (to this date) final forming of the Great Lakes.

But when the last glacier retreated it did not melt evenly. The ice was deeper in the gouged-out areas which would become lakes. It tended to melt and retreat first where it was not so thick, over the future land area of southern Michigan. This created three distinct ice lobes. The Michigan lobe over what would become Lake Michigan, the Huron-Erie lobe on the east side of the Michigan landmass, and the Saginaw lobe, which covered what would become Saginaw Bay.

As the glacier retreated, the waters of the St. Joseph, originating in the glacially formed highlands now known as the Irish Hills, as they flowed west, were obstructed by the ice of the Michigan lobe and turned southward directly into the Kankakee River and onward to what would be later called the Mississippi River, thence southerly to the Gulf of Mexico.

As the glacier retreated farther the flow discovered a channel with less resistance and turned north at South Bend to exit into Lake Michigan at St. Joseph. Eventually even Lake Michigan itself ceased to flow into the Mississippi River chain, and began to flow north, joining with the other Great Lakes on their current way to the St. Lawrence River and the Atlantic Ocean much farther north.

"The Garden of America"

It was the beauty of the river, mentioned in the 1838 gazetteer above, which also caught the eye of the early French visitors. A memoir sent to the French government in 1718 describes the valley of the St. Joseph:

> 'Tis a spot the best adapted of any to be seen for purposes of living. There are pheasants as in France; quails and paroquets; the finest vines in the world which produce a vast quantity of excellent grapes. It is the richest district in all the country.[2]

(The birds called "paroquets" are the Carolina Parakeet, which once was occasionally found as far north as the Great Lakes region. George A. Baker who offers the above paragraph in an 1899 description of parts of the river, notes that even then the birds were usually found farther south, and were common only in Florida.)

James Fenimore Cooper of New York State who is often credited with being America's first novelist, in his early book *Oak Openings or The Bee Hunter*, published in 1848, called the St. Joseph valley:

> . . . a region that almost merits the lofty appellation of the Garden of American. Here with the buffalo were found the bear, the elk, the deer, the beaver, the otter, the marten, the raccoon, the mink, the muskrat, the opossum, the wild cat the lynx, the wolf and the fox.

First Called "Riviere of the Miamis"

La Salle in writing about the river called it *Riviere de la Miamis* after the most prevalent tribe along its banks and some of the early French maps use that name. The fort he later constructed at the mouth was named Fort Miami, (sometimes with an s, Miamis) but the missionaries had, almost from the beginning, referred to the river by the name of the patron saint of travelers, Saint Joseph.

On a map drawn in 1703 by the French cartographer Delisle (see page 4) there is a river with two forks that has three dots on the lower of the two forks labeled *"Miamis,"* apparently designating a settlement of the Miami Indians. The river itself is not named unless the designation on the three dots refers also to the name of the river. It extends less than 50 miles inland, but does show a possible portage which would lead to the Illinois River.

Other rivers above it on the west coast of what would be Michigan are, south to north, *R. Noire,* the Black River at South Haven; *R. Marameg* an early French name for the Kalamazoo at Saugatuck; and *La Grande Riviere,* the Grand, which enters Lake Michigan at Grand Haven.

On a 1744 map drawn by Jacque Nicolas Bellin, (see page 7) the Maumee River which exits into Lake Erie at Toledo is called *"R. des Miamis."* The St. Joseph is labeled as *"R. S. Joseph"* but includes also *"le Fort,"* Fort St. Joseph at Niles; and *"Village de Miamis"* north of the river and *"Village de Powatwatame"* south of the river.

On this 1744 French map by Jacques Nicolas Bellin the Miamis are shown north of the river and the Potwatomi on the south bank with *le Fort* nearby. The three round dots are the source of the *Riviere de Teakiki*, the Kankakee, with *"Portage"* noted nearby.

Where Does it Come From?
Where Does it Go?

The connections of the river were not easily understood. An excerpt from *The Western Gazetteer or Emigrant's Directory* published by Samuel R. Brown of Auburn, New York, in 1817 lists among the rivers "running into Lake Michigan":

> The St. Josephs, which heads in Indiana and interlocks by its several branches with Black river, St. Josephs of Miami, Eel River and Tippecanoe. It enters the southeast end of the lake. It is rapid and full of islands, but navigable 150 miles, and is 200 yards wide at its mouth. The Pottawattimie Indians, who reside on the shore, catch prodigious quantities of fish in its waters. It runs about forty miles in the Michigan territory. On the north bank of this river stands the old fort St. Josephs, from which there is a bridle road to Detroit.[3]

The Tippecanoe River begins north of Fort Wayne, Indiana, and is the northernmost portion of the Wabash River watershed. The St. Joseph of the Miami begins very near Baw Beese Lake, the source of the St. Joseph of Lake Michigan, and some early maps show that there might have been an actual connection at one time. The southern St. Joseph River flows southwest, joins with the Maumee River and exits into Lake Erie at Toledo.

The Road from Detroit to Fort St. Josephs by land and thence to the Junction of the Illinois river with the Mississippi by water

[An accounting dated 1770 in the Haldimand Papers][4]

                                                                    Miles

From Detroit to the river Huron or Nandewine Sippy 40
N.B. There is a village of Puttawateamees of six large cabans. The river at this place is about Fifty feet wide and the water is generally from one and a half to two feet deep, when there are Floods, Travelers are obliged to make Rafts to cross it, the road in this place is bad.

To the Salt River or Wandadagon Sippy 12
N.B. There is another village of Pottawattamees of five cabans. This river is never so high as to prevent people passing it.

To one of the Branches of Grand River or Washtanon that falls into Lake Michigan 60
There is another village of Pottawattamees of eight large cabans.   112

To Reccanamazoo River or Pusawpaco Sippy otherwise the Iron Mine River
N.B. There is another village of Pottawattamees of eight large cabans. This River cannot be passed in Freshets on Rafts; at other times 1 or 2 feet deep. 75

To Prairieroude 30
N. B. There is a small lake of about ¾ of a mile wide and 11 miles long, abounding with several sorts of Fish such as Maskenongi, Whitefish

To the Fort St. Joseph 75
N.B. There is a few Pottawattamees near the fort. The road after you 180
pass the River Huron is very good being mostly on a small height of land & little wood till you come to St. Joseph's where you pass through [woods?] about a mile long and another about six miles long.

From Fort St. Joseph's you ascend that River to a carrying place 12
    (LaSalle's Portage)
From carrying place to Recankeekee 4
To the Juncture of this river with the Iroquis River. 150
To the Junction of this river with the Chicangoni River which forms the Illinois River. 45
To the Rocks or the old French Fort called Pumetewee 45
To the Mississippi 240
                                                                    541
From Detroit to the Mississippi by way of the Illinois River **833**

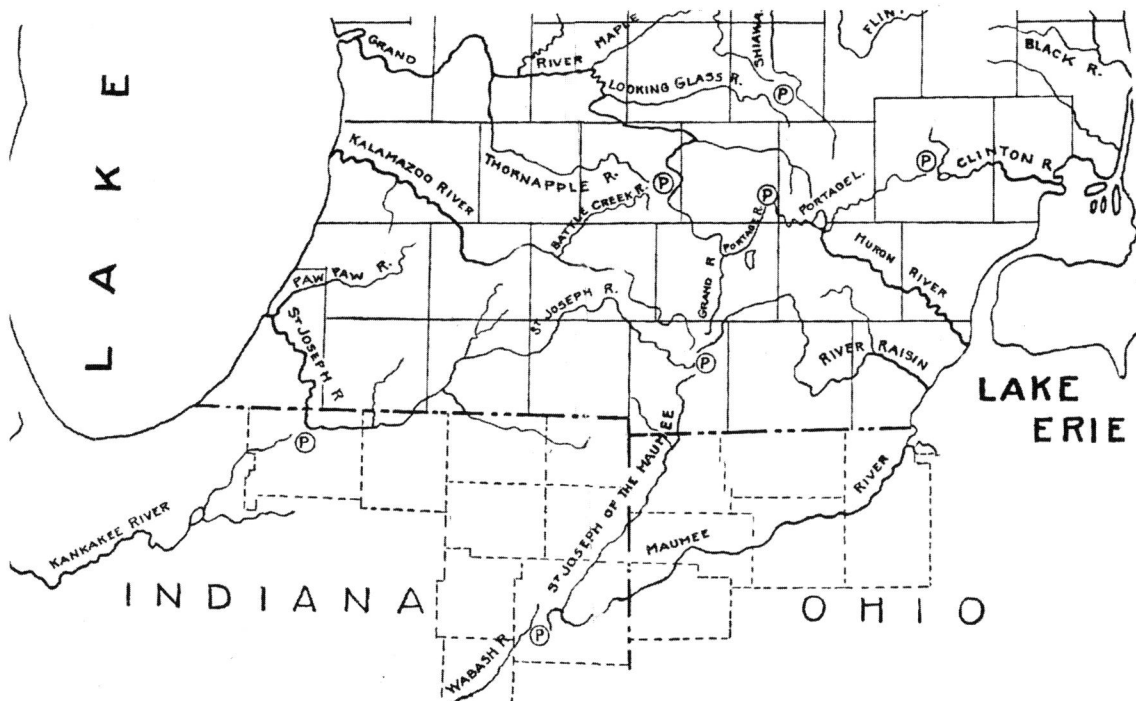

A map of early portages based on a map in Wilbert G. Hinsdale's 1931 atlas. The P within a circle marks portages. In addition to the frequently used portage from the St. Joseph to the Kankakee on the left, this map shows portages from the St. Joseph to the Kalamazoo, River Raisin, Grand and the St. Joseph of the Maumee near their beginnings.

Portages – from Here to There

In the days when rivers were the super highways of an untamed wilderness, the St. Joseph river had several interesting and useful connections.

In the Irish Hills near Jackson there is a hilly area which gives birth to most of the rivers in the southern lower peninsula. The River Raisin heads east to Lake Erie, the Grand, Kalmazoo and St. Joseph all flow west to Lake Michigan, and the St. Joseph of the Maumee flows south and connects with the Maumee River which exits into Lake Erie at Toledo, Ohio, or has a portage to the Wabash which travels southwest across Ohio and Indiana to the Ohio

River. Indians and early European travelers would use several different combinations of these rivers to reach their destinations.

One American-drawn map of Michigan Territory in 1829 shows only two portages on the entire map. One marked portage is from the Grand River into the Huron, and one portage from the St. Joseph River near the Indiana border, up the Pigeon River, north of Fort Wayne and into a tributary of the St. Joseph of the Maumee, thence into the Maumee itself and to Lake Erie at Toledo.

A trip, said to be a favorite of Territorial Governor Lewis Cass, was to travel the River Raisin west to the headwaters, portage to the St. Joseph and go west and south until they found La Salle's portage to the Kankakee near South Bend, and then go west and north for Chicago, or west and south to the junction of the Ohio and Mississippi.

Altering the River's Mouth

The harbor at the mouth of the St. Joseph River received the first lighthouse built on the east shore of Lake Michigan in 1832. (Chicago's light, the only one earlier on Lake Michigan, was built the same year, but earlier in the season.) In 1834 a preliminary study was ordered and in response to its recommendations the following year the U. S. Congress authorized expenditure not to exceed $26,000 "to build a breakwater and do other work necessary for securing a harbor of easier access and larger capacity."

The first improvement was to alter the course of the river at its mouth. The natural outlet was about 1,200 feet south of the present course, meandering southwesterly across a low sand spit which later was the site of the Silver Beach Amusement Park. In addition to the new channel, 1312 feet of pier was installed, 1,100 feet on the north and 212 feet on the south.

The channel at the new mouth was 240 feet wide, the river spreading into a basin which was 800 feet wide. There were actually two separate channels, one for the Paw Paw River which joins the St. Joseph just before its entrance into Lake Michigan, and one for the actual St. Joseph River. Later a wing dam was added to confine the Paw Paw River to its own channel.

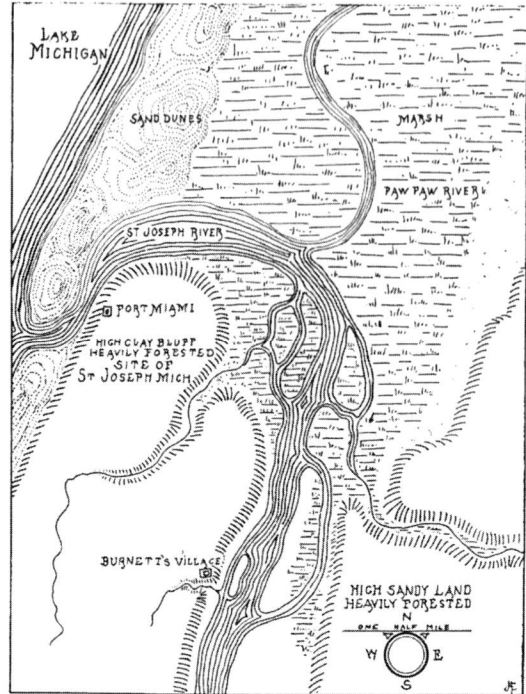

The original configuration of the mouth of the St. Joseph River from a 1781 sketch made by Joseph H. Emerson. The stream entering through the marsh at the top is the Paw Paw River.

Stream Gradient Varies

The river drops about 600 feet from its head in Hillsdale County to its entrance into Lake Michigan, but stream gradient (the drop in elevation with distance, usually in feet per mile) varies considerably on the St. Joseph River. Where the terrain is relatively flat there is often less than a foot per mile of gradient; at other areas there is over 40 feet per mile.

Nearly 75 percent of the river is classed as low gradient with a drop of less than three feet per mile. Gradient gradually decreases from the headwaters downstream toward the mouth.

Gradients between 3 feet per mile and 4.9 feet per mile constitute 18 percent of

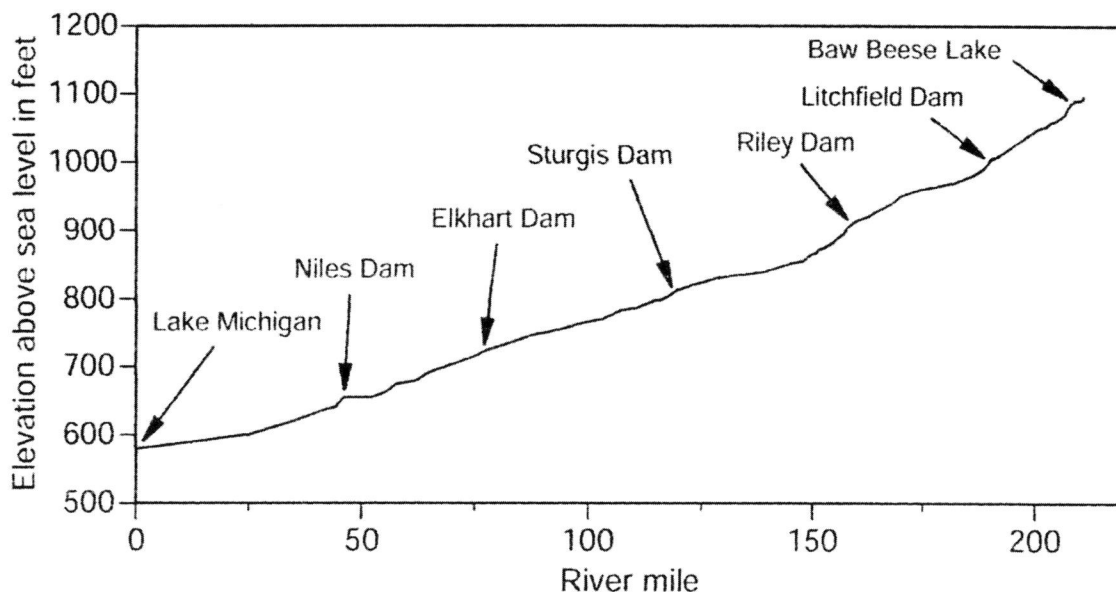

Elevation changes, by river mile, from the headwaters to the mouth of the St. Joseph River.

the mainstream, and 6.2 percent of the total mainstream is in the 5 to 9.9 feet per mile category. According to a 1999 Fisheries Department special report only 1.9 miles of the river, .9 percent. is in the most desirable gradient between 10 and 69.9 feet per mile.[5]

Today's Watershed

Today the St. Joseph River has a watershed area of 4,685 square miles. Fifteen counties in two states are entirely or partially within the watershed, and, according to the 2000 census 1,524,941 people live within that area. The watershed extends from Kalamazoo and Van Buren counties on the north, Hillsdale County on the east, Berrien County (and Lake Michigan) on the west, and Noble and Kosciusko counties, Indiana, with a small excursion into Whitley County on the south.

The river itself passes through portions of six counties in Michigan (Hillsdale, Branch, Calhoun, St. Joseph, Cass and Berrien) and two counties in Indiana (St. Joseph and Elkhart). In addition to 210 miles of the main river there are significant tributaries to the river which are 1,631 miles in length.

11

A map of the historic trails between the St. Joseph River and the Kankakee River used by Charlevoix in 1721 (top), and by La Salle in 1679 (lower).

Early Visitors

The first European to set eyes on the St. Joseph River is a matter of some conjecture and debate. Two French adventurers, Medart Chauart des Groseilliers and a companion who may have been named Radisson, later declared that they had visited the St. Joseph and much of western Michigan as early as 1654, but their claim has generally been discounted by historians.

It is possible that Father Claude Allouez, a Jesuit priest and missionary, who was ministering to the Miami Indians in 1672, followed their migration to the St. Joseph valley.

An engraving of Rene-Robert Cavelier, Sieur de la Salle done from a portrait made when he was 22, about the time he left France for Montreal..

Was Marquette an Early Visitor?

It is most likely that the first white man in the St. Joseph valley was some adventuring unnamed French explorer or fur trader who visited the banks, unnoticed and unrecorded.

Or perhaps there is some truth in the legend that the Jesuit missionary Father Jacques Marquette, and his two French voyageur companions paddled up the eastern coast of Lake Michigan in the spring of 1675, in a vain attempt to get the ill Marquette "home" to Mackinac. A statement by Marquette biographer Reuben Thwaites was partly conjecture:

> Within the mouths of several rivers did our weary canoeists camp by night or during storms -- that of the St. Joseph, also a pathway to the Mississippi, afterward used by La Salle's and many another famous expedition to the south; and those of Kalamazoo Grand and Muskegon…[6]

But the first documented visit to the mouth of the St. Joseph was by a Frenchman whose name was most often Americanized to Robert La Salle, possibly in 1672, with certainty in 1679.

La Salle Arrives in New France

Rene-Robert Cavelier, Sieur de la Salle (that is Rene-Robert of the family of

Cavelier, whose estate called La Salle was near Rouen in France) was born in 1643. He had an elder brother, Abbe Jean Cavelier, who was a priest of St. Sulpice in Canada and young Robert left France for Montreal, still a pioneering post, in the spring of 1666.

From the winter of 1869 to 1872 La Salle scholar Francis Parkman notes that the young La Salle's activities are "mist and obscurity."[7] Some historians state that it was during this period that he "discovered" the Mississippi River several months before the arrival of Joliet and Marquette in 1872. According to a version recorded by Euscebe Renadout about 1678, from a verbal account from La Salle himself: In August of 1871, he went up the St. Lawrence, with a small party into the Great Lakes, rounded the peninsula and using the Chicago River, to the Des Plaines and the Illinois, actually entered the Mississippi a short distance. On his return, according to the same account, La Salle turned up the Kankakee River and portaged into the St. Joseph River near where South Bend would later be built, and entered Lake Michigan at the mouth. He called it the *River of the Miamis* after the Indians in the vicinity.[8]

Armed with new information La Salle returned to France long enough to convince King Louis XIV that a great river really existed and if it did not lead to China, it would at least provide another useful avenue for the transport-tation of French goods. The king was persuaded to give La Salle land in the New World, and patents authorizing him to trade with the Indians and to explore the lakes and rivers of the west.

A New Boat

In 1679, in an attempt to make the transportation of his goods more reliable, La Salle ordered the construction of a 45-ton sailing ship called the **Griffon** (named for its griffin — *griffon* in French – figurehead, a mythological animal with characteristics of both the lion and the eagle).

The boat was built on Cayuga Creek near the mouth of the Niagara River in New York State. When it was finished in the spring of 1679 it was towed upstream, past the rapids, and into Lake Ontario. The **Griffon**, with La Salle aboard, visited Green Bay and found a wealth of furs which had been collected there in his absence.

To satisfy at least some of his creditors La Salle sent the **Griffon** back to Niagara with the furs, leaving from Green Bay on September 18. The captain had orders to return as quickly as possible to the southern end of Lake Michigan and meet him at the mouth of the St. Joseph River. La Salle and his party made their way south in a fleet of canoes.

Waiting for the Griffon

In November 1679 La Salle arrived at the mouth of the St. Joseph seeking

An old woodcut made of La Salle's ship **Griffon.**

In 1902 the Algonquin Chapter of the Daughters of the American Revolution erected this memorial to La Salle on the bluff at St. Joseph. The bronze plaque reads:

This glacial boulder
Found in the bed of the St. Joseph River
Was erected in 1902
To commemorate the landing of
Rene-Robert Cavelier, Sieur de La Salle
And building at this point
Fort Miamis.
1679

information about the **Griffon**, but found none. He decided to tarry there in hopes that either he would hear from the boat, or an additional group of men who were up north with his chief lieutenant, Henri Tonty, would arrive at the rendezvous point at the mouth of the St. Joseph River.

To keep the men occupied he built a fort of hewn logs 40 by 80 feet, which he named Fort Miamis. Tonty arrived twenty days later with some additional men and on December 3 La Salle left the new fort and went up the river to the portage and into the valley of the Illinois.

La Salle as Hero
Of Fictional Literature

The exploits of La Salle caught the imagination from an early day and several accounts, some more fictional, some less so, have been published over the years including:

La Salle in the Valley of the St. Joseph: An Historical Fragment
by Charles H. Bartlett
and Richard H. Lyon, 1899.

Robert Cavelier: The Romance of the Sieur de la Salle
by William Dana Orcutt, 1904.

The Power and the Glory; A Romance of the Great La Salle
by Gilbert Parker, 1925.

The French Adventurer: The Life and Exploits of La Salle
by Maurice Constantin-Wyers, 1931.

La Salle and the Great Enterprise
by Jeannette Covert Nolan, 1951

Touched with Fire
by John Tebbell, 1952.

The Wilderness Way
by Merritt Parmalee Allen, 1954.

The Golden Torch
by Iola Fuller, 1957.

He returned, this time via Lake Michigan, to Fort Miami in March of 1680. There was still no news from the **Griffon** and, just days later, La Salle and a small party set out to cross the southern peninsula on foot. The party arrived at *l'detroit*, "the straits," the narrowest place to cross the Great Lakes. They built a raft for the crossing and continued on to Niagara.

In the fall of 1680 La Salle again stopped briefly at the mouth of the St. Joseph on his way back to the Illinois. The fort was in ruin and deserted. After visiting the devastation of the Indian wars on the tribes along the Illinois he returned to the fort on January 26, 1681, having to arrive on foot because the Kankakee River was frozen over.

He was heartened to find that during his absence not only had the fort been restored but the men he had left behind had constructed a saw pit and sawed out lumber for a new vessel to sail the lakes. Near the fort stood the huts of about 50 Abnakis, Mohegan, and Shawnee Indians who sought shelter from the Iroquis. La Salle left in March, 1681, to make council with various friendly groups of Indians concerning the problems.

In December of 1681, having visited Montreal and the fort at Michili-mackinac, La Salle arrived again at the mouth of the St. Joseph. There he prepared for a long journey and left December 21 via Lake Michigan hoping that they could beat the winter ice, heading again down the Mississippi as far as they dared without encountering the Spaniards.

After a considerable sojourn in the south, and a serious illness La Salle again passed by Fort Miami in mid August of 1682, discovering several hundred Indian dwellings along the banks of the St. Joseph, tribal members gathering together to seek protection from the Iroquois and form an alliance for mutual defense. After a quick trip to Michilimackinac he again came south in the fall passing by the fort on the hill and into Illinois country.

The Final Journey

La Salle's last visit to Fort Miami would have been in November of 1683. He did not tarry but began the arduous journey to Montreal in November and then embarked for France where he gained the French king's support for a new colony near the mouth of the Mississippi River.

With 180 soldiers and settlers, La Salle left Europe on July 24, 1684, headed for the West Indies and the mouth of the Mississippi. However, the flotilla missed the delta at the mouth of the river because their course from the western tip of Cuba took them west of the Louisiana coast. La Salle was killed in March of 1687, by a disgruntled would-be colonist along the Gulf Coast, probably near the Trinity River in what would become southeast Texas.

A Glacial Tribute

In 1902 the Algonquin Chapter of the Daughters of the American Revolution used a stone found in the mouth of the river by Captain Lloyd Clark of the U. S. Coast Guard to set up a memorial to La Salle on the bluff overlooking the river and lake at St. Joseph.

LA SALLE AT 42.

During the dedication ceremonies a box containing photographs of St. Joseph in 1902, copies of local newspapers, a history of La Salle, and a list of the school children who contributed to the fund was placed beneath the boulder.

Is it the Griffon?

For over 330 years there have been "discoveries" of the remains of the **Griffon.** When portions of an old wood boat were found near Tobermory, Ontario, in 1955, a journal noted that it was the 11th possibility advanced.[9] None have proved conclusive. In 2001 Great Lakes Exploration Group announced the discovery of a bowsprit, in "northern Lake Michigan" which they believe is a piece of the **Griffon.** In 2008 a Federal Admiralty Jurisdiction was set up and scientific analysis continues with the cooperation of the Great Lakes Exploration Group, the State of Michigan and the Republic of France.

To the memory of
Father Jean Claude Allouez, S. J.
whose intrepid courage won the admiration of the Indians
and whose apostolic zeal won for him the title of
'The Francis Xavier of the American Missions'
Father Allouez was born at St. Didier in France in 1622
and died near this spot August 27th, 1689.

[Francis Xavier, 1506-1552, was co-founder of the Jesuit order, and an early missionary to Asia.]

Native Americans and Missionaries

Robert La Salle, after his trek on foot across the peninsula of Michigan wrote in 1680 that he had found the central portion of the southern lower peninsula "debatable ground between five or six nations who are at war, and, being afraid of each other, do not venture into these parts, except to surprise each other."[10]

Especially active were the warriors of the Iroquois Indians, sometimes referred to as the Sioux of the East. During the late 1600s they left their former lands in the east and invaded the western Great Lakes, attempting to gain control over the swamps of southern Michigan and the valuable furs that could be gathered there. Iroquois and related tribes rampaged through the area attacking anyone, Indian and white man, but especially the native Indians who crossed their path.

The Peaceable Potawatomi

The Potawatomi Indians, taking advantage of their superior canoe building craftsmanship, fled to Wisconsin, where they joined with other tribes to defeat the Iroquois. By the 1670s some of the Potawatomi began filtering back to Michigan and by the time the first pioneers arrived there were many Potawatomi Indian villages near the banks of the St. Joseph in several places, especially in what would be Berrien County. The settlers regarded the Potawatomi as peaceable compared with other Indian tribes, although they were warlike enough to serve as allies during the French and Indian War, 1755 to 1758, when large groups of St. Joseph Potawatomi fought the British in New York State.

Topinabee, said to be a head chief, lived in a village three miles southwest of Niles. Pokagon lived in southern Bertrand Township, west of Bertrand, on the old Chicago trail. Moccasin, another chief, some sources call him a "medicine man but not a chief,"[11] had his village on the west bank of the St. Joseph River at a place still known as Moccasin Bluff, north of Buchanan.

Topinabee whose village was near Niles was later a supporter of the Carey Mission run by Baptist Isaac McCoy.

It was into these active Indian communities that the early French missionaries came spreading the Christian gospels to them, that they might save their souls. One early settler later wrote that their work among the

Indians appeared to have been successful, for a large portion were converted to Christianity and "had become to a considerable degree civilized and accustomed to industrial pursuits."[12]

Missionaries at Fort Miami

When La Salle landed at the mouth of the river in 1675 he brought with him three Recollet priests, Fathers Louis Hennepin, Zenobe Membre and Gabriel Ribourde, whose job it was to pray for the expedition and minister to the heathen. They were expecting to rendezvous at the site with a larger party and the sailing ship **Griffon**, as noted earlier.

Hennepin wrote in a book of his travels published in France in 1683:

> . . . the approach of winter and the fear that his ship was lost, caused La Salle to be melancholy, though he tried to conceal it. We built a cabin, in which we held Divine service every Sunday. Father Gabriel and I preached alternately, taking care to use texts that would inspire courage, concord and brotherly love.[13]

The Recollect priests were referred to by the natives as "Gray Gowns" because they wore gray wool habits. After La Salle's party abandoned the area there was no further missionary activity at the mouth of the river until late in the 1600s when the Jesuits arrived and started a mission utilizing what was left of the fort.

Father Marest writing to the governor general in 1700 urges the continuation of the mission at the mouth of the St. Joseph "as a protecting influence for the Miamis Indians."[14].He calls the high bluff site that would later be St. Joseph "the most important post in all the lower lake region" and predicts that the place "will doubtless become a great city."

Father Allouez and the Niles Mission

There is some speculation that Father Claude Allouez, a Jesuit priest (and thus a "Black Robe") may first have arrived on the banks of the St. Joseph as early as 1672 following his Miami Indians as they traveled north, but this has not been proven. He had come to New France in 1658 and learned several Indian languages in preparation for ministry. He worked in Wisconsin 1667 to 1669. In 1686, at the age of 64, weakened by 30 years in the wilderness, Allouez came to the St. Joseph River area where he ministered to Indians of several tribes. One of his responsibilities was the mission at Niles where he died in 1689. A rude wooden cross was erected above the grave. It was later replaced by a granite cross. (see page 19)

A New Beginning for the Jesuits

After the death of Father Allouez the Jesuits were given a grant of land "on the St. Joseph river hitherto called the Miamis, which falls in the Lake of the Illinois and of the Outogamies." The land grant was "for the building of a chapel and residence and for the planting of grain and vegetables" and was "to be held by Father Dablon and the other missionaries, their successors and assigns in perpetuity."

By 1705 the mission had expanded to two priests, Father Aveneau who worked among the Miamis on the east side of the river, and Father Francis Chardon who ministered to the Potawatomis on the west side of the river. Father Chardon was especially well-suited for the work, according to a visitor to the mission: "He is a Missionary full of zeal; he knows nearly every Indian tongue spoke on the Lakes; and he has even learned enough Illinois to make himself understood, although he sees the Illinois only occasionally, when they come to visit his village."[15]

The mission was frequently waiting for the next priest to arrive. Charlevoix, who visited the area in 1721 wrote in his report:

> We have here two Villages of Savages, one of Miamis and the other of Pouteouatamies, they are both for the most part Christians, but they have been a long time without Pastors, and the Missionary that was lately sent hither will have no little Trouble to restore the Exercise of Religion.[16]

The work came to an end when the British took over the area following the Treaty of Paris in 1762, which ended what was popularly called the French and Indian War. About the same time there was a decree from the French government ordering the suppression of Jesuits worldwide. The decree was issued at the insistence of several members of European royalty who felt that members of the order were interfering with economic possibilities, especially in connection with the lucrative fur trade. All of the order's

Isaac McCoy

clergy were ordered to return to France on board the first vessel ready to leave for France. They were even forbidden to live in common as they waited for transportation.

Carey Mission and the Arrival of the Baptists

In 1821 Michigan Territorial Governor Lewis Cass made a treaty with the Ottawa, Chippewa, and Potawatomi Indians in southwestern Michigan which ceded to the federal government all of southwestern Michigan "except that portion of Berrien county lying between the St. Joseph river and Lake Michigan." In the treaty the government also agreed to provide funds for a blacksmith and teacher for a small group of Potawatomi Indians living on reserved land south of the river near where the City of Niles would later be built.

Isaac McCoy, a Baptist pastor and missionary, who had suggested the provision to Cass before the treaty was ratified, applied and received the position as teacher. He hurriedly made preparations to move to the area and begin the school and after a preliminary reconnaissance in May he returned to his old home in Fort Wayne to gather men and provisions. Despite the season he and 32 settlers, five cows, and 50 hogs set out with three wagons drawn by oxen and one by horses for the St. Joseph River near Niles. They arrived December 19, 1822.

McCoy named the place the Carey Mission to honor the Reverend William Carey, a noted British-born Baptist minister who was one of the first into Hindustan. Despite a frequent shortage of food, the school at Niles was open, with about 50 pupils (both Indian and French-Indian children) by May when a U. S. Army representative called at the new settlement and reported:

> By the great activity of the superintendent he has succeeded in building six good log houses, . . a school room. . . and a commodious blacksmith shop. In addition to this they have cleared about fifty acres of land, which is enclosed with a substantial fence. Forty acres have already been plowed and planted with maize, and every step taken to place the establishment on an independent footing."[17]

John L. Lieb of Detroit visited the mission in August of 1826 and reported to Governor Cass, "I was gratified with the improvement in all its departments. It is a world in miniature, and presents the most cheerful and consoling appearance."[18]

Later Robert Simerwell, who was a combination teacher-blacksmith translated several texts and catechisms into Potawatomi. The students of the mission school studied regular school subjects including geography and ancient history. The boys were taught agricultural skills and given on-the-job training on the mission farm, and the girls learned to weave and sew.

Too Many Bad Examples

McCoy came to believe that there was little chance for the Indians to learn a better way of life as long as the loose-living frontiersmen were around as poor examples, and to cheat them out of their lands and money with whiskey. In 1828 McCoy was appointed to a federal commission and began advocating a separate Indian state in the West.

In a treaty signed at Carey Mission in 1832 the Potawatomi Indians ceded all of Berrien County lying west of the St. Joseph River except a tract of land lying between the river and a direct line running from the Indiana state line to the river. This tract contained nearly 50 sections in Niles and Buchanan townships and was known as the Reservation.[19]

McCoy was appointed to assist with the removal of the Michigan Indians to Nebraska and Kansas, and one of his sons, plus a daughter and her husband moved to Kansas to continue the ministry. With few Indians left to attend the school, the Carey Mission closed in the early 1830s. McCoy moved, first to a mission on the Grand River and later to

22

Louisville, Kentucky, where he became a secretary and general agent for the American Indian Mission Association.

Early Critic

McCoy's ministry in Niles was controversial from the beginning. A small book was published in 1833 with the oversized title, *Missionary Abominations Unmasked or a View of Carey Mission containing an Unmasking of the Missionary Abominations Practiced among the Indians of St. Joseph County at the Celebrated Missionary Establishment Known as Carey Mission Under the Superintendence of the Rev. Isaac McCoy.* The writer, Timothy S. Smith, lists as his major criticisms that McCoy:

-- didn't pay the blacksmith hired under the federal program the full salary allotted and allowed him to work among the white settlers.

-- attempted to keep white settlers out of his territory and away from the pupils in his school and refused to open the school to white children,

-- practiced "vengeance" on those who gave the Indians spirits.

-- sold clothing which had been donated to his pupils and their families because it was "too good" for Indians.

-- sold to the settlers horses which had been intended to make the Indian removal easier.

The community of Niles has been both awed by McCoy's dedication and zeal to his mission, to save the souls of the Natives at whatever sacrifice necessary on his own account, and horrified in retrospect at his lack of understanding of the true needs of the Indians, and how he could serve them. In 1972 to celebrate the 150th anniversary of the founding of Carey Mission, Patricia Benson Bachman, prefaced her 16 page history:

> We have assembled on this 150th Anniversary of the founding of Carey Mission to honor those dedicated people who trudged through the agonies of winter to found the Indian mission-school which initiated the beginnings of our town, Niles, Michigan.
>
> The missionaries' plan to remove their scholars from the temptations of liquor and gambling failed.
>
> The Indians' desire to acquire a new life style and keep their lands was not respected.
>
> Their great legacy of Christian concern, political justice, and racial equality, however, have remained.
>
> Let us reunite on this historic occasion to promote the brotherhood, justice, and tolerance so conspicuously absent during the first 150 years.[20]

Today the site of Carey Mission is marked with a bronze tablet on a large boulder on the west side of the river near the corner of Phillips Road and Niles-Buchanan Road. The river landing for this site would be nearly directly opposite Fort St. Joseph south of Niles

An artist's view of Fort St. Joseph drawn from the description written by Pierre Francois Xavier de Charlevoix on a French government-sponsored trip to study existing settlements and look for sites that were good prospects for future colonization.

Charlevoix wrote in a letter dated August 16, 1721:

> It is eight days since I arrived at this Post, where we have a Mission, and where there is a Commandant with a small Garrison. The House of the Commandant which is a trifling Thing, is called the Fort, because it is surrounded with a poor Palisade, and it is much the same Thing in all other Places, excepting the Forts of Chambly and Cataracoui, which are real fortresses. There are, however in all of them some Pieces of Cannon or Patteraroes, which in Case of Need, are sufficient to prevent a Coup de Main and to keep the Savages in Awe.[21]

Fort St. Joseph

There had been a French missionary presence along the river, just south of present-day Niles, where the Great Sauk Trail met the St. Joseph River since about 1682, but it was not until 1693 that Sieur de Courmanche was sent with a small garrison of troops to the mission to construct a small military fort.

Charlevoix Visits in 1721

In 1720 Pierre Francois Xavier de Charlevoix was sent to the New World to study existing settlements and the prospects for future colonization and to explore various lakes and rivers to find a short cut to Asia. He arrived at the fort, "20 leagues up the river" at what would be Niles in August of 1721 and wrote home:

> The river St. Joseph is so convenient for the Trade of all Parts of Canada, that it is no wonder it has always been much frequented by the Savages. Furthermore, it waters a very fertile country.[22]

British Take Over from the French

In November of 1760, at the end of what was called the French and Indian War in North America, the flag of France was lowered at Detroit and replaced with the British banner. After a delay caused by lack of personnel and an especially hard winter, in August of 1761 the French flag at Michilimackinac was removed, and the same British force continued on to the small fort on the St. Joseph River.

The British were not very popular with the Indians. Unlike the French who seemed to enjoy Indian friendship, and lived peaceably, often intermarrying. The Englishman was fully aware of his assumed superiority and expected gratitude and deference from the "savages." The native people also expected regular tokens of regard, not necessarily gifts of great monetary value, but at least a ceremonial presentation from the British government.

Conspiracy of Pontiac

With Native Americans all over the peninsula chafing under the British disdain, Pontiac, an Ottawa, sought to rally the tribes and perhaps rout the settlers forever. On April 27, 1763, he unveiled his plan with fine Indian rhetoric to a large gathering of many different peoples near Detroit. However, the attack on the fort at Detroit did not go as planned.

Still, groups of Indians moved west and south and on May 16 captured Fort Sandusky on Lake Erie, and May 25 took Fort St. Joseph using the same strategy which had failed at Detroit: A small group of Potawatomi arrived at the fort and asked to speak to the man in charge of the garrison, Ensign Francis Schlosser. They told the sentry that relatives were visiting them and wished to meet the commandant. Schlosser agreed to meet with them, and the Indians departed to bring their "kinsmen."

During their absence a local French resident caught the commandant's attention and told him that the Indians had "an ill design." Schlosser was surprised, and possibly a little suspicious, since the French residents usually had nothing to do with British military personnel, but he rushed to the barracks to warn his men and found the room crowded with Indians ostensibly "visiting with the garrison." He slipped out and returned to his quarters to meet the Potawatomi kin, but a whoop sounded the beginning of the carnage. In less than two minutes all but three of the garrison of 15 were killed and Schlosser taken prisoner.

Richard Winston, an English trader, one of the survivors of the attack wrote his fellow traders in Detroit in a letter dated: 19, June 1763:

> Gentlemen, I address myself to you all, not knowing who is alive or who is dead. I have only to inform you that by the blessing of God and the help of M. Louison Chevalier, I escaped being killed when the unfortunate garrison was massacred, Mr. Hambough and me being hid in the house of the said Chevalier for 4 days and nights. Mr. Hambough is brought by the Savages to the Illinois, likewise Mr. Chim. Unfortunate me remains here Captive with the Savages. I must say that I met with no bad usage, however, I would that I was [with] some Christian or other. I am quite naked & Mr. Castacrow, who is indebted to Mr. Cole would not give me one inch to save me from death.[23]

Ensign Schlosser was taken to Detroit by his captors and exchanged on June 15 for a Potawatomi hostage held by the British. Shortly afterwards a Potawatomi leader approached the officers at Detroit assuring them that his band was "not concerned in the war, nor would be." A number of tribes withdrew at this point from the conflict, but several of them fought again when they found it to their benefit.

It is significant of the Native American attitudes that even in the frenzy of this attack, although the British were massacred, the French people at the fort were unharmed.

Fort St. Joseph and the American Revolution

Because it guarded the entrance to the portage, Fort St. Joseph was the gateway to the Mississippi River from the north.

One of the most important settlements on the British side was Cahokia on the east bank of the Mississippi River in what would later be the State of Illinois. There stood a prehistoric Indian ceremonial ground where a Christian mission had been built by the French Jesuits in 1696. The area subsequently became a major gathering place for Indian tribes, and a French colonial town with ties to the fur industry. Cahokia was garrisoned by the British in 1765 at the close of the French and Indian War and many of the French moved across the Mississippi River into Spanish territory.

In 1778 George Rogers Clark established a court at Cahokia and the 105 heads of household in the settlement swore allegiance to the Continental Congress and the independence movement in the colonies. Almost across the river from Cahokia stood the Spanish garrison at St. Louis. On the prairie nearby and along the river were many people of French extraction and language. At the same time that the American colonies were fighting for independence from the British there was unrest between Britain and Spain. In their common enemy Spain saw a common cause with the French.

In 1780 Patrick Sinclair, the British commander at Michilimackinac planned a surprise attack on St. Louis. His armies, supplemented by friendly Indians, moved southward from Mackinac, intercepting craft with provisions for the lead mines near the Mississippi River. They reached St. Louis and attacked on May 26. Shortly after the battle had begun they saw the futility of their efforts near St. Louis so they gave up the direct battle and the British and their Indian allies scattered across the countryside burning crops, killing livestock and attacking settlers. A similar attempt at Cahokia nearly across the river was also seen as a victory for the Americans.

The French Are Removed

The British were suspicious of the Frenchmen who had joined the expedition to St. Louis from the St. Joseph River settlement. On July 3, 1780, the French residents of the St. Joseph area were counted in preparation for being forcibly removed to Michiliimackinac despite guarantees which had been incorporated in the treaty which ended the French and Indian War. There were 48, including men, women and children.

In October Louis Joseph Ainsse received a commission from the British to take them to Michilimackinac. He placed them in six large canoes with French and

This map showing forts on the frontier in 1775, misses the location of Fort St. Joseph and the connection with the Kankakee, but shows the location of Cahokia and St. Louis (lower left).

Indian paddlers and took them to the mouth of the St. Joseph, then up Lake Michigan. Some remained at the fort under arrest, others left to return to Canada and still others moved south along the Mississippi toward Louisiana, stopping first at the Spanish fort at St. Louis.

Retaliation from the Mississippi

Late in 1780, at least partially as an answer to the earlier foray by the British down the Mississippi, there was an attack on the "Miamis Town" which resulted in five deaths, and the plundering of both the store, and trade stores. On January 8, 1781, Major Arent S. de Peyster, commanding the king's regiment at Detroit reported:

Since the affair at the Miamis Town something similar happened at St. Joseph's -- A Detachment from the Cahokias, consisting of sixteen men only commanded by a half Indian named Jean Bablest [Baptiste] Hammelain timed it so as to arrive at St. Josephs with pack Horses, when the Indians were out on their first hunt, an old chief and his family excepted-- They took the Traders Prisoners and carried off all the Goods consisting of at least of fifty Bales, and to the Route of Chicagou.[24]

From the Block-House known as Fort St. Joseph, which marked the site of Niles in pioneer days, there waved at different times the flags of the United States, France, Spain and England. This is a unique distinction in the historical record of this locality, hence the name:

"FOUR FLAGS"

The Four Flags Hotel opened in Niles in 1926, was one of the first to make a selling point of the community's four flags. This is a card printed by hotel manager Charles Renner.

The marauders were pursued by an Indian party led by Lieutenant Dagreaux Du Quindre who had been stationed "near St. Josephs." When the attackers refused to surrender, Du Quindre ordered a confrontation. In the fray four of the group from Cahokia were killed, two wounded and seven taken prisoner.

The Spanish are Coming!

Don Francesco Cruvat, shortly after he took command of the post at St. Louis, began planning an attack upon the British to the north. In January of 1781, there was organized a force of 65 Spanish and French militiamen, and about the same number of Indians from the western families. Don Eugenio Pirre, a captain of militia was in command with Don Carlos Tayon as sub-lieutenant.

They left St. Louis in January and were joined by Louison Chevalier, the son of Louis Chevalier who had been a trader and influential citizen at the Fort St. Joseph until his forcible removal with the rest of the French in October of 1780. It was probably through his superior knowledge of the terrain that the little army was unmolested on its trip north.

On February 12, 1781, they arrived at the fort and met very little resistance. They plundered the warehouses, sharing with the local Indians to maintain their favor. Some reports note that they remained long enough to plant the Spanish flag and claim the land in the name of King Charles III of Spain before setting the fort buildings afire and leaving for the south.

The King Was Pleased

An account in the March 12, 1782, *Madrid Gazette* a year after the event, described the attack from the Spanish point of view:

> By a letter from the commandant General of the Army of Operations at Havana and Governor of Louisiana His Majesty has advices that a detachment of 65 militia men and 60 Indians of the Otagues, Sotu and Putuami under the command of Don Eugenio Pirre arrived the second of January 1781 from the town of St. Luis of the Illinois . . . has possessed themselves of the post of St. Joseph which the English occupied at 220 leagues distance. . . they took possession in the name of the King . . . in consequence whereof the standard of his Majesty was there displayed during the whole time. He took the English one and delivered it on his arrival at St. Luis to Don Francisco Cruyat, the commandant of the post.

Jose de Galvez, governor-general of Louisiana, wrote January 15, 1782, that the King received the news with "the utmost satisfaction and gratification" and that the King:

> . . . applauded the courage and prudent conduct of the captain of militia, Don Eugenio Pirre, commandant of the detachment which formed the attack; of the sub-lieutenant of the same, Don Carlos Tayon; and the interpretter, Don Luis Chevalier, employed in the expedition; and as proof of his satisfaction with their service he has designed to confer upon the first the rank of lieutenant in the army on half pay, and on the second that of sub-lieutenant on half pay, and to command that Your Excellency shall assign to the third such a gratification as shall appear appropriate.[25]

Benjamin Franklin, who was in France helping to hammer out a peace treaty between the new nation and Britain, wrote fellow Declaration of Independence committeeman Richard H. Livingston, then serving the Continental Congress as secretary for foreign affairs, on April 12, 1782:

> I see by the newspapers that the Spaniards having taking a little post called St. Joseph pretend to have made a conquest of the Illinois country. In what light does this proceeding appear to Congress?

Franklin, John Jay, commissioner to Spain, and John Adams, commissioner to France, protested the claims, but the French supported the Spanish although nothing of importance came of it.

The little fort on the banks of the St. Joseph River was abandoned after being laid waste by the "Spanish" expedition and fell into disrepair.

Honoring a Fort

About the turn of the century there was a renewed interest in the details of the old fort and collecting artifacts. Niles resident L. H. Beeson had made an extensive collection items found at what

SITE OF FORT ST. JOSEPH, NILES, MICH.—

A memorial stone placed in 1912 to commemorate the old fort. At that time it was thought to be the actual site of the structure, as this postcard states..

was generally considered to be the site of the fort and the related buildings. In 1912, to commemorate the history of the area, a 70-ton boulder was moved from a nearby farm and erected on s rise near the river with the carved legend:

FORT
ST. JOSEPH
1697 – 1781

The eight-foot stone is on a concrete platform with two stone benches and four corner markers each listing one of the countries whose flags had flown at the site: England, France, Spain, and United States. In modern times a State of Michigan historical marker has been added to tell the story.

Archaeology at Fort St. Joseph

Archaeology began at Fort St. Joseph when the first British soldier discovered the first French artifact and has been almost continuous since then. During the 20th Century amateur archeologists and Sunday picnickers recovered baskets of old pottery shards, arrowheads, clay pipes, kettle fragments, musket balls and bits of glass. Fortunately a lot of items were collected by local men, and some of them amassed large and well cared for collections which were eventually donated to the local museum.

In 1998 Western Michigan University began the Fort St. Joseph Archaeological Project to identify and evaluate the remains of the fort. The first thing they had to do was find the location of the old fort. It wasn't under the monument. With the building of the power dam just upstream the water table had risen. To further complicate matters it was feared that the fort debris was now under an old landfill.

In 2002 the university under the leadership of Michael S. Nassaney and William M. Cremin of WMU began the search. Engineers, with a network of pipes and pumps, lowered the water table in the land and work continued. Evidence of stonework led investigators to feel that they have identified the general area of the fort, somewhat closer to the water than had been anticipated. An ongoing summer school for students in the field of archeology continues with much more to be located and evaluated.

Navigation

Native Americans early and frequently used their dugout and birchbark canoes to navigate on the river. The first vessels brought by European settlers were small boats, some purchased from the natives, and larger voyageur canoes used by La Salle and the mission priests. In 1721 Charlevoix, in a letter, noted that "The River St. Joseph is a hundred leagues long, and its source is not far from Lake Erie. It is navigable eighty Leagues."[26]

After the occupation by the English the sailing vessel, **Welcome,** called at St. Joseph with supplies in the 1770s and 1780s. This small boat was owned by fur trader John Askin who used it to collect pelts from his many outposts, but sold it to the British military in 1779. The vessel was so much a part of Michigan's British colonial history that a replica of it was constructed by the Mackinac Island State Park Commission and launched in 1980.

Trading Vessels Carry Sugar, Furs

William Burnett before 1780 established a trading post about a mile from the mouth of the river where St. Joseph was later located. He got supplies, and shipped goods, mainly sugar and animal pelts, to other markets by two sloop-sized sailing vessels called the **General Hunter** and the **Iroquois.**

One invoice for June 3, 1801, lists animal skins on the **Hunter**, Capt. Rough, Master, which were bound for David Mitchell at "McKenac" *[probably Mackinac Island]* as:

Rats *[muskrats]*	400
Minks	196
Raccoons	60
Otters	38
Fishers	6
Martens	9
Cubs *[small bear]*	5

An invoice covering a shipment in November of 1801 includes 240 buckskins, 350 doeskins, 120 raccoons, 1000 rats, 64 "cats," and 60 fox.[27]

Landing Supplies for Carey Mission

The Carey Mission at Niles between 1822 and 1833 used sailing vessels to bring supplies. The boat would anchor near the mouth of the river and the goods would be brought ashore in a small boat, then rafted up the river. Mission leader Isaac McCoy reported in his account of the mission's work the difficulty of depending on sailing ships which were unable to actually enter the river:

> Upon the failure of a vessel in the preceding spring to bring us supplies by way of the lake, as we had contracted, we took measures to have supplies brought to us by another vessel. This latter, carrying four or five hundred dollars' worth of property for us, anchored at the mouth of St. Joseph's River on the 17th of October [1823], and the captain came on shore. About this time the wind became so severe that their cable parted and the schooner was driven out to sea. About midnight, the captain, who was at an Indian house a

mile from the lake, was informed that the vessel had again come in sight. He hastened off, directing the men who were waiting to receive our property to be on the shore early in the morning. Unfortunately, they were able to land only seven barrels of flour, one barrel of salt, and two or three other small articles; the remainder of our property was carried back to Detroit, greatly to our loss and to our serious inconvenience in other respects.[28]

The first recorded entrance of a boat larger than a canoe entering the mouth of the St. Joseph River was the schooner **Savage** in the fall of 1827. Bound for Chicago with supplies for Fort Dearborn under the command of Captain Hinckley, the boat ran afoul of the weather and the captain decided to run for safety into the St. Joseph. He "jumped" the schooner over the sandbar at the mouth to shelter. There was, at that time, no one living near the mouth, but Captain Hinckley built a small hut in the shelter of the sand bank and spent the winter there. Hinckley became so sure that after settlement the harbor would be improved and much used, that he later bought property in the vicinity and became one of the proprietors of the village of St. Joseph.

Completion of the Erie Canal provided a passageway from the Atlantic coast to the Great Lakes. Traffic on the St. Joseph began to flourish about that time. Cargoes were transferred from Eastern ships to keel boats which traveled on the St. Joseph River. The riverboat also provided a commercial link to Chicago and other port cities.

Arks and Keel Boats

The era of arks and flat boats covered the period from about 1830 to 1844, when the steamboat began to rule. The important towns along the river which provided most of the freight were Three Rivers and Mendon, St. Joseph County, Michigan; Bristol, Elkhart, Mishawaka and South Bend in Indiana, and Niles and Berrien Springs, Berrien County, Michigan. From the point of the island at the mouth of the Elkhart River to St. Joseph, Michigan, by way of the tortuous stream, it is 96 miles. The trip took from several days to a week, depending on whether you were going up or down stream, and whether you were on a keel boat, or the much more cumbersome ark, which resembled a scow or large raft.

The keel boats averaged 75 feet in length and 12 feet in beam, with gunwales some 26 inches in height. They carried from 300 to 500 barrels of freight. The boats were rowed down the river with long oars, eight to a boat. On the return trip, against the current, it was necessary to pole the boat, a crew of men being used in shifts. Each boat was also rigged with a windlass and by fastening a rope to a tree the crew were able to get it over the riffles that were found in many places along the St. Joseph.

The great arks carried about 600 barrels of flour, and the equivalent in pork and produce. They were made of two pieces of timber, 50 feet long, hewn to a size 6 by 8 inches, then two sticks 16 feet long were hewn the same way, and the four framed together. Sleepers were put in lengthwise, 16 foot planks spiked crosswise and the cracks carefully caulked. Studding was fastened to

*Built at St. Joseph and first enrolled in 1879 the sidewheeler **May Graham** drew only 3.42 feet of water and ran steadily on the St. Joseph River until 1912, and occasionally for some seasons after that date.*

the gunwales. Two of the arks were fastened together, each section called a crib. Down to the mouth of the St. Joseph the coupled arks were floated, unloaded, taken to pieces and the timber sold to the captains of the lower lake vessels. Then the tired crews would make the return journey on foot through the forest.

Edward S. Moore and Abraham Prutzman established a warehouse in Three Rivers and, in the early 1830s, began shipping their flour down the river on arks they built themselves. It is said that in 1833 the fleet running between Three Rivers and Lake Michigan consisted of 10 or 11 keelboats some of which were 80 feet long by 17 feet wide with a carrying capacity of 350 barrels of flour. After 1849 the flour boats

traveled by water only as far as Niles and then transferred the cargo to the railroad. When the railroad reached Three Rivers the shippers changed to an entire rail route.

Steam Comes to the St. Joseph

Steamboats began calling at the mouth of the river in 1831, the first recorded boat was the **Pioneer**. The steamer **William Penn** arrived at the mouth in 1832, and some accounts say that she transported a detachment of soldiers from the St. Joseph valley to Chicago to fight in the Black Hawk War.

Other early commercial craft calling at the St. Joseph include the sidewheel steamer **Chicago** which had been built on the river near the mouth of Hickory

Creek in 1834-35, the steamer **G. W. Dole** which commenced operations in 1838, the **Huron** owned by Captain E. B. Ward which ran 1842-1843, and the same captain's **Champion** which continued on the run for several years. The last three boats included a large passenger traffic. It is said that there were frequently 12 to 15 stage loads of passengers awaiting transportation on the lakes to Detroit or Chicago. In good weather the trip could be made from Detroit to Chicago in 36 hours.

In 1842 the Michigan Central Railroad, which had been first proposed as a link between Detroit and Chicago via St. Joseph (the charter specified that the intermediate station be "some point in the State or Michigan, on or near Lake Michigan, which shall be accessible to steamboats on said lake"), decided to continue west from Kalamazoo and touch the lake at New Buffalo before turning south. The tracks were completed to New Buffalo in 1849 and diverted both passenger and freight traffic for a time.

Riverboats Powered by Steam

The first steam-powered craft to navigate on the St. Joseph was the **Newburyport** which ran as far as Berrien Springs in 1832. She was followed by the **Matilda Barney.** She made her first trip from St. Joseph to South Bend in the summer of 1833 and ran between these two ports for 10 years. After larger steamboats on the St. Joseph had proved impractical because of shallow water and rocks, the medium-small **May Graham** freighted fruit and passengers. There was also the little **Nettie June** owned by Andy Crothers.

In 1843 the first steamboat arrived at Constantine. In 1845 John S. Barry built a warehouse on piles over the river so that the boats could unload more easily. The **Red Foxes** were lively little craft which specialized in transportation of touring groups and passenger traffic.

An 1867 writer noted that the flow of the river had so been increased by the constant inflow of water from draining the swamps that "A steamboat called the **Schuyler Colfax**, of about two hundred tons burthen, is now plying regularly between South Bend and the mouth of the river, meeting with little or no obstruction, even at the present low stage of the water."[29]

Boatbuilding at an Early Date

There is no record that the vessel La Salle's men began in 1679 as they waited for the **Griffon** to arrive, was ever completed, but shipbuilding began almost as soon as the first settlers arrived along the banks of the St. Joseph River.

Deacon & McKalen, followed by John Griffith & Company began boatbuilding near the mouth of the river before 1832. There were also a number of vessels built at upriver sites. A 15-ton sloop called the **Dart** was constructed by L. A. Barnard at La Grange Prairie in 1832 and hauled by oxen to the river near Niles. It ran an early route from St. Joseph to Chicago. A schooner of about 50 tons was built in 1838 by Henry Depty near Bertrand. She was moved on ways to the river and floated to St. Joseph before the final fitting-out.

Before 1847 an 80-ton schooner was built on the bank of the river about eight miles above Berrien Springs. A ship yard was in operation at Constantine at an early day and it was here that the keelboat **Constantine** was built.

A Fire-breathing Riverboat

The **Davy Crockett** began work on the river in 1834. The Crockett bore a figurehead which was half horse and half alligator which was connected to the engine so that a volume of steam issued from its mouth with every stroke of the pistons. She ran for two years but in August of 1835 struck a rock seven miles above Berrien Springs, broke in two and sank.

The **Indiana,** built by John McMillan in 1843, broke all speed records on the river in 1843 when she made a passage from St. Joseph to Niles and back to St. Joseph, 100 miles, between sunrise and sunset on three successive days.

The **Mishawaka** and the **Algoma** were built at Mishawaka, Indiana, and ran to that city. For propulsion the **Mishawaka** had two wheels of about five feet in diameter and placed 16 feet apart. Over these ran an endless chain on which were fastened the buckets (or paddles). She was fast but difficult to steer, and the propelling apparatus was often broken. Finally regular wheels replaced the chain of buckets. The **Algoma** was a large steamer which also ran on the lake as far as Grand Haven.

The **Union** was a small boat built for the passenger trade. After burning out one boiler she was refitted with a horizontal boiler. On her first trip after this repair before she started from Mishawaka she was examined by Captain J. W. Brewer and branded unsafe and likely to capsize.

On the St. Joe, CONSTANTINE. Mich.

A small launch on the St. Joseph River near Constantine from a 1903 postcard.

The warning was disregarded but in passing the Mishawaka bridge she struck the pier obliquely and capsized, drowning Charles Kellogg, one of her owners.

The steamer **Niles,** a side wheeler, was one of the most successful boats on the river trade. She ran first to St. Joseph and afterwards between Constantine and Niles where the freight was transferred to the railroad. Later the **John F. Porter** was put on the route and plied between Constantine and Niles until the fall of 1851 when the railroad extended its line westward to South Bend.

The First Steamboat to Elkhart

According to an eyewitness:
    "It was a beautiful Sunday morning in the spring of 1844 that the first steamboat came puffing up the river to Elkhart. For days this event had been awaited by the inhabitants of the little

village and most of them were down to the bridge to witness the advent. A group of boys playing on the commons were startled when the sonorous whistle sounded, the cattle pricked up their ears and scudded away, as the apparition came in view around the bend of the river. . . Puffing and wheezing the boat came slowly on, but when the low wooden bridge at Main street was reached, a halt had to be made as the smoke stack could not go under the bridge. A consultation of war was held and the next morning the timbers in the middle span were removed and the boat moved through and up to the warehouses. Later the stacks were made with hinges so they could be dropped at the cry of 'Low Bridge!' "

Railroads Get the Freight

The railroad continued to bite into the riverboats' business, although rail rates were high because a single line had the monopoly on the rail freight business. Some shippers reverted to the riverboats for a while, but eventually additional railroads created competitive pricing.

During the Civil War a small steamboat called the **Union** was tied up in South Bend pending a lawsuit in the federal courts for damages because of the obstruction caused by an unusable lock which was preventing the boat from ascending the river. The courts decided a larger question and ruled that the river was no longer navigable for steamboats and that the locks need not be rebuilt and opened to them. The construction of dams at Niles and Buchanan further shortened the distance that vessels could run.[30]

Graham & Morton Transportation Company

The development of the fruit industry, beginning in the 1870s, brought new commerce to the St. Joseph valley, which was a prime orchard area. John Graham of St. Joseph joined with J. Stanley Morton of Benton Harbor and others to form the Graham, Morton and Company primarily to carry fruit grown in Michigan to Chicago and other markets, and to serve passengers (locals and tourists alike) who wanted transportation between the two places. The company reorganized as a stock company in 1879 and was renamed the Graham & Morton Transportation Company. Some of its early boats were built on the St. Joseph River by James H. Randall.

About 1858 a number of Benton Harbor businessmen, including Eleazar Morton, father of J. Stanley, asked the citizens of St. Joseph to help financially in the rebuilding of a bridge between the two communities. They were refused assistance and instead hired a Chicago company to build a canal five feet wide from the St. Joseph River into the business district of Benton Harbor. The canal was widened to 50 feet in 1865 and 75 feet in 1875. Graham & Morton maintained extensive docks along this canal. Passengers and freight from St. Joseph were usually ferried across the river. Graham & Morton continued as a major Lake Michigan operation until 1924, when the company was acquired by the Goodrich Transit Company and some traffic continued until the early years of the Great Depression.

The Graham & Morton fleet moored at their dock on the Benton Harbor Ship Canal in downtown Benton Harbor in 1906.

Later Boatbuilding

The Truscott Boat Company was founded by Thomas H. Truscott who began building boats in Grand Rapids in 1876, and moved to St. Joseph in 1892 to a factory on Ship Street. The following year the plant was moved to a brick building on the Morrison channel. The firm built mostly steam launches, sailboats and rowboats. In 1893 they provided Venetian-style gondolas and a few little steam launches to grace the lagoon at the Columbian Exposition held at Chicago. Later Truscott's was awarded a contract for 78 boats for the 1933 World's Fair at Chicago. The Truscott family sold the business in 1940, but production continued until the end of World War II building air-sea rescue boats, small tugs and submarine chasers for the U. S. Navy.

The Dachel-Carter Shipbuilding Corporation, in existence 1915 to 1945, produced boats for two World Wars including minesweepers.

The Robinson Marine Construction Company, which operated 1927 to 1955, built yachts and other pleasure boats operating boatyards in both Benton Harbor and St. Joseph.

Pleasure Steamers for the Tourists

Excursion steamers was another kind of vessel that plied various sections of the river. **Edna D.** was a small steamer which for the purchase of a 10 cent ticket would take visitors entirely around Baw Beese Lake near Hillsdale. The trip included a stop to visit "The Hermit of Cedar Island" and a marker showing the residence of the last Potawatomi Indian. The trips ended abruptly when the engine aboard the steamer, long noted for its frequent recalcitrance, suddenly exploded. The boat was a total loss, but no people were injured.

One of the best remembered boats on the St. Joseph River was the sidewheeler **May Graham**, which was built in St. Joseph by W. A. Preston and first enrolled at Grand Haven, June 11, 1879. The **Graham** was 91 gross tons, 95.5 feet long, 16 feet wide and drew only 3.42 feet of water, which enabled her to travel many places on the river where larger, or more powerful boats, could not venture. The steamer traveled a regular route between St. Joseph and Berrien Springs until 1912, when she left for at least a few seasons to work on the Grand River between Grand Rapids and Grand Haven. Her last enrollment was surrendered at Grand Haven in September of 1920 with the notation "vessel dismantled and hull to be used as scow for domestic trade only."

In Indiana the **J. C. Knoblock** built in 1882 with a capacity of nearly a thousand passengers was said to be the largest boat run on the Indiana portion of the river. For several years she gave brief, and probably very slow moving, four-mile moonlight cruises between the dams at South Bend and Mishawaka.

The stern paddlewheel steamer **Tourist** was built at St. Joseph by W. D. Preston in 1897. She was 87 feet in length, 17 feet wide, and drew 4.33 feet of water. She was first enrolled at Grand Haven on June 5, 1897, with Logan J. Drake of St. Joseph listed as owner. After two successful seasons on the St. Joseph River, running mainly from the mouth of the river to Berrien Springs, she burned near St. Joseph on September 6, 1898. Preston, her builder, bought the remains of the vessel and rebuilt, selling to the South Shore Steamship Company of Chicago, although photographs show that she sometimes ran on the St. Joseph

River until August 8, 1911, when the **Tourist** burned at Riverdale, Illinois, on the Calumet River.

Twentieth-Century Excursions

A 60-foot excursion boat, with a nine-foot in diameter stern paddlewheel called the **Island Queen** was built by Richard Hoffman at Saugatuck, Michigan, in 1956. It ran up and down the Kalamazoo River for nearly 20 years before being sold in 1975 to South Bend area investors who had created a shopping and dining complex in the old Kamm's Brewery at Mishawaka and planned excursions on the St. Joseph River.

Things did not go smoothly but the boat operated intermittently until 1983. There was a report that the old **Island Queen** fell into disrepair and at one point broke loose from her mooring, went over the dam and sank. The vessel was purchased as a hulk on the bottom by Valley Lines, a Mishawaka-based marine corporation, which restored her changing the name to the **Princess**, honoring Princess Mishawaka.

Under Captain Owen Lackey she operated between Mishawaka and Holly's Landing and South Bend's Howard Park. By 1994 low water made docking difficult at Kamm's Island and Lackey pulled the boat from the river and stored it in his back yard on Capital Avenue just south of the railroad tracks. At that site, according to a *South Bend Tribune* article, "It became a local landmark, a 12-ton sternwheeler idle in a sea of grass."

In 2003 the vessel was sold to the Alliances for Better Education Inc., and

*The excursion steamer **Tourist** on the St. Joseph River from a 1911 postcard.*

This postcard of four women and their captain aboard a river launch about 1910 promises "Half hour trips on the beautiful St. Joe River, Three Rivers, Mich."

*The **Elkhart River Queen** at her dock on the south bank in 2010.*

taken by truck to Georgia to be used for educational field trips on the Chattahoochee River.[31]

The **City of Elkhart** (later called the **Elkhart River Queen**) was built in Elkhart about 1947 by Robert "Red" Macumber and his brother William. Originally about 30 feet in length, in 1965 it was enlarged to 65 feet. The sternwheel river boat has been used for dinner cruises, and to carry groups on the St. Joseph River, going mostly north and east from its dock just above the Elkhart dam. The **River Queen** traditionally led the July Fourth Flotilla since the river parade began in 1977. The Elkhart Symphony Orchestra gave a concert from the upper deck as the boat moved down the river playing for people in the boats on the water, and riverside residents.

The vessel was placed in dry dock in 1988 and remained out of service for several years before being purchased by John Cleveland who restored the boat for service.

In 2010 the **Elkhart River Queen** was taking Sunday cruises on the St. Joseph River as well as being available for charter groups and occasions the rest of the week from June to October. The vessel is licensed to carry up to 150 passengers. There is a snack bar aboard. The Sunday cruise lasts from 2 to 4 p.m. The dock is located off East Jackson Boulevard, across the street and just north of American Park, where boat customers are asked to park. Call 574-295-1179 for reservations and information.

Floods and Other Disasters

A Nineteenth Century author wrote optimistically:

> The descent of the river from Hillsdale to Lake Michigan is gradual but constant and considerable, so that the St. Joseph, although flowing through a remarkably level country has, at almost every point, a rapid current. Being fed largely from springs and lakes, it is not subject to rapid and excessive rises nor to inconveniently low stages of water. Inundations are infrequent and unimportant.[32]

Despite his upbeat description many areas near the St. Joseph River have known water in the streets and worse. Early histories note that there was flooding in June of 1843, which was the "highest since 1836."

More Than 40 Die in 1859

The most serious flood in terms of loss of life occurred June 27, 1859, when the bridge over Springbrook, about halfway between South Bend and Mishawaka collapsed after heavy rainfall. Many of the victims only secondarily ended up in the St. Joseph River.

Springbrook was a very small stream. When the railroad was built only a small wood and stone culvert was constructed over the brook, despite warnings from local farmers about rushing freshets causing flash floods in past years, most specifically in 1841. It was midnight on a dark and rainy night. The July 2, 1859, *Mishawaka Enterprise* described the scene:

AWFUL CATASTROPHE!

The citizens of our town were aroused from their slumbers at about half past twelve o'clock on Monday night last by the ringing of the church bells, and on coming together it was ascertained that . . . an awful accident has happened but a short distance west of here to the Express Train from Chicago due at this place at 11:27 P.M. . . . The heavy rains of the evening had entirely washed away the stone culvert, and the embankment about it, leaving an awful chasm some thirty feet deep and one hundred feet in length, into which the whole train, consisting of two second class, and three first class cars were precipitated. . . . The engine and tender leaped the whole distance and buried themselves entirely out of sight at the bottom of the opposite bank, and all the cars except the sleeping car in the rear, which was thrown diagonally across the stream below the crossing, were literally smashed to kindling wood.

The water had apparently backed up behind the culvert and saturated the earth on both sides. When the weight of the train hit the debris in the chasm, the water backed up behind it was released and some of the dead and wounded were washed out into the St. Joseph River.

Since there was no passenger list it was never quite certain how many died in the wreck, but most accounts report "between 40 and 50." Shortly afterward a strong stone culvert was constructed over Springbrook.

Spinks Bridge Washed Out in 1858

The first bridge to span the river from St. Joseph to the Territorial Road which passed through what would become Benton Harbor was Spinks Bridge. It was located just northeast of the present Napier Avenue bridge where there were two islands owned by the Spinks family. A mile long trestle road was built which spanned the marsh on the east side of the river, the bridge crossed to an island in the river, then there was a marsh on the St. Joseph side, and the road climbed the bluff into that settlement.

Spinks Bridge washed out in the flood of 1858, and the trestle road was seriously damaged by a fire at about the same time. Residents of St. Joseph wanted a crossing closer to town, and felt they should not be responsible for the trestle needed to get across the marsh on the east side. It was their refusal to contribute to the cost of the long trestle, which was a catalyst for the construction of a ship canal, and the founding of Benton Harbor.

Seiche Enters River in 1893

On April 11, 1893, a Lake Michigan seiche pushed a wall of water three to five feet high up the river at St. Joseph and Benton Harbor. This raised the level of the river by four or five feet. The cause of the seiche was unknown, but has been attributed to a sudden squall or change in atmospheric pressure.

Two Bridges Succumb in 1904

Most floods in West Michigan take place during the spring thaw. The ice breaking up on the river and moving downstream is more destructive than the water. The spring of 1904 was especially notable for a large snowpack which sat on frozen soil. And then the heavy rain began. On March 7, 1904, rushing water and blocks of ice tore into the pilings of the bridge at Berrien Springs until the main bridge crashed into the river, whirling downstream and out of sight. A week later the same floods washed out the Napier Bridge in St. Joseph Township.

1908 is the Flood in Most Old Photos

But the year that everyone remembers, the year that most of the photographs depict, is 1908. There was a lot of snow that year and as early as February 15 the *Benton Harbor News-Palladium* carried the headline:

FLOODS AND STORMS ABOUND

RIVERS OVERFLOWING BANKS AND CAUSING DAMAGE IN MANY STATES

The slight thaw and rain succumbed to chilling temperatures and a major snow storm which stopped the railroads and made roads impassable. On February 25 the newspaper announced:

WATCH ICE FOR FEAR OF JAM

SHARP WATCH BEING KEPT ON ST. JOSEPH RIVER TO GUARD AGAINST DANGER

THE FLOOD OF 1908, BENTON HARBOR, MICH.

With the St. Joseph River, the Paw Paw River and Ox Creek all out of their banks in 1908 much of Benton Harbor was under water.

In 1908 there was three feet of water on Flint Avenue (South Main Street) at Three Rivers and rowboats were a common means of transportation.

A sharp watch is being kept on the big ice field above the highway bridge in order to guard against any danger of damage to the old bridge. The sudden thaw of yesterday and today has loosened the ice and it is likely that it will begin to go out of the river and harbor within the next 24 hours.

Instead on March 1, they got a sleet storm, with thunder and lightning, on March 1, which put a heavy coat of ice over everything. It was not until March 6 that the floods really began. The Niles newspaper headlined

GREAT FLOODS CAUSED BY BURST OF SUNSHINE YESTERDAY

Then it rained and things got worse. The newspaper for that day had a double column headline:

PAW PAW AND ST. JOSEPH RIVERS ARE ON RAMPAGE

HEAVY RAIN TURNS STREAMS INTO RAGING TORRENTS SERIOUS DAMAGE RESULTING

WATER RISING RAPIDLY

Ice in the St. Joseph river has broken up and today most of it has been carried out into the lake. The street railway company has kept men at work keeping the channel of the river clear and preventing the ice and debris of the river from forming a jam about the piling of the structure.

Water at Highest Point in Years

By Monday, March 9, the headline was:

FLOOD CONDITIONS WORSE; ST. JOSEPH RIVER REACHES HIGHEST POINT IN YEARS

The accompanying newspaper story noted that nearly all of the railroads were disrupted:

> In some places where bridges have been carried away by the raging waters there have been repairs made and trains are creeping along anywhere from one to twelve hours behind regular schedule. In other places the water has not receded and tracks and roadbeds are completely submerged.

Interurban service from St. Joseph to South Bend was resumed on March 8 with passengers ferried across swollen Hickory Creek. The reporter adds:

> Hundreds of twin city people took trips out to Hickory creek Sunday. The big washout appealed to the sightseers, the great gap in the road bed and the ties and rails hanging suspended in the air serving as mute evidence of the destructiveness of the waters.

Finding entertainment in the disaster the Niles newspaper reported that rowboats were docking along north Third Street, and "many citizens have taken a boat ride on N. Front and 2nd Sts., just for the novelty of the thing."[33]

Dynamite Becomes a Wintertime Ritual

Ten years later, in February of 1918, the Three Rivers newspaper, matter-of-factly stated: "Dynamite has been used to break unusually thick ice around the bridges."

The following year, Three Rivers, which usually got the worst of high water because of its three rivers, recorded that the St. Joseph River was more than three feet above the high water mark.

In 1935 they were still talking about the early 1900s and noted that the highest water level since 1915 was recorded on the Rocky River. High water had even closed Van Alstyne Drive.

Track Meet Goes Underwater

In 1943 flood waters delayed a Three Rivers area track meet as the swollen river reached within 18 inches of an all-time high mark. Twenty-five roads were closed due to high water. This may have been the year that the school board paid to have students ferried to school, and the telegraph operator at the Michigan Central Railroad had to hire a boat to get to his hotel room.

In 1947 at Three Rivers the rivers were in "heavy flood stage" by April 1 and more rain in mid-April added to the problem. In May, River Drive was closed due to high waters. On June 2 a 12-year-old boy had to be rescued when his boat was caught in a swift river current of flood waters.

The year 1948 was wet at both ends of the warm months along the St. Joseph. On March 23, the municipal power dam on the Rocky River at Three Rivers broke and caused flooding; for a time the Peale Street Bridge was in danger of collapse.

In October of 1948 a car ran into the Bennett Street Bridge near Leonidas and fell into the river. The driver a man from Sturgis was hospitalized after spending an hour trapped in his car in the water. The force of the crash made the south end of the bridge collapse.

1950 Another Benchmark Spring

Floods along the St. Joseph River tended not to be as catastrophic as those reported from the Kalamazoo or the Grand, but the potential for that kind of disaster, dams washing away suddenly, ice flowing down city streets, is always there. An article in the *Niles Daily Star*, printed September 30, 1953, reported that the water in 1950 was the "highest level in 42 years":

> Hip boots and rowboats suddenly became necessities for residents of the lower river areas as water poured through the streets. Both Island Park and French Paper Mill bridges were underwater and in danger of washing away from the pounding given by the water and the debris carried by the glutted stream.

Other high water years in the 20th Century included the spring floods of 1976, 1978, 1981 and 1985, and in June of 1989.

In March of 1982 the St. Joseph basin discharges were the largest since 1950. Two counties were declared disaster areas, and one life was lost.

Sandbags protect the riverbank during the 1908 flood in Three Rivers. Note the person sitting at the left end of the sandbags with flooding all around.

Still Battling Mother Nature in 21st Century

In mid-January 2008, there was a thaw and rain which flooded the river in Indiana. In answer flood gates were opened along the river by Indiana Michigan Power . Despite the increase in the flow, water overran the banks, and, in some cases, even sandbags stacked along the river banks.

Elkhart Emergency management and Indiana Michigan Power received telephone calls complaining that they were causing problems by "regulating the water." A spokesman for Indiana Michigan Power replied:

> This is Mother Nature. This isn't something we are doing to cause it. The Federal Energy Regulatory Commission requires all water flowing downstream to pass through the dam. A lot of people say, "Let's close the dam, so the water goes down." We can't do that. If the gates weren't open, the river would flood the homes upstream and wash the dam and the plant building away.

The high water went over the seawall at Howard Park in South Bend, and flooded Island Park. Riverside parks lost a few barrels, picnic tables and dumpsters, but the rain stopped and the flood water receded.[34] Brian Berndt of the Berrien County Road Commission pointed out the major difficulty was yet to come from the January flood.

> All the water that's filling cracks in paved roads will freeze with the return of cold temperatures and start popping the roads. We're going to have a lot of potholes in the next week.[35]

Dams and Power Plants

In speaking of the water power of the St. Joseph River at South Bend, Indiana, an 1867 author wrote:

> The fall of the river over the dam is eight feet on the west side and nine feet on the east side. The fall from the head to the mouth of the race is twenty-eight inches. Such a hydraulic power in New England would ensure the building of a city of fifty thousand inhabitants in two years. It would set the capitalists of Boston half crazy in an hour . . . who can compute its value? But when we go further and state the fact which exists today, that this is but one-half of the power now in perpetual motion at South Bend, and the additional one that for a distance of more than one hundred and fifty miles, the St. Joseph is competent to duplicate the whole of it every five miles, the senses are astounded, and every attempt at computation becomes not only futile but farcical.[36]

A 1999 St. Joseph River Assessment counted 190 dams in the St. Joseph River basin registered with the Michigan Department of Environmental Quality and the Indiana Department of Natural Resources, with 17 on the main stream. Of the 190 structures, 18 produced hydroelectric power, there were 11 retired hydroelectric dams, five for irrigation, 105 for recreation reasons (including lake level control), nine flood-control dams, four for water supply, and 19 for other reasons (private ponds, country park ponds, hatchery ponds, etc.).[37]

Starting with "The Old Mill Pond"

In the earliest days of settlement, when navigation of the St. Joseph River was still an important consideration, dams constructed to serve individual industries were usually built on tributary streams as they dropped into the St. Joseph valley. The dams were often primitive affairs built of logs and brush. They were frequently washed out by spring freshets, and rebuilt in a matter of weeks – sometimes days.

Residents begged Congress to appropriate funds for the improvement of navigation on the river. Beginning as early as 1832 petitions were sent to Washington. In 1845 and again in 1846 the Indiana legislature passed resolutions urging the federal legislators to fund the work.

In 1847 an Indiana writer editorialized:

> We have here a river coursing through two States and passing through, and in the vicinity of, an agricultural body of land without a superior in the West. For 175 miles the river distance namely from Union City to St. Joseph, steamboat navigation is greater even than the Hudson.[38]

Survey Produces Negative Results

Finally in 1879 the federal government authorized a survey of the St. Joseph River and ". . . the report was adverse to making the stream navigable and, as

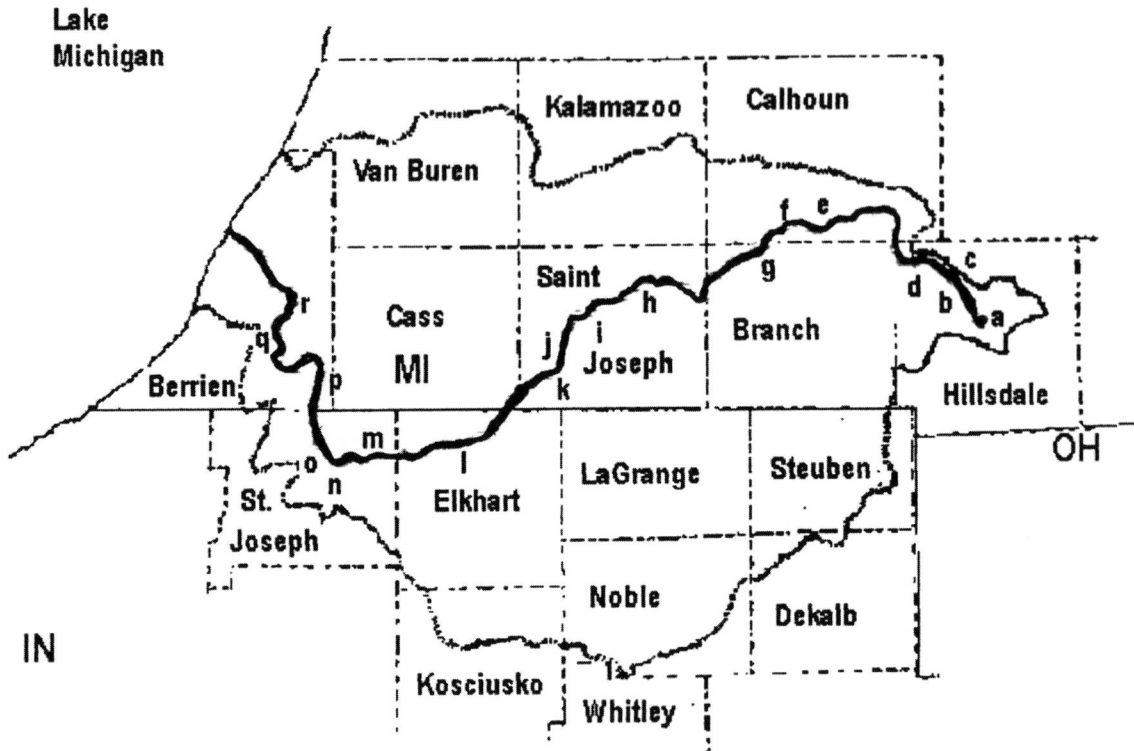

DAMS ON THE ST JOSEPH RIVER

a Baw Beese Lake
b Hillsdale
c Jonesville
d Litchfield
e Tekonsha
f Burlington
g Union City

h Sturgis
i Three Rivers
j Constantine
k Mottville
l Elkhart
m Twin Branch

n Mishawaka
o South Bend
p Niles
q Buchanan
r Berrien Springs

railroads had usurped the carrying trade to a large measure, the river was given over to power production."[39]

The first dams were for individual mills but beginning about 1890 the aim of investors and city fathers was to provide electric power not for a single industry, but for an entire community. In addition to power for mills and factories, the new dams would provide electricity for street lights, opera houses, and residences. The St. Joseph River Valley was fortunate in that from an early date the businessmen

saw the benefits to be derived from cooperation and interconnection.

But each dam has its own story:

Dams on a Narrow River

Baw Beese is a small dam which serves as a lake control device for Baw Beese Lake in Hillsdale County.

Hillsdale dam, about 20 feet high, now cascades into a small city park in downtown Hillsdale. Although it may

The old Constantine dam about 1910.

formerly have been used to power a small mill, its use today is mainly ornamental.

Jonesville dam, forming Jonesville Millpond, formerly served a mill located upstream from the present Jonesville community. In 2008 an emergency order was issued by the Michigan Department of Environmental Quality stating that the crumbling dam was "in imminent danger of failure." Further inspection showed little immediate danger to residents, although a release of sediment could threaten the river's resources. The dam is being monitored as plans are evaluated.

Litchfield dam is about 18 feet tall and although there is evidence of a race and former mill, now provides a small waterfall for a park on the outskirts of the village.

Tekonsha dam supplied a former mill, it still has a long mill race in connection with its former use, with a millpond,

which is much smaller than it was when the mill was in operation, but still of considerable size.

Hydroelectric Generating Plants

Union City's Riley Dam is the largest dam on the upper river and the only unlicensed hydroelectric facility. The State of Michigan legislation exempts the facility from any licensing procedures. It was constructed in 1923 to provide power for the area around Union City and is run by the Village of Union City.

Sturgis dam was built in 1911 by the City of Sturgis which is located 16 miles to the southeast. It still operates as a municipal hydroelectric power plant. According to the Electric Department of the City of Sturgis, the output from the dam, combined with the production of a diesel generating plant, can generate 10 percent of the city's needed electrical power. The rest is purchased from American Electric Power.

49

THE SOUTH BEND HYDRAULIC COMPANY.

This Company has recently greatly Improved the

Race on the East Side of the St. Joseph River,

at the city of South Bend, and have put in New and Substantial Head-Gates, One Hundred feet Wide. Although the Power here is not as yet developed to its full capacity, there is sufficient now available for several large manufacturing establishments in addition to those already in operation. The location is most excellent. The lots are large, and water abundant. A portion of this Power the Company propose to Lease or Sell to persons who wish to proceed with the erection of factories.

The Company has, by purchase, the right to use and draw

One-Half of the Water of the River,

which is sufficient to supply a large number of establishments with cheap and durable power.

We extract from a recent report of R. Rose, Esq., Civil Engineer, who has made careful measurements and surveys of the capacity of the river, the following statements:

"The present stage of water, (April 19th, 1866,) gives eleven thousand one hundred and fifty-seven gross horse power, the medium stage of water gives eight thousand five hundred and one gross horse power, and low stage of water, three feet below the present water surface, gives six thousand six hundred and thirty-five gross horse power. One-half of the latter power gives to the east side of river, three thousand three hundred and seventeen and a half gross horse power.

"With the present state of development of the above power, I know of no place in the North-West which affords so favorable an opportunity for creating a great water-power, at such inconsiderable expense."

Attention is directed to the class of factories and branches of business that could be advantageously pursued here. A paper mill could not fail to be a good investment. Our proximity to the Chicago and western markets, the abundance of material, (thousands of tons of straw being annually burnt and destroyed in the county,) and the cheapness of living, are inducements that cannot be ignored.

An edge tool factory, a large woolen factory, furniture factories, wagon factories, would all find a desirable location and a good market for all their products.

We would invite the attention of capitalists, East and West, to the importance, cheapness, and the superior advantages of this water-power.

Further information will be given upon application to the "SOUTH BEND HYDRAULIC COMPANY."

Reference is made to Hon. Thomas S. Stanfield, and W. G. George, Esq., South Bend, who are well acquainted with all the advantages presented by these superior mill sites.

☞ See page 60, Turner's Gazetteer of the St. Joseph Valley.

An 1867 advertisment for the South Bend Hydraulic Company then under development. The race on the east bank has been redug and is now a whitewater canoeing run.

Three Rivers dam, on the St. Joseph River is one of several on the various rivers converging in the city. The first major dam on the St. Joseph at Three Rivers was built in 1851 by the Lockport Hydraulic Company. Shortly afterwards they dug a long mill race from above the dam to the south where it powered several industries including the Sheffield Railroad Car Company. The race rejoined the river below the Broadway Bridge at the southern boundary line of the city. In 1926 a concrete dam was constructed near the Wood Street Bridge, and the following year the old river canal was closed and the river rerouted after its confluence with the Rocky and the Portage. The 601-acre reservoir has a normal water surface elevation of 797.0 feet and a total capacity of 900 kw. It is run by Grande Pointe Power Corporation and produces electrical power which is sold to the City of Sturgis.

Constantine dam was built in 1873 by the Constantine Hydraulic Company, formed in 1868 with Dr. Edward Thorne as president. The works were described in a 1928 history as "Two race-ways or canals, one on each side of the St. Joseph river, each 80 feet wide with seven feet of water having a fall of nine feet. This power had a frontage of more than 4000 lineal feet, embracing 60 acres. The dam was a good structure for its day, costing $35,000 and with the 168 acres of overflow land was estimated worth $53,000.[40] In 1912 the Constantine Hydraulic Company, Three Rivers Light & Power Company, and the Milling & Power Company of Cassopolis were consolidated to form the Michigan Gas and Electric Company. The new company completed the power house at Constantine and built a new concrete

dam in place of the old timber crib dam creating 1200 kw capacity. It is still in operation during times of peak demand, by the Indiana Michigan Power division of American Electric Power. In 2010 at the Constantine dam there was an 11 foot fall, with an elevation of 782.90 feet above sea level at the reservoir.

Mottville dam and power plant, with a capacity of 2100 kw was completed in 1920 at the cost of $560,994,48. At that time the Indiana and Michigan Electric Company lines were connected to those of the Inter-State Public Service The Mottville dam is now producing power for the Indiana Michigan Power division of American Electric Power. The dam is 23 feet in height with a normal pool level of 770.38 feet above sea level

Elkhart Dam about 1950 with the old Johnson bridge.

Elkhart, Indiana. A dam at Elkhart was first constructed in 1867 by the Elkhart Hydraulic Company. By 1870 the installation was producing 4,500

horsepower. In 1912 the old dam was replaced by a new and larger dam and a power plant which is still producing electricity, now operated by Indiana Michigan Power, a subsidiary of American Electric Power. The normal pool level at the dam is 742 feet.

Mishawaka Twin Branch dam, was three miles east of Mishawaka city when it was built by the St. Joseph & Elkhart Power Company in 1900 to transmit power to Elkhart. The dam site was originally called Hen Island after a nearby island in the river. It was placed on line in December of 1903. In 1907 the dam became part of the Indiana and Michigan Electric Company of Indiana and the name of the installation was changed from Hen Island to Twin Branch to coincide with a surrounding residential development then known as Twin Branch and Twin Branch Creek just upriver. In 1922 the entire assets of the Indiana and Michigan Electric Company were acquired by the American Gas & Electric Company, which built a large generating station at Twin Branch. The facility was still in operation in 2010, part of the Indiana Michigan Power division of American Electric Power. The installation has 21 and a half feet of fall with a pool elevation of 717 feet.

Mishawaka Uniroyal dam was constructed, probably in the 1860s, to provide power for a large factory near this site. After the factory closed in 1997 the buildings were razed. The remains of the dam were used to divert water through a new riverside park in a series of descending pools.

South Bend dam was first constructed in 1843 along the east and west races on the St. Joseph River by the partnership of Abraham Harper, William Patterson, and Lathrop Taylor organized as South Bend Manufacturing. The South Bend Hydraulic Company had ownership of the water proceeding down the east race where a steam-powered generator was later used to produce electric power for most of the cities of Mishawaka and South Bend. In 1903 the West Race was purchased by the Oliver Chilled Plow Company which constructed a power plant to provide power to the Oliver Opera House, Oliver Hotel, factories, and other Oliver properties. Today the dam has been reconfigured and forms a scenic view for the nearby Century Center. The East Race has been redug and now serves as a whitewater rafting course.

Niles dam was begun in 1866 by the Niles Hydraulic Company, but work moved slowly. In 1867 parts of the project were taken over by the Niles Manufacturing Company. French & Millard bought into the project in 1872, and the French Paper Company was still operating the power plant, located on the west bank of the river, in 2010.

Buchanan dam was constructed in 1893 and brought industry to town including an axleworks, which made steel axles for light vehicles, and later a tool company. The dam has 14 feet of fall and the elevation at the pool is 637 feet. In 2010 it was still producing hydroelectric power for Indiana Michigan Power, a unit of American Electric Power.

Berrien Springs dam, constructed in 1908, is the only existing hydroelectric dam on the river not under the authority of the Federal Energy Regulatory Commission. It has a permit issued by

The Hen Island Dam and power house east of Mishawaka from a 1909 postcard. This installation was later enlarged and renamed Twin Branch Dam.

Act of Congress in 1906. This allows the dam to operate with no control offered for the protection of aquatic resources above and below the dam, according to the Michigan Department of Natural Resources.[41] It has 32 feet of fall, with a pool elevation of 623.5 feet. In 2010 it was still producing hydroelectric power for Indiana Michigan Power, part of American Electric Power.

Cooperation Insures "Absolute Continuity of Service"

The various dams along the river which produced electricity early joined lines as a protection during emergencies. In a 1922 Three Rivers city directory an ad for the Michigan Gas & Electric Company noted that it was operating in Three Rivers, and Constantine on the St. Joseph River, plus the communities of Vicksburg, Schoolcraft, Lawton, Jones,

White Pigeon, Cassopolis, Decatur and Vandalia. The same directory further informed readers that "The transmission system is so connected with that of the Indiana and Michigan Electric Company as to insure absolute continuity of service."

After 1930, river-driven hydroelectric plants fell out of favor, bowing to steam installations which were less dependent on weather and rainfall. Many aging plants were being abandoned on other rivers in Michigan and Indiana, and, in some cases, idle dams leveled with dynamite.

Along the St. Joseph water-powered facilities were bought up by Indiana Michigan Power, a division of American Electric Power (successor to American Gas & Electric Company) and given new life. In 2010 power plants at

Constantine, Mottville, Buchanan, and Berrien Springs, Michigan, and Elkhart and Mishawaka Twin Branch, in Indiana were still being operated by Indiana Michigan Power.

Additional Dams Planned, but Not Built

In 1907 the Chapin Company announced that it intended to add to its operations at South Bend, Buchanan, and the new dam then under construction at Berrien Springs. Plans called for three "great new" dams. One would be "mid-way between Berrien Springs and St. Joseph," one at Bertrand, and one "in Indiana." The first two were reiterated in a later federal study (see below), but the dam which Chapin lists "in Indiana" may have been rendered unnecessary when the company purchased the Hen Island (Twin Branch) dam at Mishawaka and built a new power plant in 1922.

As late as a 1933 Federal survey of the St. Joseph River three places were marked for new construction of hydro-electric dams: One at Kings Landing, about mid-way between Berrien Springs and St. Joseph, one at State Line just south of Bertrand in Indiana, and one at Mendon, in St. Joseph County, Michigan.

Dams are Scenery

Beginning about 1980 municipalities began to see the river as a scenic asset to the town. Large cities and villages alike began building riverside parks and beautifying the banks. As activity-related installations gained in favor, many areas built long hiking and bicycling trails along the banks.

Planners also noticed that people like to see water spill over a dam. No matter that the water over the dam has nothing to do with the power process; it is the excess. The real power producing water enters the plant on the high side, turns a turbine to produce electricity, and exits on the low side.

But a waterfall is enticing. There is a connection to history, many communities were formed around a dam. It is a place to take the children on Sunday afternoon, and listen to the water thunder. Or watch the fish climb their fish ladder.

Green Power from Blue Water

In an effort to limit the power plant emissions that add to global warming, and at the same time increase the amount of power available, both Mishawaka and South Bend, Indiana, discussed plans in 2009 to use Federal stimulus money to build new hydroelectric dams on the St. Joseph River. An association of home owners along the river questioned in a newsletter:

> Where will they be located and will the energy output be worth the expense? The Twin Branch Dam generates enough electricity in one year to replace only two days of that generated by the Cook Nuclear Plant at Bridgeman.[42]

Similar interest was expressed by the South Bend Green Ribbon Commission which announced on Earth Day 2010 that it intended to study the feasibility of generating hydroelectric power through the St. Joseph River at old South Bend dam site near Century Center.

Fishing and Recreation

Immense quantities of fish are taken daily, but with the vast resources of Lake Michigan to draw from, the supply is never diminished. Cisco, perch, pickerel, bass of several varieties and the ubiquitous bull head are the principal kinds taken, although in some interior streams the wary speckled trout can still be lured. St. Joseph harbor is one of the few places on the Great Lakes where that prince of game fish, the white bass, can be caught. At seasons when they bite freely, the harbor presents a most animated appearance, the exciting sport sometimes extending far into the night.

From an 1893 Graham & Morton advertising brochure[43]

When the St. Joseph River was in a natural state, before dam building, it was a major spawning river for lake sturgeon. Indians speared the ancient looking fish in the Niles and South Bend area, and hook and line fishermen in the latter half of the 19th Century caught sturgeon up to 12 feet long, weighing more than 300 pounds.[44]

The subsequent chopping up of the river into segments separated by dams insured that fish would be limited in mobility, especially as far as Lake Michigan.

The Mighty Salmon Arrives

In the 1960s a small fish in the herring family, called an alewife, which had entered the Great Lakes through the Welland Canal and worked its way westward, began dying off every summer in great quantities littering the waters and beaches with dead fish. This was bad news for the tourist-led economy of Western Michigan so the DNR studied the question and decided that the best solution would be to stock the lakes with salmon imported from Oregon, which were known to have a voracious appetite for small fish like alewives.

Since salmon and their cousins, the steelhead, actually spawn annually in rivers, in 1969 the Michigan Department of Natural Resources began stocking and managing the lower 23 miles of the St. Joseph River for trout and salmon. To expand this fishery, Michigan constructed a fish ladder at the Berrien Springs Dam in 1975 which extended trout and salmon fishing opportunities an additional 10 miles upstream to the Buchanan Dam. The installation at Berrien Springs was the second fish ladder in Michigan, the first being at the Sixth Street Dam on the Grand River in Grand Rapids dedicated earlier in 1975.

Based on the success of this project, the Michigan DNR, the Indiana DNR and the U.S. Fish and Wildlife Service began discussions to develop and manage this fishery further. A formal agreement, "The St. Joseph River Interstate Cooperative Salmonid Management Plan," was signed by the three agencies in 1980.

Climbing Ladders

This $15 million dollar interstate project called for the construction of fish passage facilities at the Buchanan, Niles, South Bend and Mishawaka dams, to enable spawning runs of trout and salmon to swim upstream from Lake Michigan to the Twin Branch Dam in Indiana, a distance of 63 miles. The project also called for construction of a fish hatchery in Indiana to provide fish for Indiana's salmonid stocking in the river, and upgrades of several access facilities and sites. All of these objectives were met by fall of 1992, when all the ladders were open and fish had unimpeded access all the way to Mishawaka, Indiana.

The first ladder, the one at Berrien Springs, already had been built. It was a pool-weir, fish enter the lower end of the ladder and ascend it by jumping over the weir walls. This is the only pool-weir ladder on the St. Joseph River, but it is designed to include a sea lamprey barrier. Future modification to this ladder will include a viewing window which can be used for a manual or video count, and a modern trapping facility to collect samples more easily. Fish navigating the ladder may be viewed by the public.

The South Bend fish ladder was completed in 1988 and included a viewing window and a fish trap to allow fisheries personnel to collection brood fish to supply eggs for the hatcheries.

The fish ladder at Buchanan, 33 miles upriver, was completed in 1990 and is of a vertical slot design. Fish enter the ladder from the entrance below the dam, move upstream through a system of vertical slots, and exit the ladder in the power canal.

In 1991 the remaining two installations were dedicated. At Niles, 42 miles upriver from the mouth, a vertical slot ladder was constructed which is very deep and fish pass through the ladder and exit directly into the river channel just above the Niles dam. There is a viewing window. Also built in 1991 was the last fish ladder in the system, at the Mishawaka Dam, approximately 60 miles upriver from Lake Michigan. After passing through this ladder fish have only three more miles to go before reaching Twin Branch Dam, which does not have a fish ladder and is the end of migration.

Plus a New Fish Hatchery

Richard Clay Bodine State Fish Hatchery, a facility built in 1983 specifically to implement the St. Joseph River Interstate Cooperative Salmonid Management Plan is located in Indiana, just beyond the Twin Branch dam which marks the present end of fish migration.

The Berrien Springs fish ladder was built in 1975.

WHITE BASS FISHING ON RIVER, ST. JOSEPH, MICH.

An army of small boats full of fishermen white bass fishing on the St. Joseph River just upstream from the railroad bridge probably about 1915.

The hatchery specializes in skamania (summer run) steelhead, stocking 241,000 annually, along with 45,000 winter run steelhead. (A steelhead is a rainbow trout which has had some big lake experience and developed into a silvery fish with a steely blue head and back.) According to a Michigan 2008 report, "This strategy will enhance the already world class trout and salmon fishing status of the St. Joseph river by providing additional opportunities to catch steelhead practically year round."

The St. Joseph River fisheries project is one of only a few interstate-funded anadromous fisheries projects in the nation. Two-thirds of the cost of this project was funded through the Anadromous Fish Conservation Act, (now defunct), which was administered by the U. S. Fish and Wildlife Service, and the Dingell-Johnson Sport Fish Restoration Program (funded through the purchase of fishing equipment and motor boat fuels). The State of Michigan derived its funds from fishing license revenue and a recreational bond issue. The State of Indiana funds came from fishing license revenue and state cigarette taxes. Additional contributions came from American Electric Power, French Paper Company and the City of Niles.

St. Joseph River Rich in Fish Varieties

A 1928 history claims: "At Constantine the St. Joseph River was at one time called the best bass fish river in the state. Even today fishermen come from away to spend some time fishing."[45]

Walleye are known from Mendon downriver. They are also caught frequently in Sturgeon Lake, below

Colon, and the Sturgis impoundment. Walleyes are also a possibility and in some areas they are planted annually. The river near Buchanan has been stocked since 1984, although less in recent years. To avoid confusion in the fish genetic lines, portions of the Indiana St. Joseph are stocked with fish reared in Michigan. Also, although the minimum in Indiana is usually 14 inches, along the St. Joseph River it is 15 inches, to be the same as the minimum in Michigan.

Tournament Fishing

The river between Elkhart Dam and Twin Branch dam in Indiana has been used by bass tournament anglers. Manmade channels and gravel pits off the main flow also provide black crappie.

In 1983, to provide additional variety, the Indiana State Fish Hatchery released 5,000 Tiger Muskies, a sterile cross of female muskies and northern pike, between Twin Branch Dam and Elkhart. They are known as a fast-growing species with a 30-inch keeper limit, and have a daily catch limit of one per fisherman.[46]

Fishing is a popular sport year round nearer the mouth of the river, over the three mile stretch from I-94 to the rivermouth there are eight access sites and several marinas.

Even shore and pier anglers enjoy steelhead, brown trout and salmon in the spring; walleye, yellow perch, flathead, channel catfish and large and small mouth bass in the summer and, according to many fishermen "all of the above in the fall."

Carp, Redhorse and White Sucker

Along with the game species there is the usual collection of rough fish in all branches of the river. A Fisheries Division survey in 1987 at Union Lake in Branch County found that nearly 48 percent of the catch by weight were rough fish, primarily carp, redhorse and white sucker. These same species accounted for the vast majority of the standing crop in the St. Joseph in 1987.

The citizens of Union City, who have carefully monitored the fishing in their lake since the building of Riley Dam created it in 923, decided to take action against the rough fish. Since the early 1980s the Union Lake Association has sponsored an annual "Carp Rodeo" where teams of contestants catch, spear or shoot with a bow and arrow as many carp as possible. The first few rodeos resulted in a total carp removal of more than 2,000. More recently the prize winning catches have been approximately 300.[47]

Romantic Waters a Draw for a Century

Boating on the St. Joseph River has been a popular pastime since early days – but with a price. A 1907 history noted, "No summer season passes but that the seductive waters draw into their fatal embrace one or more victims."

On June 2, 1868, two young couples out for a pleasant paddle on the river were apparently unaware that they were launching their boat in the still waters just above the South Bend dam. Before the two men could grasp the oars after pushing off from the dock the boat was carried over the dam sideways. All four were drowned.

The South Bend board of safety for a while provided a "life-saving station" with a boat ready at any instant to go to the rescue of a person caught in dangerous currents.

Canoeing and Kayaking Gain in Popularity

In more recent years the back-to-nature movement, including non-motorized boating, has grown in popularity. The St. Joseph River is considered to be canoeable from Litchfield, in Hillsdale County, and large groups pursue the sport below Tekonsha. Most trips include the portage around one or more dams, and canoeists, collected in clubs and associations have worked to make these portages shorter, better marked and over less hostile terrain. In some places the route has previously included downtown city streets.

In Michigan the Michigan Heritage Water Trails project has begun marking river trails, and improving access. The St. Joseph River and some of its major tributaries are the pilot area for this project, opening the first water trail on August 21, 2006, in St. Joseph County, Michigan, on the St. Joseph River, the Portage River, Nottawa Creek, and a small piece of Little Portage Creek. There are 37 historical markers and a booklet available as an illustrated guide.

Canoe and Kayak Rentals

Canoe and kayak rentals, and organized trips, are available at several places along the river. In 2010 these included:

The Country Inn at Mendon, about 50 yards up Little Portage Creek at its junction with the St. Joseph, rents canoes and kayaks. Two to eight hour trips can be arranged for individuals or groups.

Liquid Therapy, or the Three Rivers Canoe and Kayak, on Main Street below the Three Rivers dam at Conservation Park, rents small craft.

Canoes are available from May 22 to October on Friday through Sunday, and holidays, from the St. Joseph County (Indiana) Parks, operating out of the Brown Barn at St. Patrick's County Park, just south of the Michigan state line. Return service from trips up the river to Niles and down the river to Keller Park can be arranged.

The South Bend Parks Department rents canoes and inflatable boats for use on the East Race Waterway, a former part of the industrial power system in downtown South Bend. In 1984 it was redug and opened as a level 2 whitewater rafting venue. The announced schedule in 2010 calls for the canoeing course to be open from June 12 to August 8, on Saturdays from noon to 5 p.m. and Sundays from 1 to 5 p.m.

Ben King of St. Joseph
Poetry for the Masses

Benjamin Franklin King, Jr., was born in St. Joseph, Michigan, March 17, 1857, and while still a child showed remarkable talent for the piano as well as for the declamation of poetic verse. One contemporary hailed him as the "drollest comic and gentlest humorist of our region" saying, "He existed as the welcome and mirthful shadow of conventional and tiresome things."

He often incorporated his piano into humorous sketches, much in the style later made popular by Danish pianist Victor Borge.

His most famous poem was "If I Should Die Tonight," which spawned a multitude of imitators. He wrote a number of poems about the St. Joseph River area (see at right) including "I Fed the Fishes" (a Nineteenth Century euphemism for being seasick), about an excursion on one of the Graham & Morton boats, and "Benton Harbor, Mich." comparing his old home to the wonders he saw at the Columbian Exposition in Chicago in 1893.

He wrote on common subjects. Most of his verses are either humorous or religious; many are both. There is a lot of dialect – German, Irish, southern, Finnish, country boy .

Verses were written with an eye to oral presentation and the author himself was a tireless lecturer. King was on a speaking tour when he was found dead by a porter in his hotel room in Bowling Green, Kentucky, on April 7,1894. He was 37 years old. The poet left a wife and two young sons. During his lifetime only one volume of poetry was published, but that was republished, in common as well as deluxe editions, several times after his death.

THE RIVER ST. JOE

Where the bumblebee sips and the clover is red,
And the zephyrs come laden with peachblow perfume,
Where the thistle-down pauses in search of the rose
And the myrtle and woodbine and wild ivy grows;
Where the cat-bird pipes up and it sounds most divine
Off there in the branches of some lonely pine.
Oh, give me the spot that I once used to know
By the side of the placid old River St. Joe!

How oft on its banks I have sunk in a dream,
Where the willows bent over me kissing the stream—
My boat with its nose sort of resting on shore,
While the cattails stood guarding a runaway oar—
It appeared like to me, that they sort of had some
Way of knowing that I would soon get overcome.
With the meadow lark singing just over the spot
I didn't care whether I floated or not—
Just resting out there for an hour or so
On the banks of the tranquil old River St. Joe.

Where the tall grasses nod at the close of the day,
And the sycamore's shadow is slanting away—
Where the whipporwill chants from a far distant limb
Just as if the whole business was all made for him.
Oh! its now that my thoughts, flying back on the wings
Of the rail and the die-away song that he sings,
Brings the tears to my eyes that drip off into rhyme
And I live once again in the old summer time,
For my soul it seems caught in old time's under-tow
And I'm floating away down the River St. Joe.

Pokagon does not wish to complain of the white man, yet he must admit he longs in his heart, again to behold the bounty of Si-bi-naw-go-naw [Paw Paw Lake] the O-de-na of his fathers. Here we killed the bear, the elk, and the deer. Here we trapped the otter, coon and beaver. But, alas, our forests have been cut down! Our woodland flowers for want of shade have faded and died! Our ancient trails cannot be traced! Our fathers' graves have been destroyed, and where our wigwams once stood and our children played, now stand the cottages of the white man. All, all has changed except the sun, moon and stars and they have not because their God and our God in great wisdom and mercy, hung them beyond the white man's reach.

Simon Pokagon (1830-1899)
Son of Potawatomi Chief Leopold Pokagon
In "Algonquin Legends of Paw Paw Lake"

Environmental Concerns

By 1925 the river from South Bend to the mouth was contaminated with sewage. In the 1930s Michigan approached the State of Indiana to improve water quality by reducing the amount of raw sewage released into the stream. At the same time Michigan took steps to alleviate the pollution caused within its boundaries with a new treatment plant at Buchanan, followed by new facilities at Berrien Springs, Niles, Benton Harbor, and St. Joseph.

However, raw sewage continued to contaminate the river until South Bend, Mishawaka and Elkhart built plants. Even the headwaters of the St. Joseph suffered from poor water quality until a new wastewater plant went into operation in Hillsdale, improving the water quality at that point by more than 80 percent.[48]

Water Quality Better, But Has a Way to Go

However, in the 1960s water quality studies looked at the resultant flow and determined that sewage contamination continues, especially after heavy rains which overwhelm sewage treatment plants until they dump raw sewage into the river. The study also revealed problems with other toxic contaminants from former manufacturing, especially papermaking plants.

Water quality continued to improve through the 1980s and 1990s with strict federal and state water quality protection laws.

Agriculture Major Source of Pollution

Based on the Michigan portion of the river, agriculture dominates the use of adjacent land, with agriculture occupying 58 percent of its banks, followed by forested land, 19.8 percent, and urban development 7.7 percent.

Agriculture is the largest source of nonpoint source pollution contributing nutrients and sediments from fertilizer and insect control sprays on agricultural fields, livestock feedlot surface runoff, livestock straying into the river floodplain, or the river itself. This results in excessive nutrient load in the water, high e.coli count and sediment in the streams, according to David Arrington, Watershed Coordinator for Le Grange County, Indiana.

Meetings with farmers near the St. Joseph River and tributary streams have resulted in management plans to provide, through Environmental Protection Agency grants, and Great Lakes Commission funds, plans and construction of barnyard fencing, and fenced crossings to keep livestock out of the stream, and off the riverbanks so that vegetation can grow and limit soil erosion.[49]

Other nonpoint source pollution comes from runoff waters from construction sites, paved areas, dumps, industrial sites and uncontrolled septic seepage. Highly erodible soils, wide-ranging channel slopes, and the presence of dams add to well-defined sediment source and sink areas. Atrazine, PCBs, nutrients, suspended solids and mercury are known contaminants in the system

Channelization, drainage of wetlands, and installation of artificial drainage systems have also altered stream temperature and decreased flow stability. Most of the large cities located within the watershed are along the mainstem of the river and have significant effects on water quality. The lower and mouth segments of the St. Joseph River basin are also threatened by increased development pressure.

The River as a Model

As a result of the Water Resources and Development Act of 1996, the U. S. Corps of Engineers (Great Lakes Region) in cooperation with the Great Lakes Commission and other regional partners has been working to develop sediment transport models of rivers which could be used by local governments and groups to minimize the erosion and sediment delivered to the rivers and harbors. "By supporting state and local measures that will reduce the loading of sediments and pollutants to tributaries, the work is helping to reduce the need for – and costs of – navigation dredging."[50]

Modeling of the St. Joseph River was completed in July of 2005. A training workshop for state and local partners took place in August of 2005. Several entities (watershed commissions, universities, etc.) have expressed interest in obtaining these models for use in future applications pertaining to the assessment of future land uses and the development of management plans. In the meantime other modeling

systems have been created and are being tested.

St. Joseph Watershed Initiative Project

This project, often called the St. Joseph Conservation Tillage Project, is funded by a Clean Water Act grant through the Indiana Department of Environmental Management. The first phase was completed in the spring of 2006.

The Nutrient, Pesticide and Sediment Reduction Project has two main thrusts. The first is a cost-share program which offers up to $3,000 to agricultural producers who commit 100 acres of productive row crop land to high-residue conservation tillage for a period of five years. The money will reimburse producers who purchase attachments for implements that are used for conservation tillage, purchase precision equipment for the application of nutrients and pesticides; and contract with crop consultants for nutrient and pesticide management on their farms

The second is an equipment rental program for conservation tillage equipment. Equipment is available for rent at reasonable prices so that producers can try it out on their own acres.

Friends of the St. Joseph

In 1994 Al Smith who had spent his youth in and around the St. Joseph River and his wife, Margaret, formed the Friends of the St. Joseph River Associa-tion as a nonprofit organization to bring together all of the many small groups formed to care for a specific part of the river, together to work toward the same goal – a healthy river system. The Friends of the St. Joseph River

FISH CONSUMPTION ADVISORY

Certain kinds and sizes of fish contain levels of toxic chemicals which may be harmful if those fish are eaten too often.

ST. JOSEPH RIVER

ABOVE STURGIS IMPOUNDMENT:
General Population: unlimited consumption of Carp under 26", Largemouth Bass under 18", one meal per week of longer Carp and Largemouth Bass. Women & Children: unlimited consumption of Carp under 26" ;one meal per week of Largemouth Bass to 18" inches, one meal per month of larger Bass to 30"; do not eat Carp over 30".

ABOVE CONSTANTINE: General Population: unlimited consumption of Carp under 26", Channel Catfish, and Walleye; one meal per week of Carp over 26". Women & Children: one meal per week of Channel Catfish and Walleye; one meal per month of Carp under 26", do not eat Carp over 26".

ABOVE BERRIEN SPRINGS: General Population: unlimited consumption of Carp and Smallmouth Bass, Largemouth Bass unlimited consumption to 18", one meal per week over 18".Women & Children: one meal per week of Large-mouth Bass 14-16"; one meal per month of Carp, Largemouth Bass 18-30" and Smallmouth Bass 14-30".

BELOW BERRIEN SPRINGS: General Population: unlimited consumption of Smallmouth Bass 14-30", and Walleye over 14"; one meal per week of Carp.

Women & Children: Do not eat Carp; one meal per month of Smallmouth Bass 14-30", one meal per week of Walleye.

same goal – a healthy river system. The group states their mission as: Association states its mission as:

> . . . to unite a diverse group of stakeholders throughout the watershed in a collaborative effort to protect restore and foster stewardship of the St. Joseph River Watershed as a critical component of the Great Lakes Basin.

The organization was awarded a $115,000 Wetland Program Development grant through the U. S. Environmental Protection Agency to foster the development and coordination of a bi-state wetland partnership between the Michigan Department of Natural Resources and Environment, the Indiana Department of Environmental Management, the Pokagon Band of Potawatomi and the Nottawaseppi Huron Band of the Potawatomi. These groups will share ideas, data and approaches to support and built wetland programs.

In this effort a Landscape Level Wetland Functional Assessment will be completed for the entire St. Joseph River watershed, to document not only the wetland loss, but the loss of wetland functions, to establish a comprehensive process to identify, evaluate and prioritize wetland efforts.

In 2009 as a means to help balance the budget the Michigan governor reunited the Department of Natural Resources and the Department of Environmental Quality as the Department of Natural Resources and Environment (DNRE.)

St. Joseph River Basin Commission

When the new fish ladders built around river-blocking dams from Berrien Springs to Mishawaka were completed in 1992, there was increased interest by sport fishermen in the St. Joseph River. Then a new concern emerged -- the quality of the water in the river and its tributaries which may need to be better protected, to insure that fish and anglers were not exposed to potential contaminants.

A new movement resulted in the St. Joseph River Basin Commission, with its primary focus on maintaining and improving the water quality. The Basin Commission is currently headquartered in the offices of the Michiana Area Council of Governments (MACOG), South Bend, Indiana.

From Analysis to Action

In 1990, the St. Joseph River Basin Commission decided to shift its activities from conducting water quality analysis on a routine basis (a task performed by other agencies) to supporting efforts related to the reduction of nonpoint source pollution in the river basin. To this end they state as the purposes of the commission:

.

--To provide a forum for discussion, study and evaluation of water resource issues of common concern in the St. Joseph River Basin.

-- To facilitate and foster cooperative planning and coordinated management of the basin's water and related land resources

-- To develop positions on major water source issues and serve as an advocate of the basin's interests.

-- To make recommendations on matters related to its functions and objectives to political subdivisions in the basin and to other public and private agencies.

-- To develop plans to improve water quality.

Source Notes

[1] Blois, John T. *Gazetteer of the State of Michigan* (Sydney L. Rood & Co.: Detroit) 1838, p. 367.

[2] Baker, George A. *The St. Joseph-Kankakee Portage* (North Indiana Historical Society: South Bend) 1899.

[3] Excerpt from "The Western Gazetteer or Emigrant's Directory," by Samuel R. Auburn, quoted in *Michigan Pioneer Historical Collection* Volume 35, facing p. 553.

[4] Haldimand Papers, *Michigan Pioneer and Historical Collections (MPHC)* Vol. 10, p. 248.

[5] Wesley, Jay K and Joan E. Duffy *St. Joseph River Assessment, Fisheries Special Report 24 (Michigan DNR: Fisheries Division) September 1999. p. 33.*

[6] Thwaites, Reuben Gold *Father Marquette* (D. Appleton & Company: New York) 1902. P. 33.

[7] Parkman, Francis *La Salle and the Discovery of the Great West* (The Modern Library: New York) 1999, p. 17.

[8] Account by Eusebe Renadout quoted in Terrell, John Upton, *La Salle: The Life and Times of an Explorer* (Weybright and Talley: New York) 1968, p. 48

[9] Snider, C. H. J. "Further Search for the Griffon" in *Ontario History* quoted on p. 81 of *The Fate of the Griffon* by Harrison John MacLean (The Swallow Press, Inc.: Chicago) 1974.

[10] La Salle quoted in Parkman, *op. cit.*, p. 121.

[11] Reber, L. Benj. *History of St. Joseph* (St. Joseph Chamber of Commerce) n.d., p. 11.

[12] *Buchanan Centennial : Commemorating 100 Years of Progress* (Buchanan Centennial Association) 1958, p. 17.

[13] Plym, J. B., ed. *Hennepin* (Fort St. Joseph Historical Leaflet No. 2 : Niles Michigan) April 1948, p.9.

[14] Reber, *op.cit.*, p. 4.

[15] Father Gabriel Marest quoted in Ballard, Ralph *Old Fort St. Joseph* (Niles Printing Co.) 1949, p. 17.

[16] Plym, J. B. ed, *Charlevoix, 1682-1761* (Fort St. Joseph Historical Association Leaflet No. 1: Niles Michigan) May, 1942, p. 7.

[17] Major Long in 1823 quoted in Ballard, Ralph *Tales of Early Niles* (Niles Printing Company) 1948, p. 69.

[18] *Ibid.* p. 72.

[19] *Buchanan Centennial, op.cit.* p. 17.

[20] Bachman, Patricia Benson *Carey Mission: Home of the Brave!* (Graphic Press: Flint) 1972.

[21] *Charlevoix, op.cit,* p.6.

[22] *Charlevoix, op. cit.* p.13.

[23] Parkman, *op cit.* p. 212n.

[24] Major Arent S. De Peyster to Brig. Gen. H. Watson Powell, January 8, 1781, Haldimand Papers, *Michigan Pioneer Historical Collections,* Vol. 19, p. 591.

[25] Weissert, Charles A. *Southwest Michigan and St. Joseph County ,* Volume 3 of *Historic Michigan: Land of the Great Lakes,* George N. Fuller, ed (National Historical Association, Inc.) n.d., p. 110.

[26] *Charlevoix, op.cit.* p.12

[27] *History of Berrien and Van Buren Counties, Michigan* (D. W. Ensign & Co.: Philadelphia) 1880, p. 40.

[28] *Ibid.* (Quoted from a narrative by Rev. Isaac McCoy).

[29] Turner, T. G. *Gazetteer of St. Joseph Valley of Michigan and Indiana for 1867 with a View of its Hydraulic and Business Capacities* (Hazlitt & Reed: Chicago) 1867, p. 15.

[30] Bugbee, W. A. "Early Navigation on the St. Joseph River," *Niles Daily Star-Sun,* March 18, 1922,

[31] Bradford, Ken "Owner sells grounded riverboat to give it new chance at life in Georgia," *South Bend Tribune,* May 5, 2003, p. C7.

[32] Turner, *op.cit,.* p. 14.

[33] Thurtell, Joel "He got forecast right, but . . ." *South Bend Tribune,* July 8, 1979.

[34] "Power company watching flood waters at dams," WSBT News recorded at www.wsbt.com/ January 11, 2008.

[35] Eliasohn, Michael "Flooding Now, Potholes Later" *Benton Harbor Herald-Palladium,* January 9, 2008.

[36] Turner, *op. cit.,* p. 60.

[37] Wesley *op.cit.,* p.35.

[38] Knoblock, Otto M. *Early Navigation on the St. Joseph River Vol. 8, No. 4. (Indiana Historical Society Publication: Indianapolis)* 1925.

[39] Knoblock *ibid.*

[40] *From a Meek Beginning: Village of Constantine, Reflections of 150 Years, 1828-1978* n.p., 1978.

[41] Wesley *op. cit.* p. 35.

[42] St. Joseph River Homeowners Association website, www.sjthoa.com/, retrieved January 18, 2010.

[43] *Echoes of Summertime Pleasures; St Joseph and Benton Harbor The Twin Cities of the East Shore and Their Multitude of Attractions* (Graham & Morton Transportation Co: Benton Harbor) 1893.

[44] Huggler, Tom *Fish Michigan: 50 Rivers* (Friede Publications: Davison, Michigan) 1995, p. 6.

[45] *From a Meek Beginning op.cit.* n.p.

[46] *South Bend Tribune*, October 5, 1983.

[47] *Michigan Department of Natural Resources Status of Fishery Resource Report 92-7,* 1992.

[48] Wesley *op cit,* p.7.

[49] Arrington, David In a speech to the 10th Annual Indiana-Michigan St. Joseph River Basin Symposium, May 21, 2010, at Fernwood Botanical Gardens near Niles.

[50] www.glc.org/tributary/models/stjoseph.html retrieved September 6, 2008.

From Beginning to End

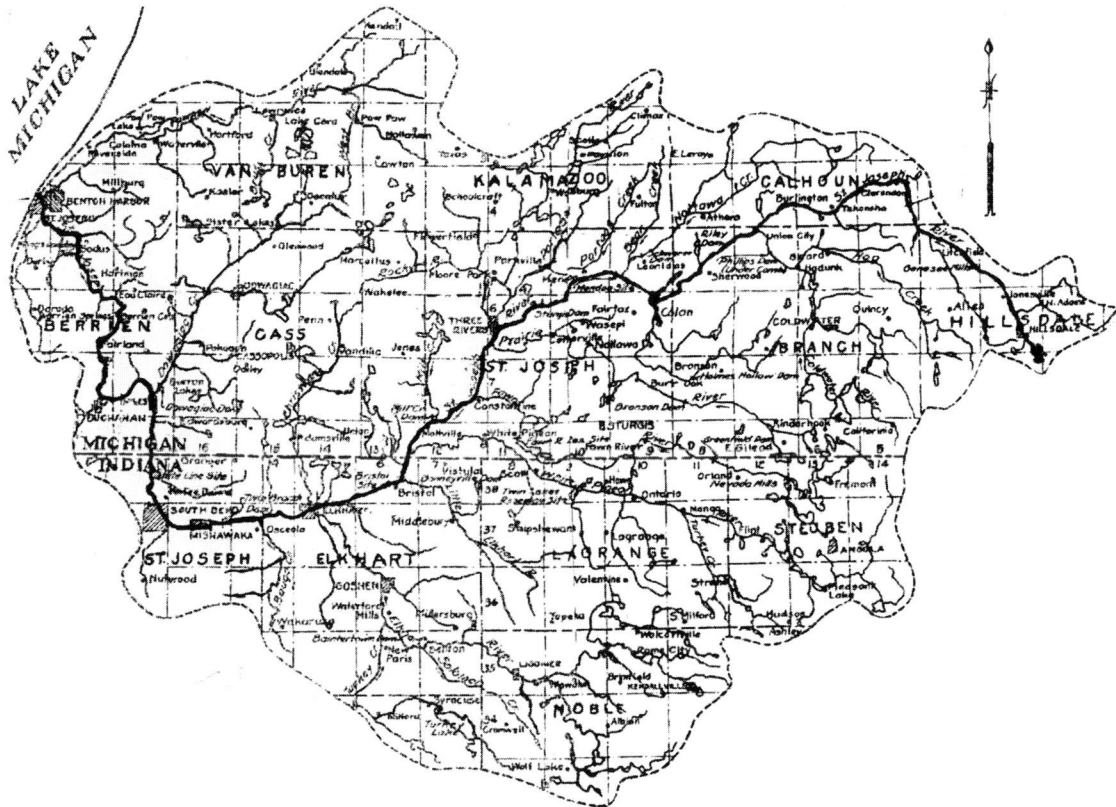

The St. Joseph River is just over 200 miles in length depending on water level and the actual source on any given day. Curves of the river often give a false idea of its true length; as the crow might fly the distance from its source to Lake Michigan is a little less than 100 miles. If the basin were entirely in Michigan, it would have the third largest watershed of the Michigan rivers. However, the St. Joseph River is a special case since about 50 miles, or about a quarter of its length, is within the State of Indiana.

This mile-by-mile view of the river is from the source to the mouth, without reference to the difficulties of canoeing some of the stretches. Mileage is based on a Corps of Engineers report which accompanied a bill in Congress in 1933.

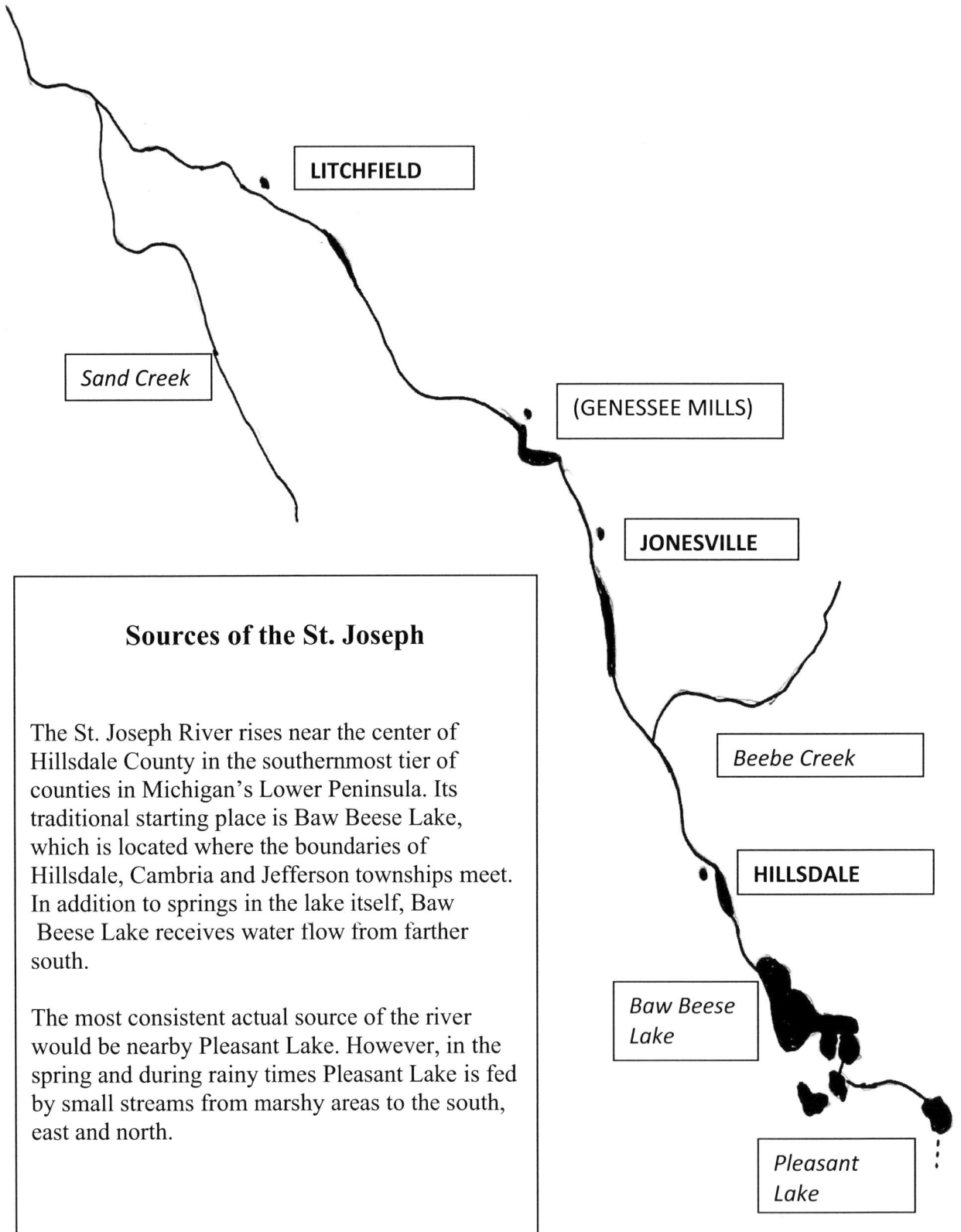

LITCHFIELD

Sand Creek

(GENESSEE MILLS)

JONESVILLE

Beebe Creek

HILLSDALE

Baw Beese Lake

Pleasant Lake

Sources of the St. Joseph

The St. Joseph River rises near the center of Hillsdale County in the southernmost tier of counties in Michigan's Lower Peninsula. Its traditional starting place is Baw Beese Lake, which is located where the boundaries of Hillsdale, Cambria and Jefferson townships meet. In addition to springs in the lake itself, Baw Beese Lake receives water flow from farther south.

The most consistent actual source of the river would be nearby Pleasant Lake. However, in the spring and during rainy times Pleasant Lake is fed by small streams from marshy areas to the south, east and north.

The Upper St. Joseph River
Hillsdale County, Michigan

208+ **Pleasant Lake**, southeast of Baw Beese Lake, is connected to it at most water levels through a series of swampy channels. Pleasant Lake itself begins in the marshy area to the south of Baw Beese Lake and the City of Hillsdale in Jefferson Township, Hillsdale County. Often Pleasant Lake is fed by marsh and small streams farther south as well as to the north. The stream that will become the St. Joseph River exits Pleasant Lake on the northwest.

207.6 Culvert. Hudson Road, U.S. 99, crosses the small stream north of Pleasant Lake in a north-south direction, and then runs parallel to it.

207.5 Culvert. Two-tenths of a mile west U. S. 99 crosses the stream northeast-southwest near a small lake and connecting stream which heads for Fourth Lake northeast of the community of Steamburg, southeast of the City of Hillsdale.

206.2 Bridge. Highway U. S. 99 crosses east west between Third Lake and Fourth Lake.

206.7 – 205.4 **Baw Beese Lake** is actually a collection of natural lakes which are joined together. The parts of the whole are known as First, Second, Third and Fourth lakes. All are at the same elevation, 1097 feet. There is a fifth lake to the southwest called Boot Lake, but it has no direct connection to Baw Beese, although there is probably seepage through the swamp. Baw Beese Lake is 414 acres with a maximum

depth of 70 feet. According to Virgil J. Vogel in *Indian Names in Michigan* the name is probably a corruption of the Ojibway word *babawasse*, "a clear piece of land, a clearing or a lake is seen through the woods." A Potawatomi chief in Hillsdale County was called Baw Beese, another possible source for the name. From the 1890s until the 1930s Baw Beese Lake was famous for its recreational opportunities with slides, beaches and resorts all around the lake and a small steamer which chugged about the water showing tourists the sights. The boat trip included a stop to visit Bud Sellers, "The Hermit of

Morlock Dam near Baw Beese Lake.

A swimming beach, complete with water slide, on the shore of Baw Beese Lake from a 1907 postcard.

Cedar Island," a fisherman and trapper who would show visitors around his island cabin displaying his neat housekeeping including an unusual pleated pattern into which he folded his bedspread. At the northernmost point of the lake is **Waterworks Park**, at Lakeview and Waterworks avenues. The park is near the Hillsdale Water and Light Plant and has playgrounds, toilets, a picnicking area and a DNR boat launch.

204.8 Enter Hillsdale Township, Hillsdale County, about the middle of Baw Beese Lake. The lake begins in Jefferson Township and crosses the northeastern corner of Cambria before entering Hillsdale Township.

204.5 The traditional start of the St. Joseph River is about two-tenths of a mile southwestward around the northern rim of the lake from Waterworks Park. Boaters should head for a tall flagpole on the grounds of the Lieghr A. Wright American Legion Post on the south bank

of the river as it leaves the lake. Waterworks Park is in the city of Hillsdale along with the north tip of Baw Beese Lake. The place where the river leaves the lake is about a tenth of a mile south of the city boundary.

204.4 Bridge. Lakeview Avenue crosses the stream north-south as it leaves Baw Beese Lake from the northwest corner. On the west side of the bridge the Mary Morlock Memorial Dam, with a drop of about a foot and a half, serves as the control dam for Baw Beese Lake. Near it is a small wooden sign which proclaims:

Headwaters of the Saint Joseph River
The Saint Joseph River begins in Baw Beese Lake,
then wanders for 210 miles through Michigan and Indiana before flowing into Lake Michigan at St. Joseph

The Hillsdale dam spilling into a downtown park in 2010.

On the back there are a number of outlined hands and the message:

"Her care is in our hands."

204.3 – 202.5 **Hillsdale** is the county seat of Hillsdale County. The first settler was Jeremiah Arnold who moved to the area from De Peyster, New York, in 1834. The town was officially platted the following year. In the early days when it was vying with Jonesville to be county seat, it was known as **Hillsdale Center** because it is near the center of the county. The first post office was established February 2, 1839, with John Potter Cook as postmaster. Hillsdale was a station on the Michigan Southern

Railroad and its growth was rapid when railroad construction was delayed and the community was the end of the line. Hillsdale was incorporated as a village in 1847 and as a city in 1869. On the 2000 census the city had 8,233 residents in its 5.6 square miles of area.

204.2 Bridge. Griswold Street crosses the river north-south. In common with nearly all of the bridges in Hillsdale, it is a culvert guarded by concrete bulwarks painted white.

203.9 Outlet from King Lake enters from the southwest.

Swans in Mrs. Stock's Park from a 1910 postcard.

Boaters on the Hillsdale millpond during "The Most Popular Fair on Earth" from an old history.

203.85 – 203.6 Hillsdale Millpond with the fairgrounds along the west bank. The Hillsdale County Fair which bills itself "The Most Popular Fair on Earth" has been held continuously since 1851. The present fairgrounds are located on the site of the original plat of Hillsdale.

203.6 Hillsdale Dam is about 20 feet high and formerly powered a mill. It spills into a small park with several benches in downtown Hillsdale.

203.6 Bridge. South Street crosses east-west within view of the dam. This bridge, in addition a concrete bulwark, ,this bridge has a wooden railing for safer viewing of the waterfall.

203.3 – 203. Mrs. Stock's Park. Just before the Bacon Street bridge, the small stream that is the St. Joseph River at this point passes through Mrs. Stock's Park, a formal Victorian-style park which was created by Wilhelmina Stock, the wife of Fredrick W. Stock who bought the grist mill across the street in 1869. Mrs. Stock planted hundreds of trees and plants, including choice varieties from other countries. One of the plants she introduced was purple loosestrife which has become a nuisance plant in Michigan in the 21st Century. There were two artificial ponds stocked with goldfish; 12 swans,(six white and six black), and three large water tanks buried to ground level and planted with water lilies. The park was maintained by the Stock family and mill employees, but was open to the public. A tennis court was added, and a redwood and stone shelter built by the Stocks' son, Alex. As the mill changed hands, maintenance was at a minimum, and some of the beauty of the park began to fade. In 2003 General Mills, owner of

TO GO A-SWIMMING
by Will Carleton

There's a red letter page that is brighter for its age,
   And the finger-marks of Time are never dimming
It has very much to say of a hot summer day,
   When we fellows ran away, to go a-swimming.
Creeping through lengthy grass while dancing shadows pass,
Threading deep haunted woods where the squirrel stows his goods,
And birds nested high teach their little ones to fly,
Where the grape-cluster shines in a wilderness of vines,
Where the mossy pillows green not a slumberer hath seen,
And the red flowers grow in a blossom-drift of snow; --
It was maybe twice as gay that we felt a bit astray
   When we fellows ran away, to go a-swimming.

And the river and the pool were so heaven-like and cool,
   With fresh baby-breezes over-skimming;
Everything well contrived for a pleasure short-lived,
   When we runaways arrived to go a-swimming.
Now all ready – now a plunge! And our bodies, like a sponge
That unduly dry has been, seem to drink the water in;
We are groping in the caves of the cold silent waves,
We are climbing to the air, flinging torrents from our hair,
And we struggle to and fro through the ripples' gentle flow,
And we duels gaily fight with the plashing waters bright,
On each other, through the gray, flinging barrels-full of spray;
   Oh! The mad and merry day we went a-swimming.

Now the moral of this rhyme is for youth's careless time,
   Full of good, sober counsel it is brimming;
In your labor or your play, your superiors obey;
   Don't you ever run away to go a-swimming.
Though the flower-jewels shine with a radiance divine,
And the daisy-blossoms creep in the meadows half asleep,
And the clouds are like a high floating castle in the sky,
And the forest-branches dumb wink and beckon you to come.
And a shady nook you know where the dainty billows flow,
Whose delicious quiet charms would fold you in their arms –
Be obedient while you may; on the shore of duty stay;
   Don't you ever run away to go a-swimming!

Will Carleton (1849-1912) was born in Hudson in Lenawee County, Michigan. He was graduated from Hillsdale College in 1869 and later worked for a Hillsdale newspaper. This poem, from a chapter called "Songs of the Rivers" in his 1902 book, *Songs of Two Centuries,* sounds a lot like young college students cutting classes to gambol in the nearby St. Joseph River. Carleton is best known for long narrative poems including "Over the Hill to the Poor-house" and "Betsey and I Are Out."

the facility, deeded the park land to the city, before selling the rest of the mill property. A major effort was undertaken in 2007-2008 and the restoration of the park to its former grandeur was capped with a dedication, and panels which show its history.

203.3 Bridge. Bacon Street crosses east-west. The stream is shallow and the bridges are small but most of the bridges in Hillsdale can be navigated by an average sized canoe.

203.25 Bridge. Carlton Street crosses east-west.

203.2 Railroad Bridge for old milling company spur crosses the small stream.

203.12 Bridge. Oak Street crosses north-south.

203. Bridge. Union Street crosses north-south. A pipe through the middle of the culvert makes this crossing particularly tricky and impossible at some water levels.

202.9 Bridge. Hillsdale Street crosses north-south.

Hillsdale College, originally called Michigan Central College, is north on Hillsdale Street. It was organized by Freewill Baptists in Spring Arbor in 1844 but moved to Hillsdale in 1853 to be nearer the railroad. In looking for a site the committee waded through the mud on the trail which would become Hillsdale Street, crossed the St. Joseph River and passed through a small elder swamp at the base of what would become "College Hill." The college buildings were the nucleus of the town east of the river.

202.75 Bridge. Manning or Maning Street crosses north-south.

202.7 Bridge. West Street crosses north-south.

202.5 Bridge. Fayette Street crosses east-west. An adjacent wooden bridge carries a bicycle and pedestrian trail over the river. The stream here is about 15 feet wide. A pleasant short boat trip can be made from the Fayette Street bridge to Jonesville.

202. Galloway Street, a former crossing, deadends at the Hillsdale Wastewater Treatment Plant.

201.4 Emery County Drain enters from the southeast, The drain begins at Lewis Emery Park and passes through Barber Lake.

201.3 Beebe Creek enters from the northeast. The creek has an extensive watershed to the southeast and has already merged with Church Drain, Shull Drain, and is the outlet for Lake Adams, Lake Bel-Air, Lacore Lake and Half Moon Lake. There is a wildlife preserve between Mauck and Moore roads along the east riverbank, which includes the mouth of Beebe Creek.

200.5 Bridge. Moore Road crosses east west.

199.7 – 199.4 **Jonesville Millpond**. The millpond is actually located about a mile south of the Village of Jonesville, and is not easily accessible by road.

199.4 **Jonesville Dam**. The dam today only provides a site for the boating race held during the town's festival days.

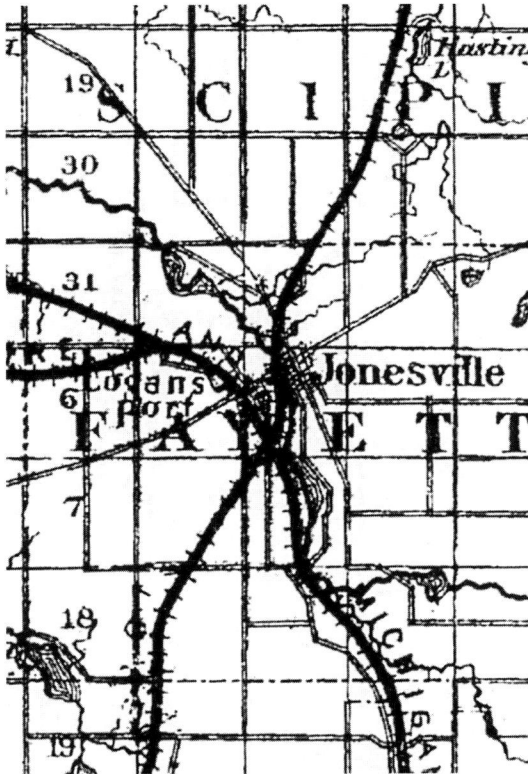

An 1873 map shows Jonesville as an important railroad junction, with a station called Logansport to the west. Just above Jonesville the wide spot in the river is the millpond for Genesee Mills.

In 2008 a routine dam inspection caused the Michigan Department of Environmental Quality to issue a warning that the structure was "in imminent danger of failure." Further inspection revealed that the "hazard potential for the dam was low" but the situation continues to be monitored. The individual who owns the land on both sides of the river at that point is regarded in law as the present owner of the dam. According to a newspaper story he was not aware that he had any responsibility for the dam until notified by the state of its problems.

198.5 Bridge. Chicago Road (U.S. 12) crosses southeast-northwest in downtown Jonesville. A small park is

located upstream from the crossing. This is the approximate site of the old Sauk Trail, an old Indian trail from Detroit to Chicago, which the river will cross two more times on its way to Lake Michigan at Mottville and again south of Niles.

198.8 – 198.2 **Jonesville**. Benaiah Jones from Painesville, Ohio, visited the area in 1828, and, with his brother, Edmund, bought land in 1829. The village was platted and named Jonesville in 1831. It was the first village in the county and the first county seat. Elisha P. Champlin was the first postmaster in 1841. Jonesville was incorporated as a village in 1855. An 1873 railroad map shows the Lake Shore & Michigan Southern Railroad, both the east-west line and the Lansing Division, and the Fort Wayne, Jackson and Saginaw Railroad. West of the tracks and south of the river is a railroad station called **Logansport**.

198.3 Enter Scipio Township, Hillsdale County

197. – 196 .6 **Genesee Mills**. The remains of a mill pond which once served the mills at the community of Genesee Mills still provides a wide spot in the river. There is also evidence of a mill race which goes off to the right.

196.9 **Way-Back-In** A campground on the south bank of the river caters to canoers and kayakers. The site also has RV hookups, rustic cabins, and canoes for rent to its customers. It is located at 3590 Jonesville Road: 1-800-491-3031.

196.6 Bridge. Genesee Road crosses east-west.

196.6 Enter Litchfield Township, Hillsdale County.

195. Bridge. Rainey Road crosses north-south on the township line. At this point the river is about 30 feet wide.

194.3 Bridge. Until 2004 the Sterling Road bridge which crosses the stream east-west was a Pratt through truss bridge built in 1893. It was an especially prized early example of the Michigan work of the Smith Bridge Company of Toledo, Ohio, particularly notable because of the ornamental details on its portal cross bracing. In 2004 the Hillsdale County Road Commission decided to replace the span with a modern standard concrete bridge and slated it for demolition. Bridge preservationists requested and received permission to move the iron bridge, renovate it and re-erect it on M-156 at Morenci in Lenawee County just north of the Ohio border where it serves as a pedestrian crossing. It sits next to a renovated 1935 beam bridge, which handles the vehicular traffic,

193.3 Bridge. Cronk Road crosses the stream north-south.

192.8 Bridge. Herring Road crosses east-west.

192.55 – 192.4 **Litchfield Millpond**.

192.4 **Litchfield Dam**. The concrete dam is about 20 feet high.

192.6 – 192.4 The **Litchfield Fire Fighters Park,** between the dam and the highway bridge, has toilets, drinking water and a playground.

192.45 Pedestrian bridge. An arched wooden pedestrian bridge takes visitors to a small peninsula to view the dam and climb wooden steps up to view the pond.

191.7 – 190.8 **Litchfield**. The town was settled by Samuel Riblet and Henry Stevens in 1834, and a village named **Smithville** was platted in 1836 by Hervey Smith and his son, David Lewis Smith. Hervey Smith became the first postmaster of an office named **Columbus** on February 3, 1837, and it was renamed Litchfield on August 12, 1837, after the former home of some of the early settlers from Connecticut. Litchfield was incorporated as a village in 1877. On the 2000 census it had a population of 1,458 with an area of 2.4 square miles.

191.3 Bridge. Anderson Road (M-49) crosses the river southeast-northeast and enters downtown Litchfield.

191. Bridge. West St. Joe Street crosses east-west on a bridge constructed in 2002. The section of river from Litchfield to Tekonsha has the greatest drop per mile (other than sections including a dam).

188.65 Sand Creek enters from the southwest. The creek begins east of Hillsdale at South Sand Lake.

188.5 **Saratoga**. The small unincorporated community of Saratoga is located on the northeast bank of the St. Joseph just downstream from the mouth of Sand Creek, along Mosherville Road. Today there is little left of Saratoga but an old cemetery.

188.3 Bridge Hadley Road crosses north-south.

The dam at Litchfield is no longer used to create power, but makes a pleasant waterfall in a roadside park on the edge of downtown.

A wooden pedestrian bridge over the St. Joseph River allows park visitors a closer view of the dam and millpond..

HOMER

Homer Lake

BURLINGTON

CLARENDON

TEKONSHA

Union Lake

UNION

Tekonsha Creek

Coldwater River

Soap Creek

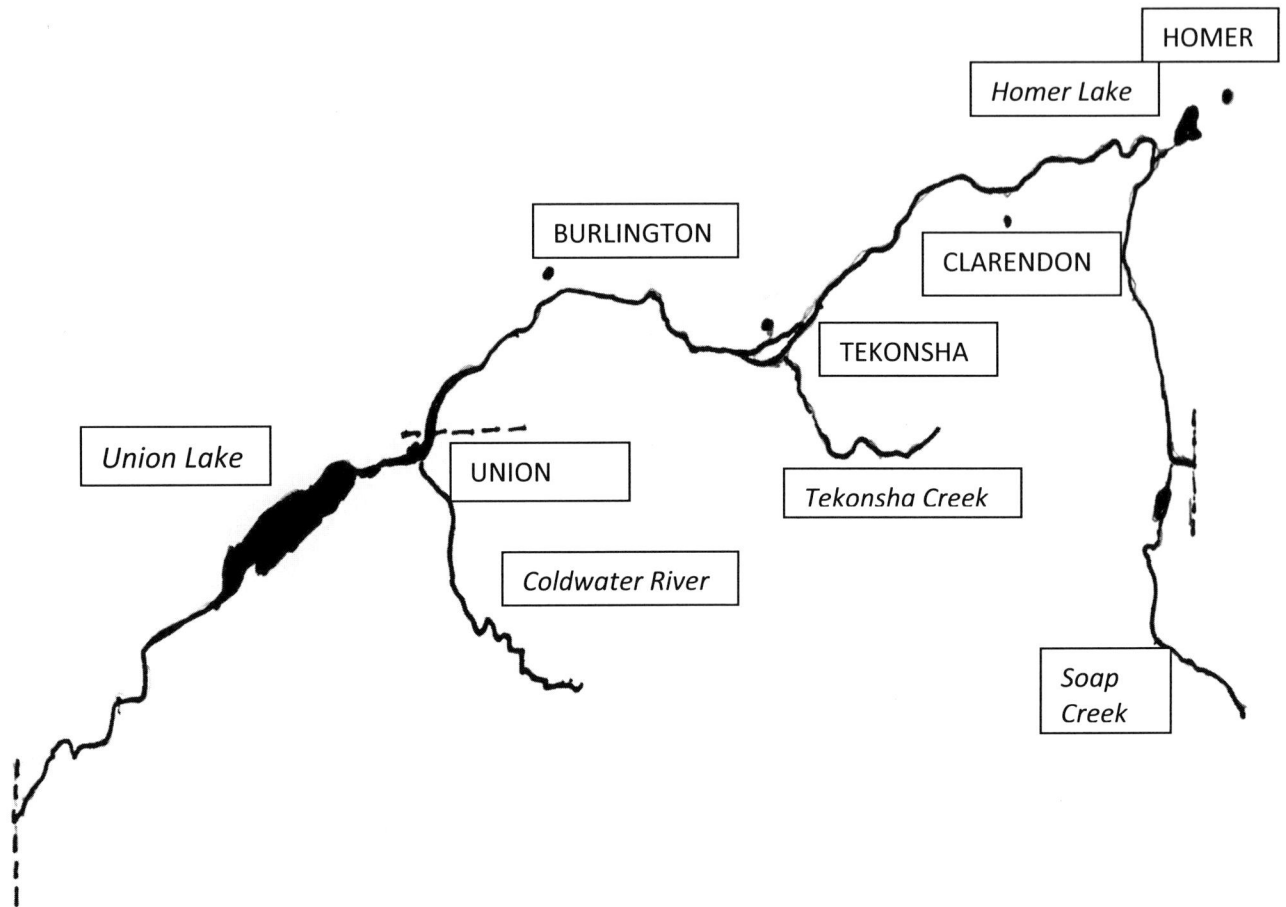

The river leaves Hillsdale County (at the far right of this map) and cuts across a small corner of Branch County where it turns abruptly north. Just across the Calhoun County boundary it picks up Soap Creek.

The St. Joseph receives the flow from Homer Lake, and turns west, reaching its northernmost point just past Twentytwo and Onehalf Mile Road. Within the boundaries of Union City the river returns to Branch County, where Riley Dam created Union Lake in 1923.

At this point the river is still small, often only about 25 feet wide, and passes through a dense wooded terrain, before entering St. Joseph County, Michigan, at the left hand side of this map.

Upper St. Joseph River
Branch and Calhoun Counties, Michigan

187.4 Enter Butler Township, Branch County. The river crosses a small corner of Butler Township.

186.4 Enter Clarendon Township, Calhoun County.

186.4 Bridge. South County Line Road crosses east-west on the county line.

186.2 Soap Creek enters from the south after passing through Quaker Lake.

184. Bridge. T Drive South crosses east-west. **Bentley's Corners** is a mile west of the river.

182.6 Bridge. R Drive South crosses east-west.

182.4 According to canoeists, downstream from R Drive bridge there is a bridge made from two semi-trailers with wheels and tires still in place, in the southwest corner of section 13

182. – 181. An old ox-bow flows toward the east until it is only about a mile west of Homer Lake (which it drains but the former channel has filled in until it is no longer navigable). A mill race was dug across the narrowest part of the oxbow, and a 1916 plat map shows a small mill pond still in place on the race. Canoes and small boats may sometimes use the old mill race and cut nearly two miles off of the trip. The river which had been traveling north makes an abrupt turn to the west. Homer Lake is less than two miles from the west branch of the Kalamazoo River at Homer.

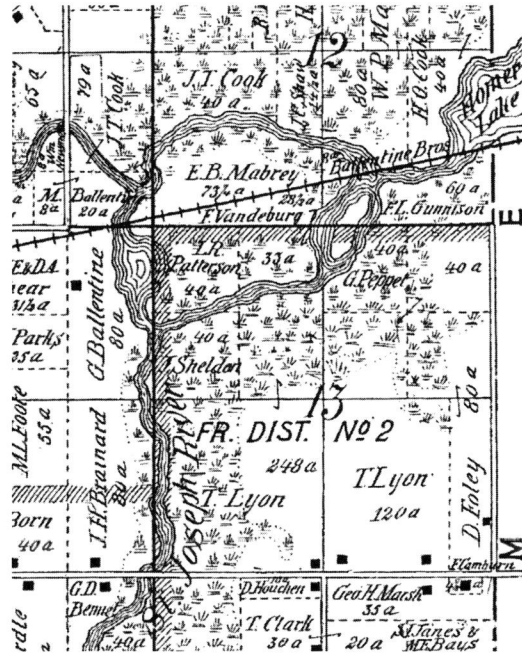

The circular stream on this 1916 map started out as an old oxbow which served as an outlet for Homer Lake. A mill race was cut across the neck of the oxbow and this map shows the old mill pond on that race. At left, west of what is now the Twentytwo and Onehalf Mile Road bridge is the northernmost point of the St. Joseph River.

179.5 Closed Bridge. Twentytwo and Onehalf Mile Road formerly crossed the stream in a north-south direction on a Pratt Truss, riveted not pinned, built in 1906 by the Elkhart Bridge and Iron Company of Elkhart, Indiana. It is the only known surviving example of this type of bridge built in Michigan by this company. In 2010 the bridge was still standing in disrepair, but access was blocked. The road it served is unpaved.

In the summer of 2010 the TwentyTwo and Onehalf Mile Bridge over the river near Clarendon was closed and in need of repair, but still standing.

179.45 The northernmost point on the St. Joseph River is just west of Twentytwo and Onehalf Mile.

178.5 Bridge. Twentytwo Mile Road crosses north- south and enters Clarendon on the south. This is a State Reward Bridge constructed under the State Reward Act of 1919 which required that the Michigan Highway Department pay half the cost and supervise the construction of all bridges on State Reward Roads. It is a low concrete bridge built in 1920 by A. R. Morrison of Port Huron. The second half of the cost was provided by the Calhoun County Road Commission.

178.5 **Clarendon.** Settlers from New York State arrived in 1832 and named their little town **Cook's Prairie** after a family named Cook. On July 25, 1840, a post office opened there named Clarendon. **Clarendon Centre** postoffice was opened June 14, 1854,

with Warren L. Deming as postmaster, in the center of Clarendon Township on the main road between Homer and Tekonsha. The township had been named for Clarendon, Orleans County, New York, the former home of

By 1913 the Clarendon post office had been moved from the original settlement near the school to the railroad depot.

82

Although the dam was lowered after the mill burned in 1953, water still passes down the mill race and under the old gristmill foundation at Tekonsha.

many of the new settlers. In 1871 the office was renamed Clarendon and moved a mile south to the Michigan Central Railroad depot at **Clarendon Station**. The track is now abandoned. The post office operated there 1871 to 1877, and 1883 to April 30, 1910. There is also an old river gauging station at Clarendon.

175.6 Bridge. Twenty Mile Road crosses north-south.

175.5 Clarendon and Eckford Drain enters the river from the northeast.

Just before the next bridge there is a flooded gravel pit. Boaters should hug the north bank to stay on the main river.

174. Bridge. Eighteen and Onehalf Mile Road crosses north-south. It is a 1930s style bridge of concrete with iron railings.

173.6 Enter Tekonsha Township, Calhoun County.

172.2 – 170. **Tekonsha Millpond.** The millpond, which is almost entirely northeast of town, is much smaller and swampier than it was when it was in active use.

170. **Tekonsha Dam**. In 1835-1836 the early settlers of Tekonsha dug a long mill race north of the river and built a dam. Thus they were able to avoid the curves in the river and bring a large

83

An 1870 map of Tekonsha shows the meandering river, the mill race built in 1837, and the large millpond which once powered both a gristmill and a sa mill. This map shows separate junctions for Tekonsha Creek, and the outlet from the Shedd lakes, which join the river after the race leaves the main river at the dam and before it rejoins it near the bridge.

proportion of the river's water down the race where it initially powered a sawmill and a gristmill. Only remnants of this dam exist today. The two streams come together again just before the Main Street bridge on the south edge of Tekonsha, where there is a second, smaller dam.

170. – 168.8 **Tekonsha**. Darius Pierce located land in the region in 1832, but sold to Timothy Kimball who became the first settler in 1833. Harris C. Goodrich became the postmaster of an office called **Wirt** on February 15, 1836. The office was renamed Tekonsha in June of the same year. Tekonsha was considered the halfway stop for travelers going from Marshall to Coldwater. In

1871 it became a station on the Michigan Central Railroad. Tekonsha was incorporated as a village in 1877. The first flour mill was built on the race in 1849 by Dr. Campbell Waldo, and later sold to the Randall family. The mill burned in 1921 and was replaced. At its peak production much of the flour was sold to customers in Virginia, South Carolina and North Carolina. In later years a major customer was the Drake's Batter Mix Company of Jackson. The mill burned in 1953. The only building left was a tall, red metal-sheathed, wheat storage building, made of two by four lumber laid flat for added strength. This interior of this remaining structure was seriously burned about 2009. The population of Tekonsha in the 2000 census was 712, with a land area of .7 square miles.

A plaque affixed to a stone near the river by the community in 1926, explains the origin of the name:

The old Randall gristmill on Main Street in Tekonsha about 1940. These buildings replaced the structures which burned in 1921. They in turn were destroyed in a second major fire in 1953. Because of the continuing difficulties of bringing in wheat, by rail, the company chose not to rebuild after the second fire.

84

In commemoration of
TE–KON-QUA-SHA
1768-1825
Chief of the Pottowatomies
This village – Tekonsha
named in his honor is located
on the site of the old Indian village
governed by that chief.

169.35 The mill race and the main river merge just before the bridge.

169.3 Bridge. Main Street, crosses north-south and goes into Tekonsha.

169.25 **Friend's Landing Park** on the northwest corner of the bridge has a small fishing dock suitable to launch a canoe or kayak. The park honors the memory of Jerry S. Friend.

169.1 Tekonsha Creek, having already merged with Tamarack Creek and the outlet from the three Shedd Lakes (West, East and South), enters the river from the southeast.

168.5 Bridge. Twin bridges carry Interstate 69 across the river north-south.

166.8 Outlet from Wilder Lake enters from the south.

166.6 Bridge. Fourteen Mile Road crosses north-south near Stony Point Hill which rises to an elevation of 990 feet on the south bank near the road.

165.9 Railroad Bridge. Old Conrail track crosses the river east-west.

164.7 Bridge. Thirteen Mile Road crosses north-south. The bridge has concrete railings.
163.7 Enter Burlington Township, Calhoun County.

163.7 Bridge. Twelve Mile Road crosses north-south at the township line on a bridge constructed in 2001 which replaced a 1907 concrete arch bridge.

162.9 Remains of the old Burlington dam. There is a fork in the river, the main river on the left (south) going over the razed dam. The old race on the north is blocked off to boat traffic.

162.6 Bridge. Marshall Street (called Eleven Mile Road in the township) crosses north-south and enters Burlington to the north.

163.4 – 162.5 **Burlington.** The settlement was founded in 1833 by William and Ansel Adams. There were several residents who had served in the War of 1812 and the town was named for the gunboat Burlington which had served on the Great Lakes. Levi Houghtaling was the first postmaster in 1838. **Burlington Station** was located a little over a mile to the south between 11 and 12 Mile roads on the Michigan Central Railroad.

Burlington from an 1873 map with Burlington Station to the east and south

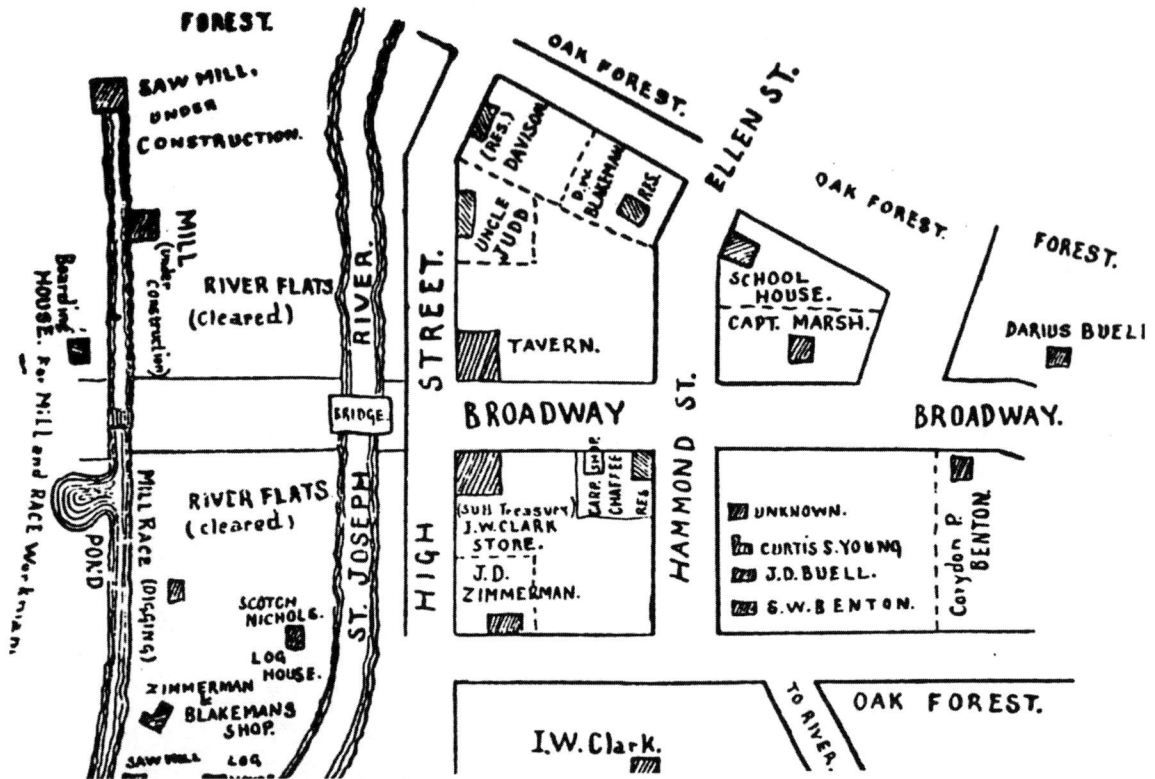

An old map of "Goodwinville" dated 1838-39. Note that the sawmill and mill race (from the Coldwater River to the St. Joseph) are both under construction/ At left is a boarding house labeled: "For Mill and Race Workmen."

Burlington was incorporated as a village in 1869. The population in 2000 was 405 with a land area of .7 square miles.

161.4 Bridge. Ten and Onehalf Mile Road crosses the river north-south. On the upstream side of the bridge there is sometimes a small set of rapids created by the remains of an old dam.

159.6 Bridge. Nine Mile Road crosses north-south.

158.6 Burnett Creek enters from the south just east of the village.

158.55 Enter Union Township, Branch County.

158.8. – 157.4 **Union City**. The area was surveyed by Robert Clark in 1826, but Isaiah W. Bennett bought the first land in 1831. Justus Goodwin bought 600 acres in 1833, dug a mill race, and was named the first postmaster of **Goodwinville** in 1834. When the settlement was platted in 1835 it was named Union City, probably because of the union of the Coldwater and St. Joseph rivers at that point. The post office changed its name to Union City in 1840. Union City was incorporated as a village in 1866. The population in the 2000 census was 1,804, with an area of 1.5 square miles. A home at Union City, now owned by children's author Patricia Polacco, was a stop on the underground railroad and was said to have been visited by Abraham Lincoln. The village

Riley Dam at Union Lake photographed in the summer of 2010.

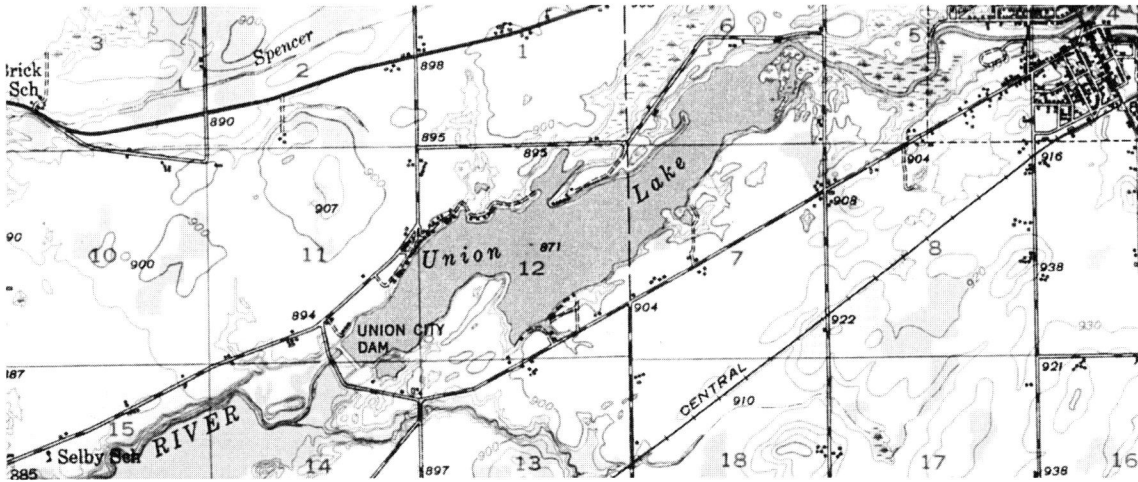

Union Lake is downriver from Union City (at upper right of this 1950 U. S. Survey Map). There is a large lakeside community on the southern shore.

is partially in Burlington Township, Calhoun County, but mostly within Union Township, Branch County.

158.2 Coldwater River, which begins near Coldwater Lake, enters the river from the southeast in downtown Union City, having already picked up Fisher

Creek (sometimes called the Sauk River) from Marble Lake, Cold Creek, Hog Creek and the outlet from Hodunk Pond.

158.1 **Veteran's Memorial Park** on a high bluff just before the bridge on the north bank. The park includes a large boulder with a plaque dedicated in 1979 to the memory of the dam committee, the eight men who worked out the plans for the building of Riley Dam and Union Lake in 1922.

158. Broadway Street crosses north-south in downtown Union City.

158. – 157.6 **Riverview Park** on the south bank has sports fields, play-grounds, picnic areas and river access.

157.8 Bridge. Park or South Street crosses north-south, where there is canoe access and parking.

157. Bridge. Arborgast Road crosses north-south at the east end of Union Lake.

156.8 – 155. **Union Lake** is about two and a half miles long. There is a public access site off Tuttle Road near a bayou on the north side. Elevation of the lake is 872 feet.

156. Enter Sherwood Township, Branch County. The township line divides Union Lake almost in half.

155. **Union City Riley Dam**. Union City had an early power plant near downtown, built on a race from the Coldwater River to the St. Joseph. By 1914 there was no longer enough power to satisfy the needs of the village and during World War I electricity was rationed. In 1920 John Moore, village president, advocated building a new hydropower source at a different location. Many sites were viewed and rejected. It was at this point, according to a local historian, that "someone remembered a barefoot high school boy who had spent much time on the river

and had casually noted a spot on the St. Joe for a dam." The dam and new power plant were dedicated August 3, 1923. Since that time three diesel generators have been added to the plant, and an agreement was signed in 1954 with Consumers Power for additional power when needed.

155.2 **Union Lake Association Fish Rearing Pond**. A fish hatchery was located on the south bank below the dam as early as 1922, the Michigan Department of Conservation helped some, but later when the local people felt the lake needed restocking they asked fishermen to donate a part of their catch of bluegills and sunfish to the pond for brood stock. Later the species raised were northern pike and walleye with some funds granted by the Fish America Foundation and the Michigan DNR.

155. Bridge. Riley Road crosses north-south just past the dam at the eastern end of Union Lake. Near the bridge is a boat launch, access area and a parking lot.

154.7 Riley Creek enters from the south having already picked up Buell Drain, Lee Drain and County Drain 58. Riley Creek and road were named for early settler Daniel Riley.

152.6 Blackwell Drain enters from the southeast.

152.5 Bridge. Athens Road (old M- 78) crosses the river north-south.

151.4. Spencer Creek enters from the north, having passed through Kenyon and Oliverda Lakes and Spencer-Kendig Drain, and Kilbourn Drain enters from southeast.

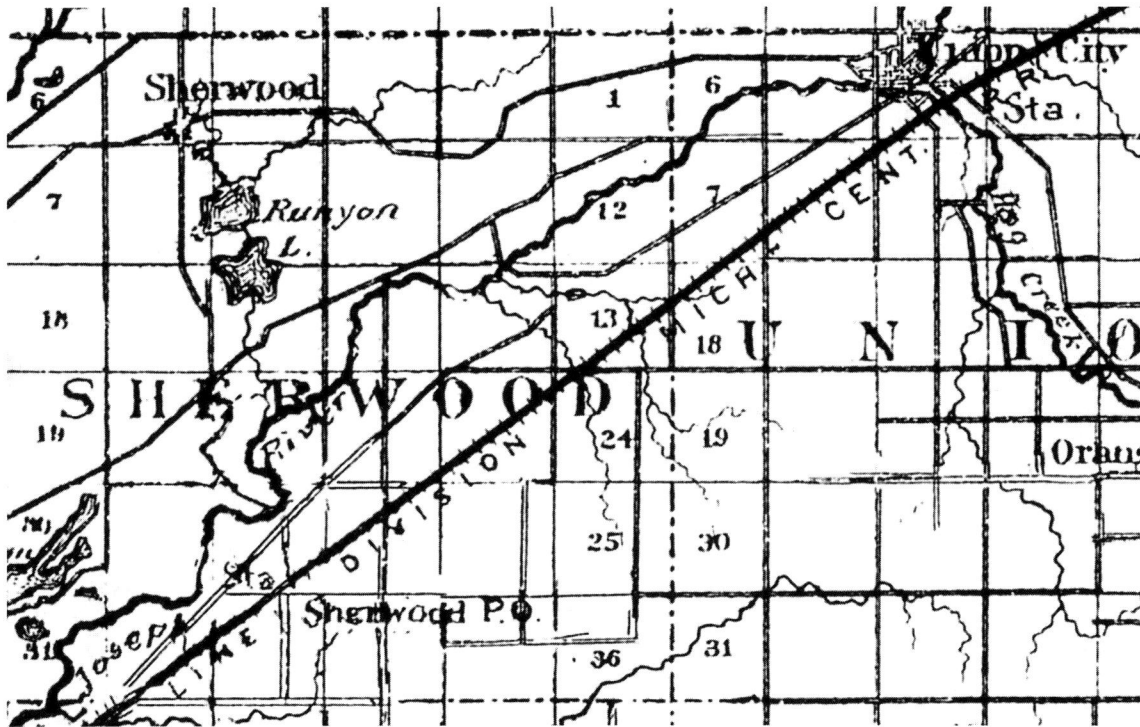

An 1873 map shows Union City (right) before the dam was built and two communities called Sherwood (left).The Coldwater River (right) is labeled "Hog Creek.".

151.3 Bridge. Arney Road approaches the river going east-west, makes a right turn across the bridge and enters the Village of Sherwood.

Sherwood There was a settlement named **Hazenville** laid out on the farm of E. F. Hazen in Sherwood Township west of Union City. A post office named **Durham** opened there March 8, 1833, with Lot Whitcomb as the first postmaster. In 1839 it was renamed Sherwood to honor its first settler, Alexander E. Tomlinson, who had come from Sherwood Forest, England. Elsewhere in Sherwood Township there was a post office named **Newstead** which opened on February 13, 1867 with Ryon Williams as the first postmaster. By 1873 there was still a settlement named Sherwood near the northern boundary of Sherwood Township, but the post office had been transferred to a place on the Michigan Central Railroad near the southern boundary of Sherwood Township. Later maps show little remaining of the northern Sherwood but an old cemetery. The later Sherwood, to the south, incorporated as a village in 1887. In 2000 the village had a population of 324 and included about one square mile.

146. Island in the river from old oxbow.

142. River Lake is attached by a short channel which enters from the north just before the river turns south. A series of small lakes including, Blossom, Goodrich, Havens and Adams, which form a semi-circle around River Lake, drain eastward into Sturgeon Lake.

139.2 Enter Matteson Township, Branch County.

Rocky River

Portage Creek

Little Portage Creek

Nottawa Creek

MENDON

Sturgis Dam

COLON

Big Swan Creek

THREE RIVERS

Prairie River

Fawn River

CONSTANTINE

MOTTVILLE

Pigeon River

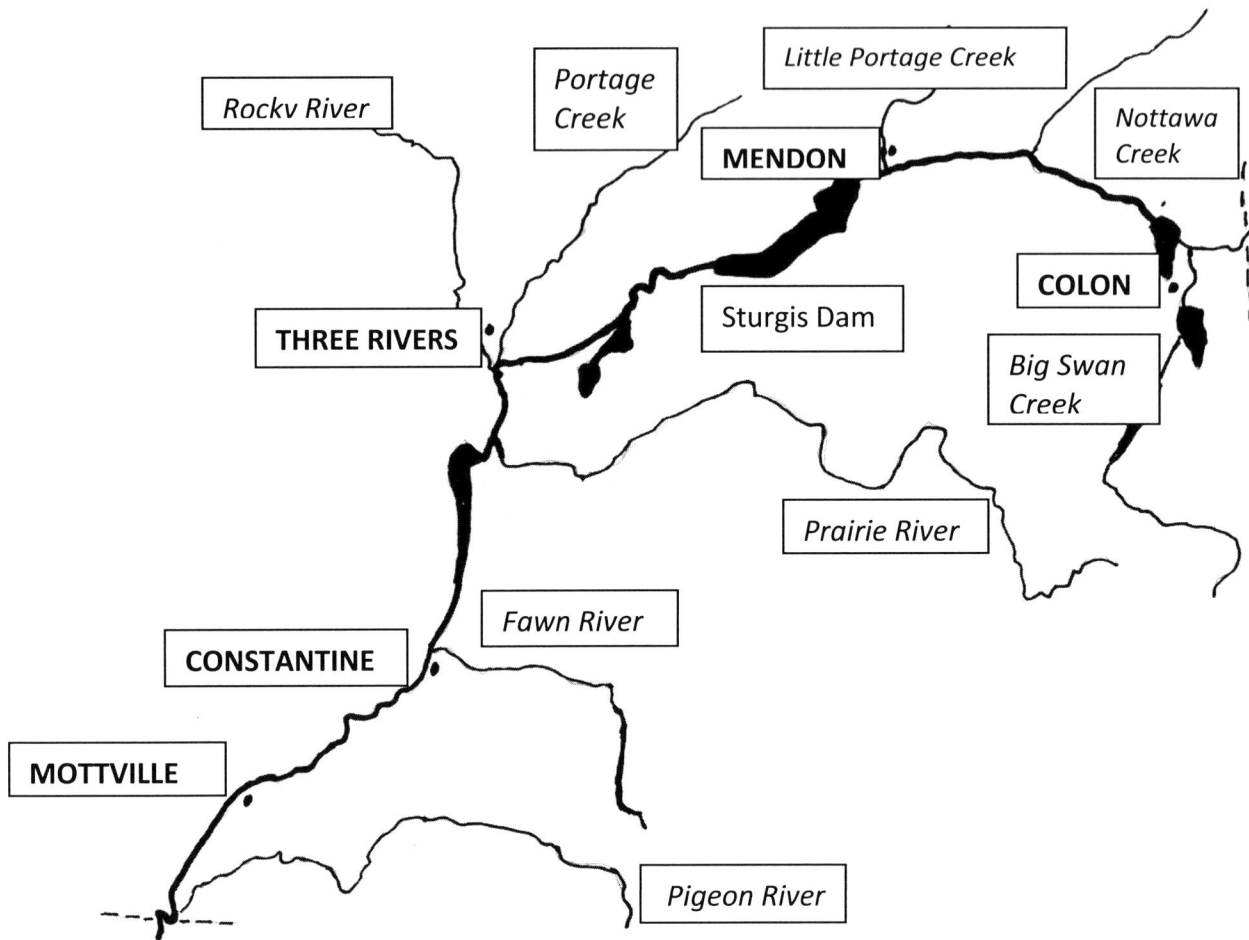

The St. Joseph River in the county named for it in Michigan is marked with plentiful feeder streams and several hydropower producing dams. The municipalities of St. Joseph County were also among the first to recognize the river as a major asset and to design canoeing routes, boating brochures, and, in 2006, dedicated the first Michigan Heritage Water Trail in the state.

The county is often known as "River Country" because it has more miles of navigable rivers and streams than any other county in Michigan. The river enters the county from Calhoun County (dotted line at far right) traveling east-west and exits to the south into the State of Indiana at the dotted line at the lower edge of this map.

Middle St. Joseph River
St. Joseph County, Michigan

138.1 Enter Colon Township, St. Joseph County.

137.25 Closed Bridge. Stowell Road crossed the stream north-south. In the summer of 2010 this crossing was blocked pending the possibility of work on the bridge. Stowell Road is the halfway point of the total 518 foot drop of the river from source to mouth.

136.8 – 135.5 **Colon**. The settlement was founded by Lorancie Schellhous in 1831. According to village sources, Schellhous and associates were trying to find a name for the new village and he "took up an old dictionary and the first word I put my eyes on was 'colon.'" He looked at the definition and it said "a mark of punctuation indicating a pause almost as long as that of a period . . . we called it Colon." At that time, before the damming of Swan Creek formed Palmer Lake, the configuration of lakes in the area, resembled a colon. A post office called Colon was established January 15, 1836, with Schellhous as the first postmaster. Colon was incorporated as a village in 1904. The famous magician Harry Blackstone (1885-1965) had a cottage there where he perfected his shows and offered residents a free glimpse before heading out on tour. In partnership with an Australian magician, Percy Abbot, he formed a company to produce illusions and other "magical" devices, a company which is still the most prominent and productive company in the world of magic. Both Harry Blackstone and his son, Harry Blackstone Jr., (1934-1997), a prominent stage and TV magician, are buried in Lakeside Cemetery, Colon. The town has an annual magic festival in the summer. Colon had a population of 1,227 in 2000 and an area of 1.7 square miles. On maps the village limits of Colon touch the St. Joseph River to the north in several places. However, the land that is north Colon is heavily wooded, privately owned and isolated. No public roads reach the northern boundary.

At Colon (dotted lines) the St. Joseph River comes from the east and enters Sturgeon Lake (upper left) barely touching the northern boundary of Colon. Swan Creek comes from the south and passes through Palmer Lake before joining the river at the northern boundary of the village.

91

Swan Creek pouring over Palmer Dam in downtown Colon in 2010.

136. Swan Creek passes through Palmer Lake to the south of the town, then continues northward through Colon and enters the river from the south at the north village limits. Big Swan Creek begins in Morrison Lake north of Coldwater, by the time it arrives at the St. Joseph it has already incorporated Little Swan Creek. Palmer Lake is a manmade lake controlled by Palmer Dam on Swan Creek in downtown Colon. The reinforced concrete dam was reconstructed in 1997.

135.5 Sturgeon Lake. The St. Joseph River enters Sturgeon Lake at about the midway point of the eastern shore. Sturgeon Lake Access is south of the river junction, just north of downtown off Blackstone Road. There is a memorial stone near the ramp which states:

Dedicated to all past CAAA members who helped stock area waters with walleye.
In memory of our friend and founder Jim Smith, 1952-2002.

135.2 Ainsley Drain passes through Havens and Adams Lake and enters Sturgeon Lake from the northeast just before the river exits from the lake.

135 The St. Joseph River exits Sturgeon Lake from the northwest corner.

134.5 Bridge. Farrand Road crosses northeast-southwest. There is small boat access at the downstream side of the Farrand bridge.

134.2 Remains of Old Farrand Bridge. The first bridge near this point was built in 1840, followed by a sturdier model which served until 1965. About 1988 the iron framework of the old bridge was removed and sold as scrap.

134.2 Enter Leonidas Township, St. Joseph County

133.5 McCauly Drain enters the river from the north.

133.6 Remains of old railroad bridge. Concrete pilings are all that is left of an

1889 railroad bridge which served the Battle Creek & Sturgis Railroad.

132.5 En Gedi Campground and River Resort The 40 acres that make up the campground, with 3,000 feet on the north bank of the St. Joseph River, has been a campground since the 1940s when it was developed as Baumann Farm Camp. It went through a succession of owners and purposes as Conestoga Horse Camp, Yehuda Youth Camp, Green Acres Campground, until new owners in 2005 began the development of En Gedi Campground and River Resort. The plan for the camp calls for 85 campsites, and a number of deluxe cabins and bath houses.

131.9 Olney or Mathews Bridge. Bennett Road, called West Jacksonburg Road on the north shore, crosses the river southwest-northeast. The present bridge was constructed in 1972. There is small boat access on the downstream south side of the bridge.

131.5 Remnants of an old dam used for power by the Becker Lard and Co. are visible just as the river bends left. Earlier there was a sawmill at about this point, and there are still signs of the old mill race.

131 Nottawa Creek enters from the northeast after passing through Kings Mills. Nottawa Creek begins near Leonidas, and on the way to the St. Joseph picks up Bear Creek and Pine Creek. Leidy Lake State Game Area, centered on Leidy Lake, is less than half a mile south of the river at this point. About a mile up Nottawa Creek from the St. Joseph is Rawson's Mill Park, where there is a mill which contains portions of

a building constructed in 1840. It is currently being restored.

130.5 Enter Mendon Township, St. Joseph County.

130.5 Bridge. North Sturgis Road (M-66) crosses the river north-south on the township line. River elevation at the bridge is 840 feet. This is the approximate site of Vandemark's Ford, in the early days the best fording place between Colon and Three Rivers. There is boat access on the southeast side.

130.2 Mendon dam site. A Federal study conducted by the Corps of Engineers in 1933 recommended that for additional water power in the area a dam be erected at approximately this site. Nothing was ever built.

128.3 Bridge. Nottawa Road crosses north-south and goes into downtown Mendon to the north.

Nottawa Bridge with an overlook from Reed Riverside Park, site of the annual Mendon Riverfest in August.

A postcard view of the old bridge at Mendon, date uncertain.

128.25 Reed Riverside Park on the north bank in Mendon just past the Nottawa Road bridge has a boardwalk which overlooks the river, picnic facilities and toilets. A large entertainment gazebo is a venue for the annual Mendon Riverfest held in August.

128.7 – 127.6 Mendon was a French settlement inhabited first by fur traders Peter and Gabriel Godfrois in 1829 and Francois Moutan in 1831. The first true settler was Leander Meatha (sometimes written as Metty) who arrived at the village site in 1834. The place was called **Wakeman** in 1843, named for early settlers Hiram and Mark Wakeman , but some local sources say it was platted as **Puddleburg** in 1844. The name Mendon was suggested by two early citizens, Benjamin F. House who came from Mendon, New York, in 1837 and Moses Taft who had arrived from Mendon, Massachusetts, in 1835. The name became official in 1845. The Mendon post office was established December 17, 1858 with William Pollett as postmaster. It was a station on the Grand Rapids & Indiana Railroad. The town became a stopping place for travelers because it is half way between Detroit and Chicago. It was incorporated as a village in 1875. Population in 2000 was 917 with an area of .8 square miles.

128 Little Portage Creek enters the river from the north near downtown. The **Mendon Country Inn,** formerly the Wakeman House, sits at 440 Main Street, Mendon, about 50 yards up the mouth of Little Portage Creek. An early hotel, built in 1843, it has been refurbished to serve as a bed and breakfast, and also has its own canoe and kayak dock on the creek with boats for rent. A variety of trips on the water can be arranged. Phone: 269-254-9291 or 1-800-304-3366.

127.45 Marantette Manor House. On the south bank on the top of the bluff stands the well-preserved home of Patrick and Frances (Mouton) Marantette built beginning in 1835. It was built at the approximate site of a trading post run by the Godfrois

The Marantette Manor house in Mendon

94

The Marantette bridge photographed in 2010. The structure has been closed for several years awaiting plans for its restoration.

An old railroad bridge at Mendon with the old Marantette bridge in the foreground.

Brothers. Marantette Farm was especially known as breeders of prize horses. Madame Marantette (born Emma Peck, 1849-1922) was a noted horsewoman, winning awards for high jumping and racing, all while using a sidesaddle. She also performed for a few years with a circus, both in the U. S. and in Europe. Local tradition has it that one day the Madame had been tippling and went out for a ride without any clothes, Lady Godiva style. When not on horseback Madam Marantette could be seen riding about town in a carriage drawn by her trotting ostrich.

127.63 Between the Marantette home and the bridge, near the fence on the south bank, there is a small stone memorial which states:

Father Hennepin
Landed Here
1680

Father Louis Hennepin was part of La Salle's expedition, and visited the area with La Salle during the winter of 1680-1681. Hennepin is said to have remained near Mendon for four years in a small cabin on Little Portage Creek. Some-where nearby, historians disagree about the exact site, is a ford the Indians called Grey Robes Ford.

127.6 **Marantette Bridge** is a picturesque, and often photographed, steel Pratt through truss bridge which was built in 1900 by the Massillion Bridge Company of Massillion, Ohio, the second bridge constructed at this site. It is no longer in use and efforts are being made toward restoration.

127.6 – 127-5 DNR boat access site at the end of Railroad Street in Mendon has a concrete ramp and toilets.

127.5 An abandoned railroad bridge, formerly part of the Grand Rapids & Indiana Railroad constructed in 1873, crosses parallel and just downstream from the Marantette Bridge. The railroad bridge can be accessed for fishing and photography by a pathway to the left of the toilet in the access site.

125.4 Bridge. Prairie Corners Road (Wakeman Road on north bank) crosses southeast-northwest as the river begins to widen as a backwater of the Sturgis Dam. There is small boat access on the northwest corner of the causeway.

125.3 Enter Nottawa Township, St. Joseph County.

123.2 Bridge. Angevine Road crosses north-south.

121.2 Enter Lockport Township, St. Joseph County.

121.1 **Pahl Point Park** on the north bank off Sturgis Dam Road, at the end of the causeway, has hiking trails, picnic tables, toilets and parking.

New entrance to Langley Bridge.

The Langeley covered bridge now spans less than a third of the total river above the Sturgis Dam. It was built in 1887, raised in 1910 to accommodate the increase in the width of the river when the Sturgis Dam was built, and refurbished extensively in 1951.

121. **Langley Covered Bridge**. Covered Bridge Road crosses the river southeast to northwest, partially on a covered bridge, the longest of Michigan's few remaining covered bridges. The length of the old bridge, shows the pre-Sturgis-dam width of the river at this point. The bridge was built in 1887 by Pierce Bodner of Parkville using white pine for the frame timbers and is of Howe truss construction, 282 feet long with three 94-foot spans. The bridge's name honors a pioneer Centreville family. When the Sturgis dam was built in 1910 the bridge was raised eight feet with a causeway extending to to reach shore. In 1950-51 extensive repairs were carried out by the St. Joseph County Road Commission including the insertion of steel I-beams under the structure for added strength. There is an historical marker on the southeast end of the bridge. Across the road from the south entrance to the bridge is the old Gardner School, built in 1852. The school was closed in 1945.

120.5 – 12 0. **Covered Bridge Park** is on the south bank above the dam. It has a launch ramp, parking, picnicking facilities, playground, walking trails, a fishing area and toilets. Below the dam there are many islands, the main channel of the river flows to the north.

120.0 Sturgis Dam. The City of Sturgis, located about 16 miles to the southeast of this point, owns and operates this dam to generate power for the city. It was built in 1911. According to the Electric Department of the City of Sturgis, about 20 percent of the needed power is produced by the Sturgis Dam and a city-run diesel generating plant. Any

The dam at Three Rivers on the St. Joseph River photographed in 2010.

additional power needed is purchased from American Electric Power. Sturgis is planning a celebration in 2011 for the centennial of the dam.

119.2 An abandoned steel bridge marks the approximate site where John Leland settled in 1834. He dammed Indian Run, a small creek just downstream from the old bridge, and began to manufacture reapers and threshing machines, including the V Sickle Harvester. Canoeists need to stay to the righthand bank and not get caught in the circle around an old oxbow.

117.8 Davis Bridge. Schweitzer Road (M-60) crosses east-west on the Davis Bridge. The river widens into a backwater at this point.

115.2 A large bayou goes off to the south. The main river channel goes to the north. There is a boat ramp and other facilities at **Stump Bay** on the south bank of the upper part of the bayou and a similar ramp and facilities on the northwest bank of **Noah Lake** which is at the deadend of the bayou off South River Road (County Highway 128) which crosses the water between Stump Bay and Noah Lake. There is a causeway with only a small bridged opening between the two parts of the bayou.

113. Jefferson Street goes along the west border of Riverside Cemetery on the north bank and deadends at the river where there is a small boat launch with accompanying parking.

113 – 11 0.8 **Three Rivers** T he first town platted at the confluence of the St. Joseph, Rocky and Portage rivers was created by Christopher Shinnaman in 1830 and named **Moab**. The following year George Buck and Jacob McIntefer platted a town named **St. Joseph** nearby, but it did not develop after they lost the

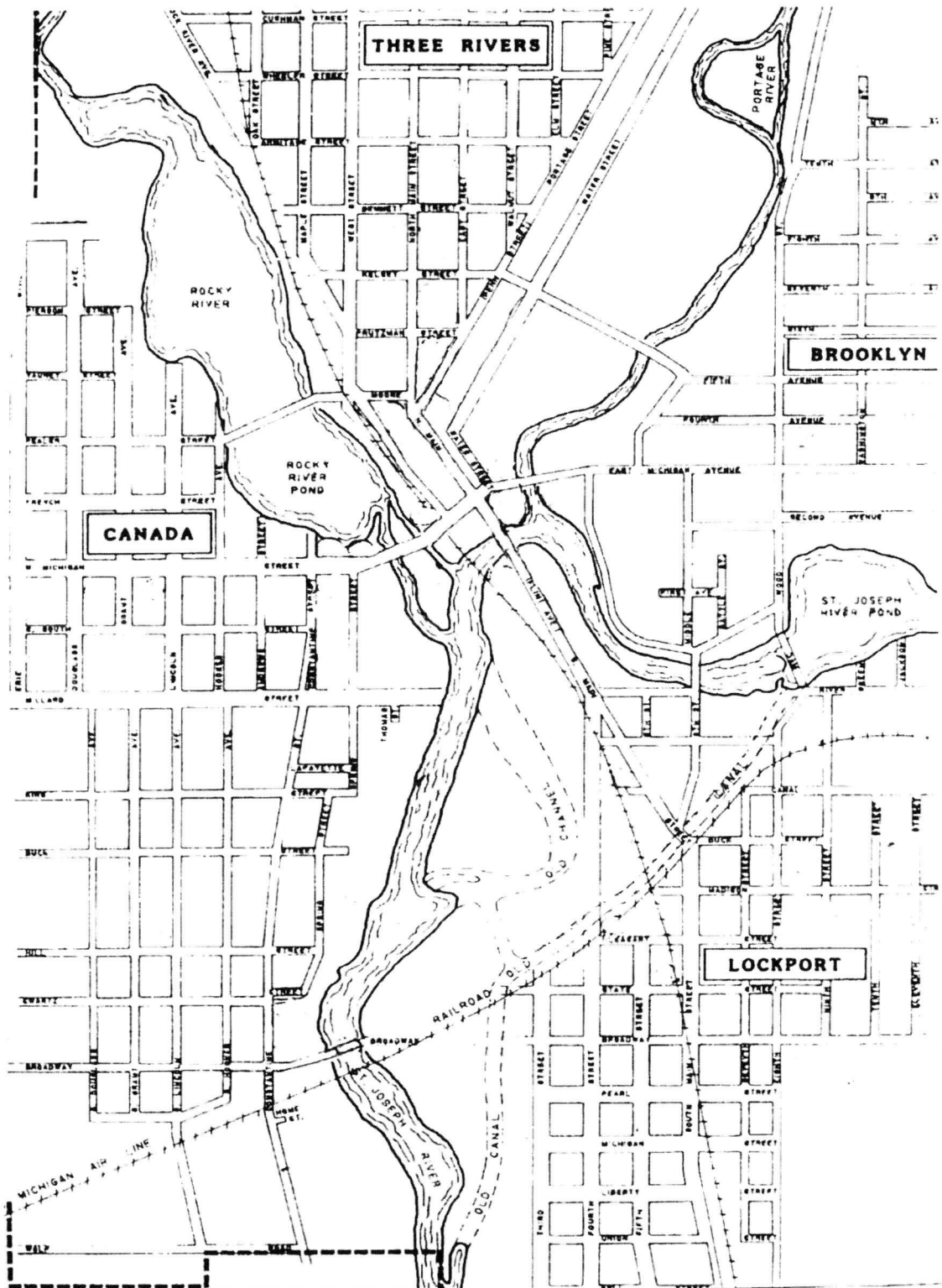

A map of Three Rivers showing the four main parts, Brooklyn, Canada, Lockport and Three Rivers, formerly called Moab, which joined together to form the town and the old Lockport canal bed and connections.

Sheffield Car Co, ❄ ❄ Three Rivers, Mich....

Manufacturers of ● ● ●

Hand Cars, Contractors Cars,

❖ ❖ ❖ **Plantation Cars,** ⌐ining Car Wheels ·· · · · · and Axles.

Steel Wheels. ◎ ◎ ◎ Chilled IronWheels, Etc.

Advertisement for Sheffield Car Co. of Three Rivers from a 1932 publication. Note the train running alongside the railroad canal and the old river channel in the background.

bid to be the county seat. John H. Bowman platted a new village which he called **Three Rivers** in November, 1836. In December George Buck and his associates platted **Lockport** to the southeast, naming it for their projected canal and waterpower projects. A post office, called **Bucks** was established October 10, 1831 with George Buck as its first postmaster, later called Lockport and, after Burroughs Moore became postmaster, the name was changed to Three Rivers in 1840. In 1871 the corporation limits of Three Rivers were extended to embrace all of the former plats, Lockport, in the bend of the St. Joseph River to the southeast; **Brooklyn** between the St. Joseph and the Portage rivers on the east, and **Canada** between the Rocky River and the St. Joseph on the west. Three Rivers was incorporated as a village in 1855 and as a city in 1895. In a 2008 census the population was 7,129 with 4.7 square miles of area.

112.8 **Three Rivers Dam**. Built in 1851 of wood and dirt, the structure was improved in 1879 with cement. The Wood Street bridge was built just upriver from the dam in 1911. The bridge cost $10,000 to build and $91,000 to demolish in 1984. The dam has a 750-foot earthen embankment on the right and a 200-foot embankment on the left, separated by a 283- foot gated spillway section. The 601-acre reservoir has a

The long bridge near the dam at Three Rivers about 1912.

100

normal surface elevation of 792.40 feet. The dam is operated today by the Grande Pointe Power Corporation and produces electrical power which is sold to the City of Sturgis.

Lockport Canal. (See map of Three Rivers on p.99) Beginning near the south approach to the current dam the Lockport Canal was built to bring power to that community in 1851 by the Lockport Hydraulic Company. The canal left the St. Joseph impoundment at the dam and traveled southwest reconnecting with the main river south of the Broadway bridge near the present city limits of Three Rivers. The canal was later filled in, but there is a depression which shows part of its path. The Sheffield Car Company, which made specialized electric railroad cars was one of the most successful industries along the canal. A Sheffield car was one of the first pieces of railroad equipment to cross the German lines into Lorraine at the end of World War I.

112.6 Bridge. Sixth Street crosses north-south. The first bridge at approximately this site was built in 1903 on Sixth Street. It was moved in 1925. Sometimes called the Middle Street bridge.

112.5 Portage River enters from northeast. The most distant source of the river is Portage Lake in Charleston Township, Kalamazoo County. The stream flows in a largely southerly direction and picks up Dorrance Creek, the outlet from a series of lakes near Vicksburg, Brown Creek which flows into Portage Lake, St. Joseph County, Garman Foster Drain, Felker Drain and Parkville Drain, before entering the St. Joseph River.

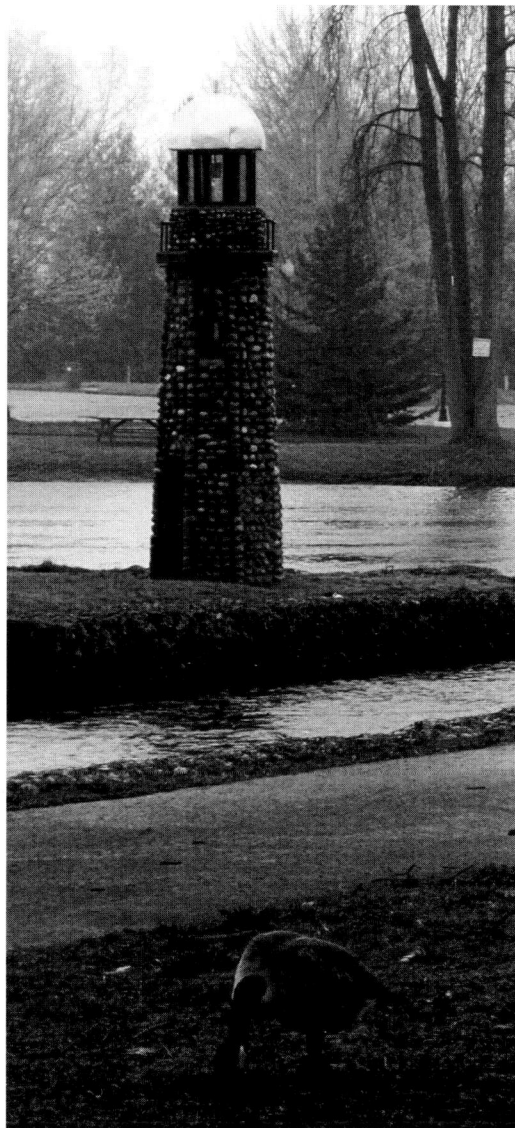

A stone lighthouse built at Scidmore Park in Three Rivers in the 1920s by former caretaker Estey Griffin.

112.45 **Riversby.** Between the mouth of the Portage River and the Main Street Bridge, is a large brick home called Riversby by the Silliman family, which built the structure around 1876 to serve as a blacksmith shop. Later they occupied the upper floors as a residence. Sue Silliman, a local librarian and historian, was its last resident. After her death in 1945 it was opened as a museum with a restored blacksmith shop and other displays of Three Rivers history.

112.4 Bridge. Main Street crosses north south and goes into downtown Three Rivers. The original bridge at this site was constructed in 1838. The present bridge was built about 1920 as a five-span concrete-arch bridge. The concrete fascia is molded to look like masonry blocks. The original orange pipe railings were replaced in 1952. At a site nearby there was said to be a Jesuit mission, possibly as early as 1667. On the southeast bank of the river between the Main Street Bridge and the railroad bridge stood the Magnetic Spring and Bathhouse, a popular tourist draw about the turn of the century.

112.35 Railroad bridge. An active railroad track runs behind the stores on Main Street in downtown Three Rivers crossing the St. Joseph River northwest-southeast.

112.3 Rocky River (some early references call it Rock River) enters from the northwest having already picked up the outlet from Huyck Lake, Sheldon Creek, and the outlet from Spring Lake, in Cass County. In St. Joseph County the Rocky River is joined by, the outlets from Cranberry and Ayers lakes, Four County Drain, and Flowerfield Creek which has already picked up Spring Creek. The dam on the Rocky River has been largely removed, leaving only a small mill pond with Memory Isle, a city park, in the middle of it. This was the site of an historic battle between two Native American tribes in 1802. The old mill race still runs under a brick building which was once used as a power plant and is now a

The settlement of Eschol on the river between Three Rivers and Constantine, on an 1838 map.

restaurant, giving the Rocky River two channels into the St. Joseph.

112.2 – 111.8 **Conservation Park**. On the peninsula on the south bank of the St. Joseph, across from the confluences of the Portage and Rocky rivers, this park includes a boat ramp, picnicking facilities and a canoe livery.

After joining with the Portage and Rocky rivers the St. Joseph River makes a 90 degree turn to the south.

112.3 – 111.6 **Scidmore Park** is on the west bank of the St. Joseph at the corner of West Michigan Avenue and Spring Street, just south of downtown Three Rivers. It has picnicking facilities including four shelters, a playground, restrooms, a petting zoo, and old cages left from a former exotic zoo. There is a lot of stonework, and a fieldstone lighthouse, most the work of Estey Griffin, a former caretaker. Oldtimers will remember Old Joe the talking crow, which often rode on Estey's shoulder. In 1977 the city bought additional riverfront to construct the River Walk Pathway which begins in Scidmore Park and continues in nearby Memory Isle Park.

111.3 Bridge. Broadway Street crosses east-west. The original bridge at the locality was built in 1878 and replaced in 1924. Between the Broadway Street bridge and the crossing at Constantine Road, the river marks its halfway point in mileage.

111.3 **Eschol**. In 1832 Benjamin M. King, a shoemaker by trade, and his wife Martha, were the first settlers at Eschol on the east bank of the river below Three Rivers. The following year the site was platted by Charles B. Fitch and Asa Wetherbee from a survey made by John S. Barry of Constantine. The dam went out in 1840 and was not rebuilt, so the settlement died, although it is included on *Farmer's Rail Road & Township Map of Michigan*, printed in 1863. In 1888 the former site of Eschol was described as "on the east bank of the St. Joseph, where the new bridge crosses the stream."

111.25 Railroad bridge. An old Penn Central bridge, just south of the Broadway bridge is no longer in use.

109.5 Prairie River enters from the southeast having already picked up Colon Ditch, Nottawa Ditch, and Spring Creek.

109. Bridge. Constantine Road crosses the river partially on a long peninsula in a north-south direction.

108.5 Enter Fabius Township, St. Joseph County. The river in Fabius Township is wide and quite marshy.

107. Enter Constantine Township, St. Joseph County

106 **Florence Bridge.** Withers Road crosses east-west on the Florence bridge. There is access for small boats and parking.

105.7 **Florence**. A post office called Florence a short distance east on Roys Road was opened July 29, 1837, in a tavern run by Lyman Vean, who had come to the area from Maine in 1834. It was named for the township, which had been named for Florence, Italy, by Michigan Territory representative from St. Joseph County Neal McGaffey. The post office closed in 1902.

Florence Station and post office shown on an 1873 railroad map before the building of Florence bridge. On this map Three Rivers and Lockport were still separate settlements. There are still townships called Lockport and Florence.

H. H. Riley of Constantine
Early Michigan Humorist

Henry Hiram Riley (1813-1888) was a Constantine attorney who, under the pseudonym of Simon Oakleaf , wrote a number of articles for *Knickerbocker Magazine* set in the fictitious Michigan town he called "Puddleford."But residents of Constantine, and other nearby parts of the St. Joseph River, would sometimes recognize the locale – and occasionally themselves. Riley was born in Great Barrington, Massachusetts, in 1813 and had worked on New York newspapers until 1842 when he moved to Kalamazoo. He studied law for six months and moved to Constantine where he worked as a lawyer, served as St. Joseph County prosecuting attorney and in the Michigan State Senate in 1850 and 1862. The sketches published in *Knickerbocker Magazine* were gathered and published in *Puddleford and Its People* in 1854 and went through several subsequent editions and revisions. Riley died in 1888 in Constantine.

(Above) An illustration from the book depicting a conversation with Jim Buzzard as he rests in his fishing boat on the river. Note the river steamboat in the background.

The rivers that watered this waste were large, and flowed from still deeper solitudes toward the great lakes. The sun, as ancient as they, rose and set upon them now as it did centuries ago. The forests upon their banks sprang up, flourished, waxed old, and died; and still the river ran, and new forests rose upon the ruins of the old, and the glory of the new stood implanted in the grave of the old. The bison, moose, and bear drank from the sources of these rivers, driven upward by the noise of civilization. But they had an interest to me beyond all this: they were the inlets of Christian missionaries more than a century ago. It was up these streams that the French Jesuit,* with his eye aloft, and the cross erect, paddled his solitary canoe among the aborigines. Here he built his camp-fire beneath the stars, and told his rosary in the awful presence of his God — how awful, indeed, in such a spot, at such a time! We can almost see the venerable man, and hear the dip of his oar; the water-fowl scream, scared, and dive along before him, and the Indian stands upon the bank in his presence, like a monument in wonder.

The foot-prints of the Jesuits are still found upon the bluffs of these rivers. Mounds, which were thrown by them into square and circular forms, now roofless and silent, and matted all over with vines, still bear witness to their devotion. Yet, how little is thought of them now! Because the Jesuits did not till the earth, and sow, and reap, and swell the commerce of the world: but did n't they sow? They sowed the seeds of everlasting life among the simple children of the forest; and *they* have sown from age to age since, and many an Indian still offers the prayer which was taught his forefathers so long ago.

Such, reader, were the woods around Puddleford, and such

* Father Hennepin and others.

Above, a page from the 1854 edition of Puddleford and Its People *giving H. H. Riley's observations on the work of the early missionaries in the valley of the St. Joseph River.*

The Constantine power house erected in 1902. This photo is from a 1908 postcard.

103 **Constantine Dam** Although there had been earlier dams in the area it was not until 1868, when navigation began to wane, that a company was organized to improve the water power in Constantine. A "substantial" dam was built across the St. Joseph River with a raceway on each side of the river. A city power house was erected in 1902. The operation is still in use as part of the Indiana Michigan Power unit of American Electric Power.

102.5 Fawn River (earlier known as Crooked Creek) enters from the east, picking up Sherman Mill Creek just before the confluence.

102.4 – 100.3 **Riverview Park** with a boat launch is on the south bank. Access by car is from Riverside Drive. Park facilities include a playground, picnic tables and grills.

102.3 Bridge. Washington Street bridge carries U.S. 131 across the river northwest-southeast and goes into downtown Constantine. At the east end of the bridge a large rock marks **Shelby's Park** at Riverside Drive. A gazebo and park benches are located along the river.

103-101.5 **Constantine** The first settler in the area of Constantine was William Meek who came in 1828 and built a sawmill on the Fawn River, and the place was known as **Meek's Mill**. Niles F.Smith, businessman and lawyer, had the name changed in 1835 to honor the Roman Emperor Constantine the Great. The original plat of Constantine was created in 1831 by William Meek when there were only five families on the site. John S. Barry, later a state senator and governor opened in a store in 1834 until his death in 1870. He was the town's first postmaster when the office was established January 15, 1836. Historic industries include two casket companies and The New World Washing Machine Company. Constantine was incorporated as a village in 1837. The Lake Shore and Michigan Southern Railroad was compelled, by the terms of its charter, to make the St. Joseph River a point on its line, so a station was established at Constantine in the early 1850s. The village is largely on the south bank. The population in 2000 was 2,095 with a land area of 1.7 square miles. Constantine was the home of H. H. Riley, a well-known attorney, judge and author. (See pages 104-105.)

100. Access on the east bank with a paved parking area and boat ramp.

98.2 Black Run enters from the north having already picked up Hassinger Drain.

97.6 Enter Mottville Township, St. Joseph County, after a brief dip into Mottville Township the river turns northward and re-enters Constantine Township before turning southwestward back into Mottville Township, although the north bank remains in Mottville Township nearly to the dam.

97.1 **Mill Creek Park** stands on land owned by the Indiana Michigan Power unit of American Electric Company, but managed by Mottville Township. A small parking area provides walking access to the area below the Mottville Dam on the north bank.

97 Mill Creek enters from the north having already merged with Profile Lake Drain and the outlet from Little Wood Lake.

96.4 **Mottville Dam**. Just past the dam on the south bank is the Mottville Canoe Park, with a boat launch, picnic tables, toilet, and a marked portage. Dam and park may be accessed by road from Riverside Drive on the south side of the

The bridge at Constantine from a 1909 postcard showing the Constantine power plant at the far right.

The Mottville power plant was still in active use in 2010..

river where there is a parking area. The dam at Mottville was constructed in 1920 at the cost of $560,994 connecting the Indiana and Michigan Electric Company with the lines of the Inter-State Public Service Company. Herman L. Hartenstein, U. S. Representative, initiated a bill in Congress granting the right to erect the dam. It is now producing electricity for the Indiana Michigan Power division of American Electric Power. The dam is 23 feet in height with a normal pool level of 770.38 feet above sea level

96.5 – 95.8 **Mottville** was first settled by Joseph Quimby who arrived in 1828. The village was platted by George Risdon and John R. Williams in 1830. Hart L. Stewart was the first postmaster in June of 1830. Mottville Township, a part of White Pigeon Township until 1837, was named after the settlement which was named after early settler Alva Mott. The community is unincorporated and is mostly residential.

96.2 Former bridge site. The Great Sauk Trail, originally an Indian trail which connected Detroit and Chicago, crossed the St. Joseph River at a shallow spot nearby. Responding to a pioneer desire to push into the interior of the peninsula the federal government surveyed the old trail and, in 1825, opened it as the Chicago Road. The first bridge to cross the river at Mottville was erected in 1833-34 and was replaced by a pile supported bridge in 1845. In 1867 this was replaced with a covered Burr arch truss structure. The crumbling shore abutments are visible in the river and on the shore at this point.

96.2 Pedestrian Bridge. In 1922 the Burr arch truss bridge which had been just upstream was replaced with a reinforced concrete girder camelback bridge designed by the Michigan State Highway Department. The structure is 270 feet long with three 90-foot spans. It is a classic example of a type of bridge built mainly in Michigan and Ontario

108

and was constructed by Smith & Nichols of Hastings. When a modern bridge was built just downstream in 1990, the old camelback bridge was refurbished and converted for use by pedestrians.

96.15 Bridge. The new U. S. 12 bridge crosses the river southeast-northwest.

96. The township boundaries are irregular at this point and divided by the river. The northwest bank is in Porter Township, Cass County, and the southeast bank in Mottville Township, St. Joseph County, to the Indiana-Michigan state line.

92. Pigeon River from White Pigeon enters from the east, just north of the state line, having already picked up Pigeon Creek, Turkey Creek, Fly Creek and Buck Creek. The Pigeon River begins near Shipshewana, Indiana.

91.5 After receiving the Pigeon River the St. Joseph flirts with the state line, with the south bank even partially entering Indiana at this point before a last loop in Michigan, and a southward plunge into Indiana.

The concrete girder camelback bridge at Mottville, probably photographed shortly after it was built in 1922. A new bridge was built in 1990 for vehicles, but the old camelback was refurbished and is open to pedestrian traffic.

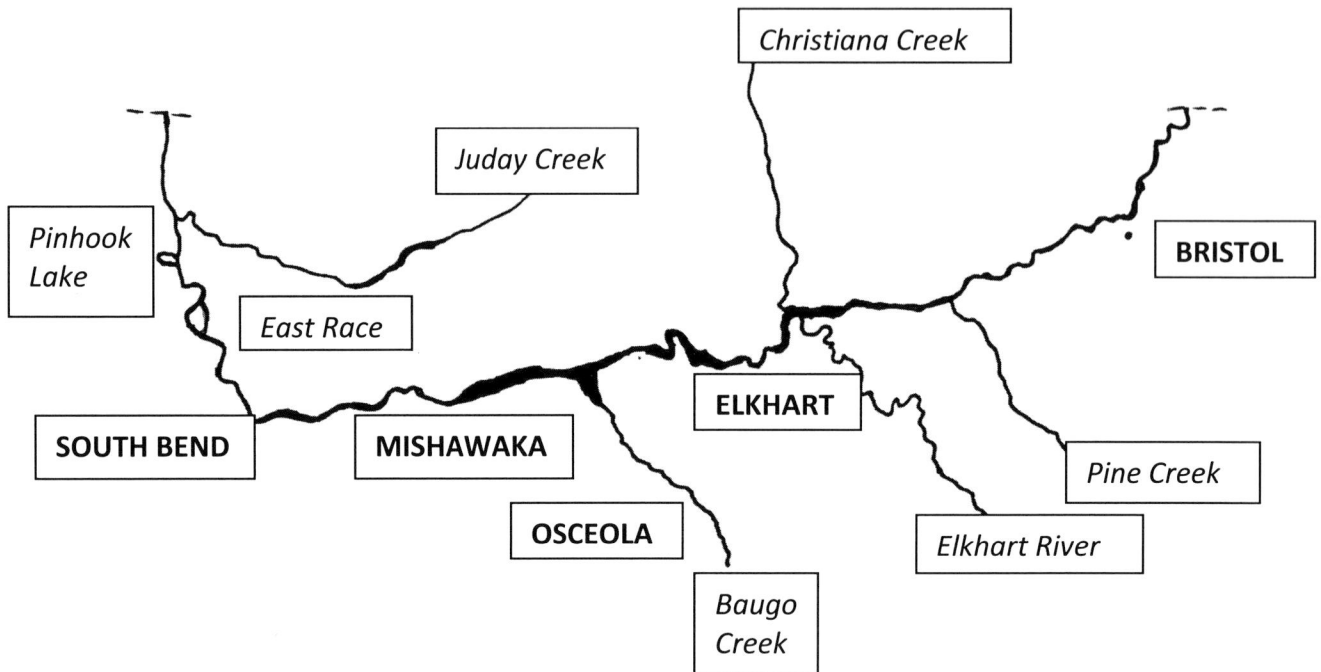

The St. Joseph River begins in Michigan and ends in Michigan. Only about 50 miles, or 25 percent of its length, dips southward into the State of Indiana, but it is the most populated portion of the river. On the 2000 federal census the three largest cities in Indiana on the St. Joseph totaled a population of 206,220. The three largest cities on the river in Michigan are St. Joseph, Benton Harbor and Niles, all in Berrien County, and their combined population in 2000 was only 32,175.

The Indiana stretch of the river was the area where power produced from the stream was most used for large scale industry. Big volume industries included the Ball Band/ Uniroyal plant at Mishawaka, a Studebaker factory just south of the Elkhart River junction with the St. Joseph, and other major manufacturers of musical instruments, toys, plows, sewing machines and household appliances. This led to prosperity for the region, but, it would be discovered later, at a cost to the environment.

Today no municipalities along the river have worked as hard to create parks, pedestrian bridges and river hiking and biking trails as those in Indiana sometimes using former industrial sites.

The Middle St. Joseph River
Elkhart and St. Joseph Counties, Indiana

91.1 Michigan-Indiana state line. After the St. Joseph River touches Indiana at about mile 91.5, it turns northward back into Michigan for nearly a half mile before heading south and entering Washington Township, Elkhart County, Indiana.

89.3 Trout Creek enters from the northwest. Trout Creek begins in the southeast corner of Cass County, Michigan, and merges with Mud Creek just south of the state line.

88. Bridges. The Indiana Toll Road (I-80 and I-90) crosses the river east-west on twin bridges.

87.3 Little Elkhart River enters from the east via Middlebury having already picked up the Rowe Eden Ditch, Haarer Ditch, Hostetler Ditch, Emma Creek, East Lake Ditch, Mather Ditch and the outlet from Cass Lake in La Grange County.

87.6 – 86. **Bristol** In 1834 when Dr. Henry H. Fowler arrived at the little settlement near the junction of the Little Elkhart and the St. Joseph rivers, already about a dozen families were in the area. He laid out a town on the west side of the Goshen Road and called the place **Sydneyham** after his birthplace in England. That same year Samuel P. Judson, a merchant of Buffalo, New York, but a native of Indiana, set up a town on the east side of the Goshen road which he called Bristol. The two settlements were part of the incorporated Town (village) of Bristol in 1869.

Population of Bristol in 2000 was 1,382 with an area of 2.5 square miles.

87.5 – 87.1 Hermance Park is five acres in area and located on the southwest bank of the St. Joseph where the Little Elkhart River enters the larger river. The park was presented to the town by the Bristol Conservation Club in 1959 and is named for Farnham "Bud" Hermance (1898-1975) who, according to a plaque, "devoted his entire adult life to the betterment of this community." It is the center of an annual Bridge to Bridge Canoe race in September and other canoeing events throughout the summer. Hermance Park hosted the U.S. Canoe Association annual event in 2008. It has picnic facilities, toilets, playground, and a pavilion which may be rented. Adjacent to the park is a public fishing site and an Indiana DNR river access site with two boat ramps and a gravel parking lot.

Washington Township and the Town of Bristol from an 1876 atlas. The stream going off to the right is the Little Elkhart River.

87.4 – 87..2 **Congdon Park** is a four acre park on the northwest river bank on a peninsula which juts into the river, just before several islands. It was acquired by the municipality in 1987 mainly to serve as a site for the Harvest Celebration or Homecoming Festival which had been held every summer since 1883. Although the festival now has a new venue, Congdon Park hosts the annual Storytellers Festival each September. The park is named for Earl Congdon, whose family for three generations owned the Congdon Drug Store in Bristol. Facilities include a playground, picnicking tables, a paved walking path and a wooden fishing platform at the south end. The park is accessible on land from North Division Street northeast of the bridge.

The old Beardsley grist mill on the north bank of the river at Elkhart. The mill race ran from Christiana Creek on the north into the St. Joseph River.

87.2 Bridge. North Division Street crosses the river south-north and goes into downtown Bristol on the south bank.

87. **Cummins Park** A three acre park located in downtown Bristol on the south bank of the river directly behind the Elkhart County Historical Museum, which is located in the Rush Memorial Center, a former school. The name honors Cloyce Cummins, a long-time Bristol resident and former fire chief. From the parking lot which serves both museum and park, there are paths to the river, tennis and basketball courts, and a small playground. The flintlock/tomahawk reenactment is held at Cummins Park each August. The old Cathcart Cemetery, with burials from the 1830s to the 1850s, is contained by a white picket fence on the east edge of the park.

85.7 Bristol dam site. A federal survey of the St. Joseph River in 1933 recommended a site in this area for a dam to provide additional hydroelectric power. It was never built.

84.2 **Nibbyville.** A small unincorporated community called Nibbyville is located near a spot on the north bank of the river where several tall power lines cross.

83.3 Sheep Creek enters from the southeast.

82. From this point the township boundaries of Osolo Township on the north and Concord Township on the south, both in Elkhart County, bisect the river.

Looking north up Main Street in downtown Elkhart from a 1910 postcard.

81.5 Pine Creek which enters from the south, begins in Middlebury Township as a north and south fork. After the two branches merge it picks up Indian Creek.

81 -- 80.5 **Garden Village,** an unincorporated area, shows on some maps on the north bank, with a short canal which serves as a marina.

80.5 -- 73.2 **Elkhart** In 1829 a post office called **Pulaski** was established on the north side of the St. Joseph River. Two years later Dr. Havilah Beardsley moved to the area from Ohio and purchased one square mile of land from a French-Indian named Pierre Moran, and started a rival village which he called Elkhart. The origin of the city's name is uncertain. One source says it is after the city's Island Park, in the middle of the St. Joseph River, which looks like an elk's heart. Another story claims that the city was named for Shawnee Indian Chief Elkhart, cousin of Tecumseh, and the father of Princess Mishawaka, the namesake of the City of Mishawaka, eight miles up the river. Industries began in Elkhart using water-generated power include the Conn Company and other musical instrument factories, the Miles Medical Company, and, in 1932, the Studebaker car plant. The city was a major producer of early travel trailers and, in 1949, was declared "Trailer Capital of the World." Elkhart was incorporated as a town (village) in 1858, and as a city in 1875. In 2000 Elkhart had a population of 51,874 and a total area of 22.3 square miles.

113

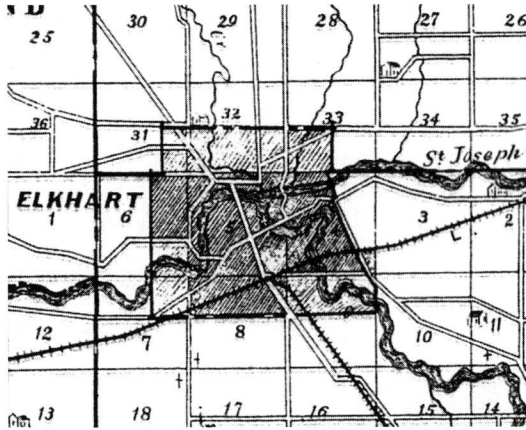

A map of Elkhart from 1876, the Goshen Road cuts diagonally through the town. The Elkhart River is at lower right.

79. Putterbaugh Creek enters from the north. The creek begins at Heaton Lake to the northeast.

78.5 Lilly Creek enters from the north.

Just after Lilly Creek the river continues south now entirely in Concord Township, Elkhart County, Indiana.

78.45 **Martin's Landing**. A small park run by the City of Elkhart on the south bank where the river comes very close to East Jackson Boulevard at Crescent Street. There is a dock for fishing and picnic tables.

78.4 Dock of the **Elkhart River Queen** on the south bank. The vessel in 2010 was taking Sunday cruises up and down (although there is little "down" because the dock is less than a mile above the Elkhart Dam) the St. Joseph River as well as being available for charter groups and occasions the rest of the week from June to September. The boat was constructed in 1947 and ran for nearly 20 years at about half of its present size. It was lengthened to 65 feet in 1965 and is licensed to carry up to

150 passengers. The Sunday cruise lasts from 2 to 4 p.m. The dock is located at 110 Bower Court off East Jackson Boulevard across the street and slightly east of **American Park** where customers are asked to park. Call 574-295-1179 for reservations.

77.8 **Elkhart Dam**. In 1867 the Elkhart Hydraulic Company built the first dam in this area across the St. Joseph River. By 1870 the installation was producing 4,500 horsepower for the residents and industry of the town. In 1912 the old dam was replaced by a new and larger dam and a power plant which is still producing electricity, now operated by Indiana Michigan Power, a subsidiary of American Electric Power. Elevation at the dam is 742 feet.

77.75 Bridge. Johnson Street crosses the river north-south, just west of the dam. Until 2010 this bridge was a metal riveted Warren deck truss bridge built in 1918, although it had been considerably modified. The old bridge was entirely removed in the summer of 2010 and a new multi-lane span was under construction.

77.6 Remains of old railroad bridge, dismantled.

77.3. Christiana Creek (called Christian Creek on some maps) enters from the north, coming from a series of lakes including Eagle, Juno and Christiana lakes, near Adamsville, Michigan. The first mills in the area were powered with a long race from Christiana Creek to the St. Joseph River constructed by Havilah Beardsley in 1840.

77.3 – 77. **Island Park**, in the river near the mouth of the Elkhart River, is

114

New Power Plant, St. Joe River, Elkhart, Ind.

The Elkhart dam and power plant not long after its reconstruction in 1912.

New Bridge over the St. Joe River, Bristol, Ind.

The Johnson Street all-riveted Warren deck truss at Elkhart after its construction in 1918. The structure had been widened and changed several times although it was still considered an historic bridge worth saving when it was demolished and replaced in the summer of 2010.

accessible by a bridge from Sycamore Street on the south bank. The city purchased the island for $200 in 1881. It is connected by footbridge to **Lundquist Bicentennial Park** on the south bank, named for Eldy Lundquist, a former local sportscaster and later a state representative. Facilities at Lundquist include walking trails, toilets, and picnic tables.

77. Ruthmere. Now a museum, the mansion called Ruthmere was built in 1908 for Albert and Elizabeth Beardsley to the design of E. Hill Turner, a Chicago architect. It is in Beaux Arts style with Prairie accents and is considered one of the finest of the large homes that line much of the St. Joseph riverbanks in Indiana. The building was restored by the Ruthmere Foundation and members of the Beardsley family and was opened to the public in 1973. The home of Dr. Havilah and Rachel Beardsley, the founding family of Elkhart, was acquired by the Ruthmere Foundation in 2007 and is currently under restoration nearby. Ruthmere is on the north bank opposite Island Park at 302 East Beardsley Avenue.

77. Elkhart River enters the St. Joseph River from the south. The Elkhart is a major Indiana river. The north branch and the south (or Rimmell) branch begin to the southeast near Albion, Indiana. After the two branches join they continue westward and merge with Turkey Creek which comes from Lake Wawasee, Solomon Creek, Rock Creek and Yellow Creek before joining the St. Joseph, where there is also a gauging station.

76.9 Beardsley Park on the northeast corner of the Main Street bridge in front

of Ruthmere is a neighborhood park in the shadow of downtown. Near Beardsley Street is a National Historical Chemical Landmark sign which celebrates the development by Miles Laboratory of the first test strip, a test for glucose needed by diabetics. "This led to the development of other strips to test for protein and other substances."

76.8 Bridge. Main Street Memorial Bridge crosses north-south in the middle of downtown Elkhart. It is dedicated to the veterans of the area, and includes memorial pylons to World War I members of the armed forces. The south end of the first bridge across the St. Joseph was in the same location as the present Main Street Bridge, but the northern end extended about seventy-five feet farther east, so that it was at right angles with the current. Ice breakers were constructed on the east side in order to break up ice packs as they came sweeping down the river. Built about 1840, the first bridge was designed to be a covered bridge, but it was never completed so, after about 15 years, the timber rotted away and one span was carried down with the current. Local legend relates that when it was replaced downtown businessmen fought to have the new bridge cross the river at the foot of their street. As a compromise it was decided to build the bridge from the alley between two streets. A concrete deck arch bridge was constructed at this point in 1927.

76.4 Bridge. Sherman Street crosses east-west and becomes Bower Street west of the river. There is a DNR public access site on the southwest corner.

76.2 Bridge. West Lexington Street crosses the river east-west. A three-span concrete bridge was first constructed at this site in 1926 by the M. E. White Company.

75.3 Bridge. Bridge Street crosses the river east-west. It is a concrete stringer bridge and was originally constructed in 1939 by H. L. Maddocks Company. Elevation just above the bridge is 717 feet.

74.5 – 75.25 **McNaughton Park** is a city park located just past the Bridge Street bridge on the north bank off Arcade Avenue. Facilities include two boat launches, playground, picnic tables, sports fields, tennis courts, toilets, fishing area, concession stand and walking trails. It was a gift to the city by John McNaughton.

75.2 Bridge. Nappanee Street (State Road 19) crosses north-south near the sewage treatment plant.

75.2 Enter Cleveland Township on the north bank and Baugo Township on the south bank, both in Elkhart County. The township boundary bisects the channel eastward to the county line.

73.3 **Treasure Island County Park** is a four acre site run by the Elkhart County Parks and Recreation Department on the south bank. It has picnic facilities, a fishing area and good access for canoes and kayakers. By road the park is located on Road 16, eight-tenths of a mile west of State Route 19. The park gates are closed November 30 to April 1.

73. – 71. There is a two-lobed peninsula jutting out into a river bend with several short canals and marinas.

Oddly shaped peninsula in the St. Joseph River near the west edge of Elkhart County.

70.7 Cobus Creek enters from the north, having already picked up Gast Ditch.

69.6 Enter Penn Township, St. Joseph County, Indiana.

69.6 Bridge. Ash Road crosses the river north-south on a concrete bridge first constructed in 1929 by the Rieth-Riley Construction Company, William S. Moore, engineer.

69. Baugo Creek enters the river through the broad Baugo Bay on the south. The bay was created when the water level

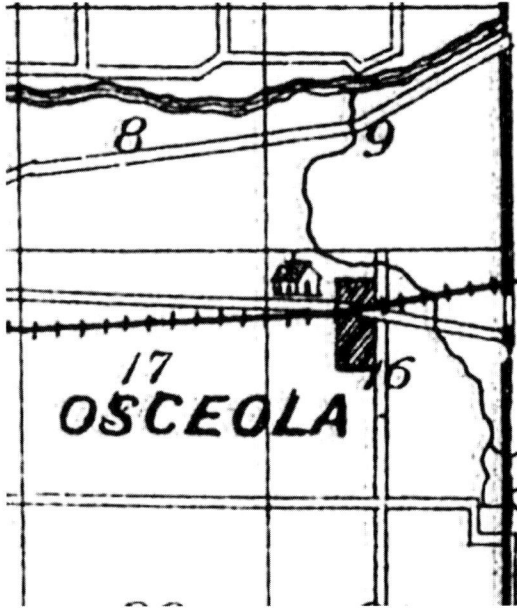

Osceola was begun in the 1830s nearly a mile south of the river on Baugo Creek. This map is from an 1876 atlas.

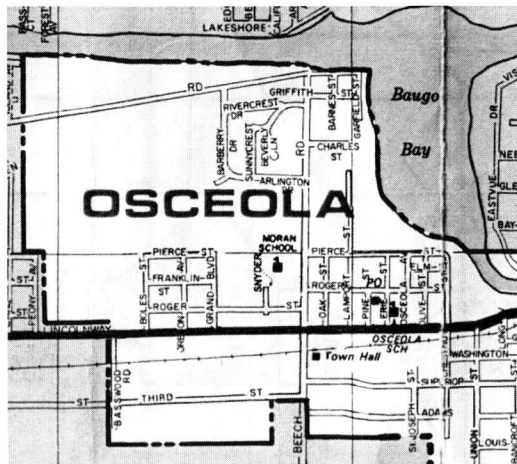

When the Hen Island (Twin Branch) dam was built in 1903 the water level rose on Baugo Creek to create a large bay east of town. The town then expanded to the north acquiring river frontage.

rose as a result of the Twin Branch Dam in 1903. At the south end of the bay along the creek is the 214-acre **Ferrettie/Baugo Creek County Park**, located on County Line Road, north of U. S. 933 in Osceola. The park is

recycled from a former dump site. The facilities include an 18-hole disc golf course, picnic tables, innertubing in the winter and a boat launch on the south end of Baugo Bay.

69. – 68.3 **Osceola,** according to some sources, was originally called **Bancroft's Mill**. It was begun along Baugo Creek just under a mile from its junction with the St. Joseph River, where a dam formed a millpond for the first flour mill. It was first platted in 1837, but replatted by William Thrall in 1856. The town is named after a part Indian man born Billy Powell in Alabama in 1804 and later known by his Indian name, Osceola, derived from *os-y-o-hol-la*, a ceremonial drink. He was influential with the Seminole Indians of Florida during their fight to avoid the American government's efforts to relocate them in the 1830s. To get him out of the way government representatives invited him to a meeting, arrested him, and threw him in prison where he died in 1838 from malaria. The name was suggested for the town by John A. Hendricks, who is said to have been a friend of U. S. General Thomas Sidney Jesup, who had captured Osceola. The place grew rapidly after the Indiana Railway Company ran its tracks into the community in 1851 and, in 1900, erected a powerhouse for the interurban. The community expanded in all directions and now has just under a mile of frontage on the St. Joseph River west of Baugo Bay between Elkhart and Mishawaka. The population was 1,859 in the 2000 census with 1.4 square miles of area.

68.7 **Eagle Point**. On some maps the southwest corner of the entrance into Baugo Bay is designated Eagle Point.

118

The Mishawaka Woolen Mills from a 1918 postcard. Note the white pipe extending from the righthand building which is sending waste directly to the river. The old mill was bought in the 1950s by the Uniroyal Corporation.

67.4 – 62. **Mishawaka**. The town was founded in 1832 by Alanson Hurd who, with his partner William Earl, built the first blast furnace to process the local bog iron in Indiana. In July of 1833 he laid out and platted the village of **St. Joseph Iron Works**, on the south bank of the river about four miles above South Bend. They built one of the first bridges across the St. Joseph River in the summer of 1836 where there was a shallow ford. In June of 1836 Joseph Bartlett and James R. and Grove Lawrence laid out the town of **Indiana City** on the north bank opposite the Hurd settlement. When a post office was established in 1834 it was called Mishawaka and eventually included both settlements as well as additional territory. In the late 1800s it was nicknamed the "Peppermint Capital of the World" because of the vast crop of

that plant in the nearby swamps. In 2000 Mishawaka had a population of 46,557 with a land area of 16 square miles.

The name Mishawaka is one of those Indian names complicated by semantics and tied up in legends. One writer claims it is derived from *m'she-wah-kee-ki* said to mean "country of dead trees" and might have something to do with the Indian practice of girdling trees to create farmland, or perhaps the smallpox epidemic which ravaged the Potawatomi village at that site. Others relate it to a Potawatomi word meaning "swift rapid" or "swift river." The legend is that the town was named after Princess Mishawaka, daughter of Shawnee Chief Elkhart. She was taken prisoner by the Potawatomi during the battle at Three Rivers in 1803. The lady was in love with the white hunter Dead Shot,

Hen Island (later called Twin Branch) dam and powerhouse from a 1910 postcard.

but had to struggle with Gray Wolf who tried to "save" her from the inter-racial marriage. The municipality leans toward the second explanation and is often called "The Princess City."

67.8 Bridge. Bittersweet Road crosses the river north-south on a modern concrete bridge.

67.5 – 67. **Margaret Prickett Marina Park**, named for a former Mishawaka mayor, is a 15 acre park on the north bank between East Jefferson Boulevard and the river. It has a pavilion for rent, playground, picnicking facilities, fishing piers and two boat launch ramps.

67.1 **Richard Clay Bodine State Fish Hatchery** was built in 1983 specifically to implement the St. Joseph River Interstate Cooperative Salmonid Management Plan. Accessible off Jefferson Boulevard between Bittersweet and Currant Roads. The hatchery specializes in skamania (summer run) steelhead, stocking

241,000 annually from Mishawaka's Merrifield Park, along with 45,000 winter run steelhead, creating a nearly year-round steelhead fishery. It is named for an Indiana legislator and sportsman who was instrumental in passing legislation creating the interstate management plan.

67.1 Lang's Bayou, on the south bank, extends a lake-like presence into east Mishawaka.

67. **Twin Branch Dam**. The dam site was originally called Hen Island because an old settler made a living raising and selling chickens on a nearby island. Since chickens don't fly well, and were surrounded by water, there was no need for fences. The dam began generating power in December of 1903. The plan of its investors, the St. Joseph & Elkhart Power Company, was to transmit this power to Elkhart. In 1907 the dam became part of the Indiana and Michigan Electric Company and the name of the installation was changed from Hen Island Dam to Twin Branch Dam to coincide with a surrounding residential development then known as Twin Branch. In 1922 the entire assets of the Indiana and Michigan Electric Company were acquired by the American Gas & Electric Company, which built a large generating station at Twin Branch. The facility is still in operation in 2010, part of the Indiana Michigan Power division of American Electric Power. Elevation at the site is about 717 feet, with a fall of 21 ½ feet.

66.9 Twin Branch Creek enters the river just past dam from the south.

66.8 – 66.6 **Laing Park** This 2.4 acre park is on both sides of Eller Creek near its junction with the St. Joseph on the south bank. It is reached off Lincolnway, practically in the shadow of the Capitol Avenue bridge.

66.7 Eller Creek enters from the south through the **Frank Zappia Public Access Site.** This is a favorite fishing area within sight of the Twin Branch dam. It is named for a Mishawaka businessman at the suggestion of his son, Joseph Zappia, a former Mishawaka city council member.

66.65 Bridge. Capitol Avenue crosses the river north-south at the southern boundary of the access area.

66.1 – 65.4 **Eberhart-Petro Municipal Golf Course.** Eighty-nine acres of open space is provided by this golf course which is located on both sides of the river. The golf course began in 1929 as a nine hole course on the south side of the river. In 1949 it expanded to Petro Park north of the river and added nine more holes. The 5502 yard layout is a par 70 course. The signature hole is #18, a 489-yard, par 5, requiring a long downhill tee shot over the river to an extremely narrow landing area. The river comes into play on three other occasions, and a creek meanders across some holes on the back nine. Entrance is at the north end of State Street, east of Mishawaka Avenue. There is a parking area and a boat launch on the downstream left end of the golf course where there is an old stone bridge. A small wooden bridge serves the upstream portion of the course. The combined course is named for benefactors Frederick George Eberhart and Mason L. Petro.

65.4 Miami Island (often called Monkey Island, though nobody is quite sure why) is a five acre island park in the river,

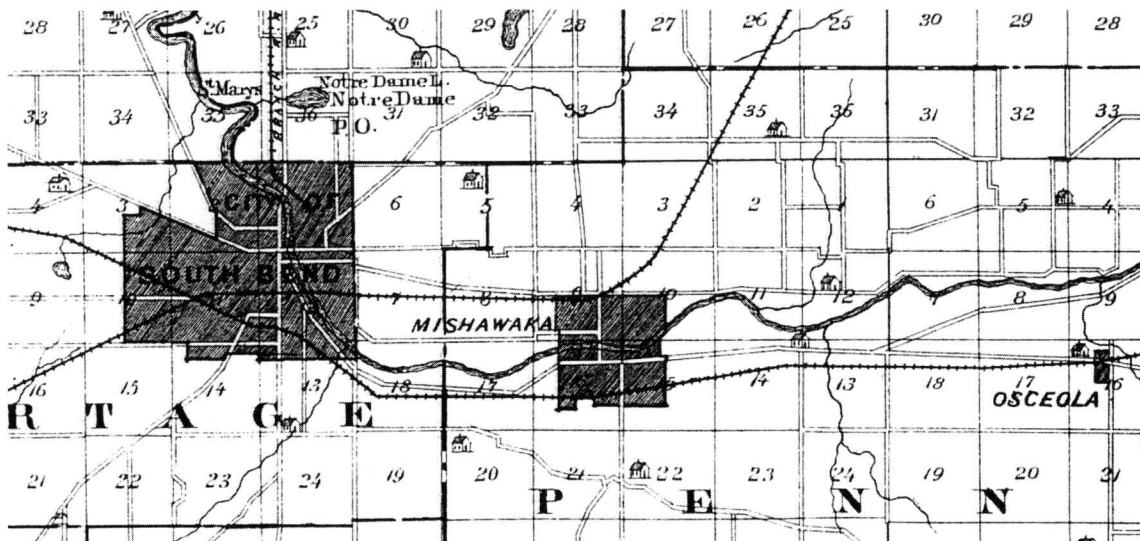

The three towns in St. Joseph County, Indiana, on this 1876 map (four if you include the Notre Dame post office) were several miles apart. The distance from Mishawaka to South Bend was more than four miles. All were linked, however, with an electric railway which ended in Osceola.

A modern pedestrian bridge carries the Mishawaka Riverwalk across the river at the west end of Beutter Park. Note bas-relief panels flanking the south entrance.

reached from North State Street at the north end of the Eberhart-Petro Golf Course, where there is also a stone bridge which crosses the main river. The island has a boat launch for small boats, playgrounds, picnicking facilities and toilets.

65.3 Willow Creek enters the river from the north passing first through portions of the golf course.

64.4 – 63.6 **Merrifield Park** on the southeast bank, has Indiana Avenue to the east and the river to the west and north. Its 25 acres are bisected by East Mishawaka Avenue. The southern section includes a splashpad, lighted basketball courts, playgrounds, picnic

areas and an open-air pavilion available to rent. In the northern section are sports fields, playgrounds, an ice skating rink, an Olympic-sized swimming pool, a lodge called Castle Manor and a boat launch. This is where steelhead are planted annually. The park is named for George C. Merrifield, a pioneer school teacher who became a State Legislator after he retired from teaching.

64. Bridge. Mishawaka Avenue crosses the river east-west and provides access to Merrifield Park. It is a concrete deck arch bridge first built about 1924 and reconstructed in 1987. In the summer of 2010 it was again under reconstruction.

63.3 Bridge. Cedar Street crosses north-south.

63. **Mishawaka Uniroyal Dam**. Constructed to serve the Uniroyal factory which was located on the south bank where Beutter Park now stands, power is no longer produced here. Instead the water has been redirected down a descending series of pools in Beutter Park.

63. – 61.9 **Mishawaka Riverwalk**. A scenic three-mile loop along both sides of the river was planned in 1991 and the final section dedicated November 7, 2009. The loop runs from just west of the dam through Central Park and Battell Park on the north bank, across the Logan Street Bridge and through Kate's Garden, Kamm Island and Beutter Park on the south bank. The path is designed to accommodate walkers, joggers, cyclists and rollerbladers with a 10 foot paved path with no vehicle crossings.

62.8 – 62.6 **Central Park** on the north bank, in addition to supplying a portage path around the dam includes playgrounds, lighted sports fields, a pavilion and other picnicking facilities and is part of the Mishawaka Riverwalk. Fishing for the handicapped is available along the entire river wall, and a fish cleaning station is located west of the restrooms and pavilion area. A fish ladder constructed in 1991 is the last in a series which allows fish to swim upriver as far as the Twin Branch dam. .

62.65 Bridge. Main Street crosses the river north- south and goes into Mishawaka . At this point both banks of the river are part of the Riverwalk project.

62.65 **Ball Band Monument Park**. On the north riverbank on the west side of the Main Street bridge is this tiny (one acre) park dedicated to all the Ball Band Workers of Mishawaka. It overlooks the

site of the former Mishawaka Woolen Company which began in 1868 making flannels, later invented an all wool knit boot, and, in 1898, added a rubber department to manufacture the Ball Band (Red Ball) work shoes. The factory was very active during World War I making boots and clothing for the military. In the 1950s the factory was bought by Uniroyal and when it closed in 1997 was making life jackets, bowling balls and tennis shoes. A gazebo in the park was donated by the Kiwanis Club of Mishawaka in honor of Ball Band employees and was dedicated Memorial Day, 2003.

62.65 – 62.7 **Beutter Park**. A seven acre park on the south bank built on the site of the former Ball Band/Uniroyal factory. It was named for Robert C. Beutter, mayor of Mishawaka 1984 to

The old race which served the Ball Band/Uniroyal factory has been redirected to form a series of descending pools in Beutter Park, decorated with modern sculpture and colorful landscaping.

The Logan Street bridge, built in 1925 and reconstructed in 2007,

2003. The main focus of the park is the river. The race which separates the park from the mainland, has elliptical-shaped overlook weirs and fiberoptic underwater lighting. Other features include a found-object sculpture called *Shards* and an 800-foot perennial garden. Beutter Park is located just west of the Main Street bridge, and is accessed by land from North Spring Street, or by turning west off Main Street. It is a popular place for summer concerts.

62.7 Pedestrian Bridge. A modern-style pedestrian bridge with artistic embellishments is located at the west end of Beutter Park .

62.5 – 62.6 **Battell Park** is located on the north bank. This 11 acre park is reached off West Mishawka Avenue. Facilities include picnic tables, tennis

and basketball courts, playgrounds, a terraced rock garden, Civil War statue, a gazebo (popular for weddings and photographs) and an historic bandshell which features summer concerts. The park was a gift from Anna Battell in 1880. Many features were built during the Works Progress Administration program of the 1930s.

62.4 – 62.5 **Kamm Island** is considered one of the most picturesque places in Mishawaka. This 7.5 acre island park is near the south bank to which it is linked by a foot bridge. It is part of the Riverwalk and is a favorite fishing site

62.3 – 62 **Lincoln Park** is on the south bank, where there is a public access, a restored restroom facility originally built by the Works Progress Administration during the 1930s, and a monument to

124

Princess Mishawaka. Some local sources say she was buried there.

62. – 61.9 Kate's Garden. Just west of the Logan Street bridge on the south bank is a small park which honors Catherine "Kate" Kosanovich, a community leader who loved flowers. In addition to flower gardens and a gazebo, the park contains *Educators* a sculpture by Tuck Langland. The sculpture was dedicated in 2000 "as a tribute to teachers, mentors, parents and the educators who have had such a positive influence on our lives and our community." Kate's Garden is located at 1202 Lincolnway, adjacent to Lincoln Park.

61.9 Logan Street crosses the river north-south on a bridge decorated with black coach lights. It was first built in 1925 and reconstructed in 2007.

61.9 – 61. River Park. On the map accompanying a 1907 history of St. Joseph County, there is a village called River Park between Logan and Ironwood streets on the north bank of the river. River Park was platted in 1892 by Albert J. Horse and Benjamin F. Dunn, and was later expanded to include the **Fordham** and **Berner's Grove** plats. It was incorporated as a town in 1900, and was the home of the South Bend Watch Company from 1903 to 1929. In the summer of 1918 River Park asked to be annexed to the City of South Bend in order to obtain a better water supply and more acceptable fire protection. When the City of South Bend seemed less than eager, River Park officials took their proposal to Mishawaka, which sent South Bend scurrying back to the negotiating table. South Bend officials

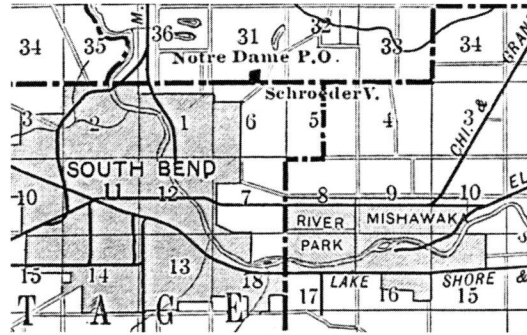

River Park on a map accompanying a 1907 history between Mishawaka and South Bend..

were quoted in the August 18, 1910 *South Bend Tribune* as remarking, "Such people as these are what South Bend wants." Amd River Park was annexed to South Bend.

61.9 Enter Portage Township on the north bank. Between the Logan Street and Ironwood bridges the township boundary bisects the river with Portage Township on the north and Penn Township on the south.

61.9 On the north bank leave Mishawaka and enter the city limits of South Bend.

61.9 – 53.2 South Bend A fur trading post brought the first settlers to the south bend of the St. Joseph River about 1820, to a post called **Big St. Joseph Station**. In 1829 the settlement applied for a post office, and Lathrop Minor Taylor, a fur trader, was named postmaster of **Southold**. The following year the name was changed to **South Bend** to alleviate confusion with other Midwest communities named Southold. In 1831 the town was laid out as the county seat and one of the four original townships of St. Joseph County. Much of the early development was centered around an industrial complex of factories which were powered by races built on either side of the St. Joseph River. Steam locomotives reached the city in 1851 and interest began to build for inter-city streetcars. In 1882 the South Bend Street Railway Company tried the first service of electrified streetcars in the world. Initially a failure, the electric current problems were solved and the line was extended to Mishawaka. Local industries included Singer Sewing Company, the Oliver Chilled Plow Company, Honey-well, the South Bend Toy Company, and the Bendix Corporation. South Bend was organized as a town (village) in 1835 and incorporated as a city in 1865. The population of the city in 2000 was 107,789 with an area of 2.8 square miles.

61.5 The southernmost point of the St. Joseph River, from which South Bend gets its name, is located opposite 31st Street in South Bend on the north, and Alabama Street in Mishawaka on the south.

61. Bridge. Ironwood Street crosses the river north-south a small park along the river is located at its northwest end. The concrete deck arch bridge was constructed in 1940.

61. From this point both banks of the river are in Portage Township.

61. -- 60.6 **Former Site of Playland Park**. Development began on the south bank here before 1890, when much of the land was purchased by the Chicago, South Bend and Northern Indiana Railway for a place to turn trains around, and then expanded into a destination park. In 1896 features were a bicycle track, grandstand and a lake "filled with clear water." A casino was added in

1909 and a rollercoaster and exhibition hall in 1912. In 1925 the park was taken over by private ownership and renamed Playland Park, a name selected in a contest. Renovations in the 1930s include a merry-go-round imported from Germany, a large swimming pool, and a ballroom with major dance bands. The South Bend Blue Sox played some of their games at the park into the 1950s. In 1962 the area was converted into a nine hole par-three golf course with an attached miniature golf course. After the golf courses closed the land was unused for several years until purchased by Indiana University at South Bend as its River Crossing campus. The only reminder of the old amusement park is the cement grandstand and some of the old lightpoles of the ballpark.

60.4 Pedestrian Bridge. A bright red pedestrian and bicycle bridge connects the two parts of the Indiana University at South Bend.

60.45 The remains of Springbrook, a small creek, the site of a serious railroad accident in 1859, enter the river from the south.

60.6-60.3 **Veterans Memorial Park** (formerly North Side Boulevard Park) on the north bank has restrooms, picnic facilities, a playground, a lighted softball diamond, and a boat access.

The river begins to angle northward

60.2 Bridge. Twyckenham Drive crosses north- south. A distinctive bridge with four arches and 15 obelisks, built in 1929 and restored in 1981-81. It was again under reconstruction in the summer of 2010 for repair of piers,

A pedestrian and bicycle bridge which connects the new part of the campus on the south side of the river on the old site of Playland Park, now used mainly for housing, to the libraries, offices and classrooms on the north side.. Red and white letters on the side of the bridge spell out "INDIANA UNIVERSITY AT SOUTH BEND."

In the summer of 2010 all that was left of the old Playland Park was this cement stadium with lights and loudspeaker on tall poles. Until the 1950s the South Bend Blue Sox played some of their games here.

The ornate seawall at Howard Park, South Bend.from an old postcard. The park has been used for recreational purposes since before 1878, and was formally named Howard Park more than a century ago in 1894.

columns and beams and the installation of new lighting and railings "to restore the bridge to its original appearance and historical significance." A memorial to World War I veterans had been removed but was expected to be returned. An *eruv*, a symbolic wire which acts as an "enclosure" for a Jewish community located on the south end of the bridge, was left in place during reconstruction.

60.2 – 59.3 Northside Boulevard Park is a long narrow stretch of green which runs from Twyckenham Drive bridge to the Sample Street bridge, between Northside Boulevard and the river next to a walking path.

59.5 Railroad bridge. Grand Trunk Western remains in big letters on the steel portion of the structure. It was built about 1938.

59.3 Bridge. Sample Street bridge with stone abutments crosses the river southwest-northeast. The Sample Street bridge was originally constructed in 1900, and reconstructed in 1971 by St. Joseph County. It connects to Eddy Street and Beyer Avenue on the north.

59. Bridge. Osbourne Street (or Cooper Street) crosses southwest-northeast and connects to Eddy Sreet. The road is designated Indiana Route 23.

58.8 Viewing Park The narrow parkland continues on the north side of the river along Northside Boulevard to Howard Park. A small overlook on the north bank allows pedestrians a view of the bridges crossing the river nearby.

58.4 Pedestrian and bicycle bridge crosses the river east-west affording walkers and bicyclers access to the other bank and the downtown area. There is also a narrow strip of parkland along the west bank between the footbridge and the bridge at Jefferson.

58.4 – 58.2 **Howard Park** on the northeast bank is a park nearly as old as the city. This neighborhood was once part of an unincorporated community known as **Lowell**. Originally swampy low ground, it first was flooded in the winter and used for ice skating. In 1878 the city council passed a resolution to review the area for improvement, and purchased a few lots before setting the boundaries of the park. Fill dirt was added to create gardens and pathways and a sea wall was built along the riverbank. In 1894 it was officially titled Howard Park after the councilman who wrote the 1878 resolution. The park was enlarged in 1902 and beautified by the gifts of an electrified fountain from John M. Studebaker and a bronze fountain from Calvert Degrees, as well as public drinking fountains. During the relief programs of the Depression a stone and slate administration building was constructed, along with a new fieldstone river retaining wall, stairways and viewing stands. The park came full circle with the building of an ice skating rink. In recent years running trails and some modern sculpture have been added.

58. Bridge. East Jefferson Boulevard crosses the river east-west. The bridge was built in 1905 during a campaign known as the "City Beautiful Movement," encouraging structures which would "enhance the aesthetics of the city" rather than being purely functional. It has four broad arch spans supported by piers designed to resemble chalices and other sculpted details. The

bridge was reconstructed 2003-2004 by the St. Joseph County Board of Commissioners and Engineering Department and reopened in time for its 100th birthday.

58.01 **South Bend Dam** The first dam at approximately this site was erected in 1844, and provided water for two races. Today the west race has been filled in, but the east race has been redug and functions as a rafting course. The water cascading over the roller-type dam today is prized for its scenic value. Normal pool elevation is 680 feet. The two sides of the dam are at different angles with *Keepers of the Fire,* a Mark di Suvero sculpture, in the middle.

The dam near the Century Center is in a v-shape with a piece of modern sculpture erected at the center.

58.01 The **Century Center Convention Center** on the west bank was designed by noted architects Philip Johnson and John Burgee. The facility opened in

The East Race Waterway at South Bend has been restored and is used on summer weekends as a whitewater rafting course.

1977. This center features over 75,000 square feet of convention space. The main building contains a 30-foot, two-story high glass wall with a view of the St. Joseph River.

58.1 **Seitz Park** is located at the entrance to the East Race Waterway, and is the area of the portage. It is also the access to a viewing area for the fish ladder which the Indiana DNR uses to allow upriver access to the steelhead and salmon and keep tabs on the number and varieties of fish in the river. There is a floating dock for canoes and other small boats. Also at Seitz Park is a statue dedicated in 2004 to the members of the South Bend Fire Department "who gave their lives protecting the life and property of the citizens of this city."

58.1 **East Race Waterway** The East Race on the St. Joseph River, formerly used for factory power, was restored and turned into a whitewater rafting and kayak course in 1984. It was the first artificial white water course in North America and one of only six in the world. Its rapids are said to rival those of the Colorado River and waves can be generated over six feet in height. The facility is open June through mid-August administered by the South Bend Parks and Recreation Department. The East Race Waterway is 1,900 feet long and takes about five minutes to traverse at moderate speed. Rafts, safety vests, helmets and paddles are provided. The water speed can be adjusted during contests, but during regular rafting hours is a class 2 whitewater. At scheduled times the waterway is used by the Indiana River Rescue School to teach rescue squads, firemen and other emergency works techniques for "swiftwater rescue."

57.8 Bridge. Colfax Street crosses the river southwest-northeast sloping downward from downtown to the north bank.

57.8-57.7 **Bicentennial Park** on the west bank provides a pleasant viewing area on the river between Colfax and La Salle Street bridges.

57.6 Bridge. La Salle Street crosses southwest-northeast. Built in 1907 the La Salle Street bridge is one of the oldest concrete arch bridges in South Bend.

57.4 Dock and access on the northeast bank where the millrace rejoins the river.

JEFFERSON STREET BRIDGE, SOUTH BEND, IND.

The Jefferson Street bridge in South Bend, built in 1905 as part of a "City Beautiful Movement."

La Salle Street Bridge, South Bend, Ind.

The La Salle Street bridge in downtown South Bend from a 1910 postcard.

E 5335 Pin Hook. Scene on St. Joseph River. South Bend, Indiana

The west side of the old Pinhook bend in the river from a 1918 postcard. It was from a point nearby that La Salle and others landed on the west bank and picked up their boats for the portage to the beginnings of the Kankakee River.

There is also a minimum style access on the south bank.

57.4 – 56.8 **Leeper Park** is on the southwest side of the river next to the North Pumping Station. It is an old park built from a swampy area which had a number of artesian wells, and still features lagoons and duck ponds. The Navarre Cabin, thought to have been built in 1820 by Pierre Navarre, the first European to permanently settle in what would become St. Joseph County, was relocated there in 1904, although the cabin has since disappeared. The park has a nationally known tennis center which hosts tournaments as well as a city-run tennis school. It is named for David Rohrer Leeper, a former mayor of South Bend, who resided nearby. The park is divided into three sections, one

east of Michigan Street, and two west of Michigan Street.

 56.9 Bridge. Michigan Street crosses northwest-southeast. This is an ornate arch three-span bridge built in 1914 by the Kuert Construction Company of Indianapolis.

56.4 Bridge. Angela Boulevard crosses southeast-northwest. The plaque on the bridge lists its construction date as 1940 by the H. L. Maddock Company. It was associated with the Public Works Administration of the Depression. **Brownsfield Park** is across Riverside Drive at the west end of the bridge.

56.3 Railroad bridge. A metal deck girder span, formerly a part of the Norfolk Southern Railroad, crosses the river east-west. This bridge is no longer used for trains.

56.3 At this point although it is Clay Township on the east bank, the entire river is within Portage Township, both townships are in St. Joseph County.

56 . – 55.4 **Holy Cross College** on the east bank is a Roman Catholic, co-educational, residential institution of higher education founded in 1966 and administered by members of the Congregation of Holy Cross. It was formerly a junior college.

55.4 Outlet from St. Mary's Lake enters the river from the east. St. Mary's Lake is located on the campus of the **University of Notre Dame** to the east. The flow leaves the lake near the Our Lady of Fatima House and Shrine off U. S. 31/33 and enters the St. Joseph River between the Holy Cross campus and Saint Mary's College.

55.4 – 54.9 **Saint Mary's College**, on the east bank of the river, is a private Roman Catholic liberal arts college founded in 1844 by the Sisters of the Holy Cross. Saint Mary's is one of the oldest institutions of higher education for women in the country. It was the first school to offer graduate degrees in theology for women. All three colleges are located in an unincorporated area known as Notre Dame, northwest of the City of South Bend.

55.3 **St. Joseph County Canoe Landing**, at the bend near a utility station on the west bank, is a grassy area with access for canoes and one small paved ramp.

55.3 – 55.2 **Keller Park** is on the west bank just beyond the utility station, with access from Riverside Drive. Facilities include a playground, tennis courts, bank fishing, and a series of stone guardrail supports featuring bronze relief sculptures of cattails.

54.6 Enter Clay Township on the east and German Township on the west. The township line goes down the middle of the river including the former river ox-bow at Pinhook Lake which is now landlocked. Both townships are in St. Joseph County, Indiana.

54.3 – 54. **Pinhook Park**. Pinhook Lake was formerly an ox-bow on the

La Salle Landing marker shows where La Salle and party crossed the land in 1679 on the way to the Kankakee.

133

West bank of the St. Joseph River. It was from the westernmost point of the ox-bow that the portage trail began which Robert La Salle and others used to portage into the headwaters of the Kankakee River about three miles west and thence into the Illinois and Mississippi. Today the old ox-bow that was once a part of the St. Joseph is cut off from the river by a causeway which runs along the river bank, and the park is chiefly located within the old bend of the river where there is a pavilion, picnick-ing facilities, toilets and fishing areas. Also the Angel of Hope Memorial Gardens. The lake is stagnant and weedchoked.

53.4 **La Salle Landing** located on the west bank on the outside of the old bend in the river. There is a small park marking the place where the early explorers actually picked up their canoes and started west to the Kankakee. There is a memorial stone and bench to mark the place off Portage Road just past the north boundary of Riverview Cemetery. The stone reads:

Rene-Robert Cavelier Sieur
de la Salle
French scholar and explorer
first white man to visit the region
portaging from the St. Joseph River to
the Kankakee River
crossed this land
December 5, 1679.
To commemorate the visit of LaSalle,
the Board of Parks Commission
erected this tablet
on land donated for that purpose
by Robert O. Myles.

53.6 Bridge. The Indiana Toll Road, I-80 and I-90 crosses the river east-west.

53.55 Bridge. Cleveland Road crosses the river east-west, in the shadow of the Indiana Toll Road.

53.4 Juday (sometimes misspelled Judy) Creek enters the river from the east. Classified as a coldwater trout stream it was re-routed to build a golf course near the Notre Dame campus. Juday Creek begins in St. Joseph County south of Granger where there is a Juday Creek Golf Course.

54.5 – 53.2 **Riverside Park**. A city park, on the west bank across the river from Juday Creek, runs along the riverbank. There is a DNR boat access nearby.

53.4 – 53.2 **Izaak Walton League Park** runs from the mouth of Juday Creek to the Darden Road bridge on the east bank. It is a private facility operated by the St. Joseph County Izaak Walton League which was chartered in 1924. The Izaak Walton League is an American environmental organization founded in Chicago in 1922 which promotes natural resource protection and outdoor recreation. They proclaim themselves "defenders of soil, air, woods, water and wildlife." They are named for early fishing enthusiast Izaak Walton (1593-1683) known as the "Father of Flyfishing" and author of *The Compleat Angler* first published in 1653.

53.4 **Darden Road Pedestrian Bridge.** Part of the Riverwalk hiking and bicycle trail this bridge is a former downtown bridge which from 1885 to 1906 spanned the St. Joseph at what is now La Salle Street. In 1906 the bridge was removed and floated down the river to Darden Road where approach spans were added and it served vehicle traffic until 1970. The metal bridge has two Pratt through truss spans which are metal pinned. It was built by P. E. Lane of Chicago in 1884. When the structure was moved the original builder's plaque was removed and cast in a concrete stand near the new site, and a modern substitute installed on the portal. It is the only known truss bridge in St. Joseph County, Indiana.

53.2 Bridge. Darden Road crosses east-west.

52.5 – 53. **Clay Township Park** is a large park on the eastern bank with sports fields, playgrounds, picnic tables, toilets and hiking trails to the river bank. It is accessed by road off Laural Street.

52. Bridge. Auten Road crosses the river east-west.

52.3 Sheffield Creek enters from the east.

51.2 State Line Dam Site. This spot is identified in a 1933 federal study as a potential site for a hydroelectric dam. The plan had earlier been discussed by the South Bend Power Company in 1900 but no construction was ever begun.

50.7 – 50.3 **St. Patrick's County Park** on the east bank has canoe rentals, restrooms, picnic facilities, and refreshment sales. At some seasons canoers or kayakers can put in at St. Patrick's and arrange for a shuttle to meet them on arrival at the canoe landing at the Niles dam five miles to the north. The state line is about a hundred yards north of the boat ramp at St. Patrick's, where canoes and other

The Darden Road pedestrian bridge began life in 1885 as a downtown crossing and was moved to the north edge of the city in 1906 to facilitate movement of traffic across the river north of Notre Dame University

boating equipment can be rented at the Brown Barn. From here there is also the possibility of boats traveling south to Pinhook Park or the County Canoe Landing at Keller Park, a distance of 4.5 miles. Or the two trips can be combined, beginning at Keller Park to the Niles Dam, 9.5 miles, about four hours on the river. Turn north from Auten Road onto Laurel Road, which deadends at the park entrance onto Billy C. Hankins Parkway. In season there is a fee for entrance to the park.

50.05 **State Line** Some modern maps show an unincorporated community called State Line just south of the Michigan state line on the east bank of the river.

50. **Indiana - Michigan State Line**

Lake
Michigan

Paw Paw River

BENTON
HARBOR

Pipestone Creek

ST. JOSEPH

Hickory Creek

Love Creek

Lemon Creek

BERRIEN SPRINGS

Lake
Chapin

Dowagiac River

NILES

BUCHANAN

Brandywine
Creek

BERTRAND

McCoy Creek

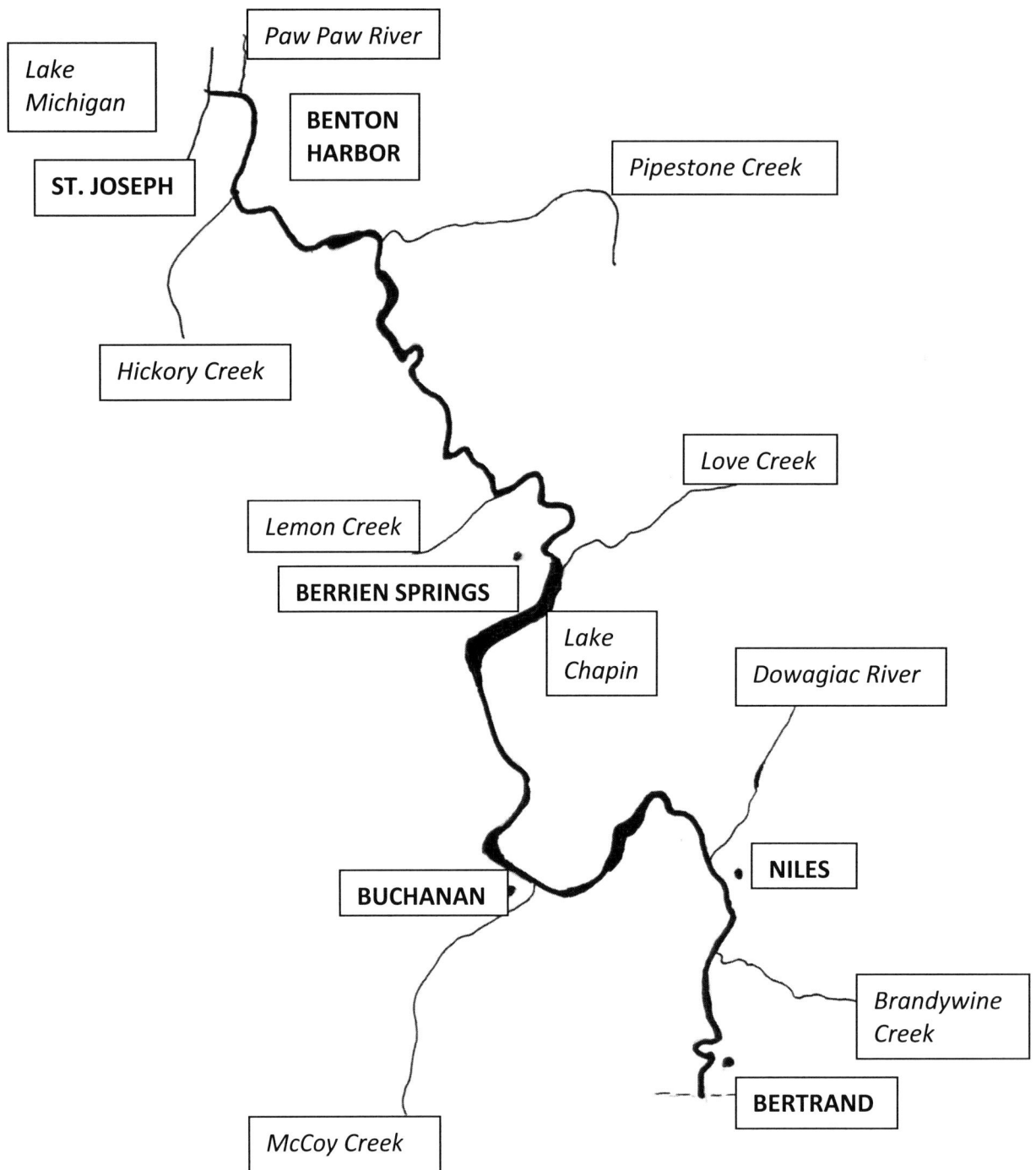

The lower St. Joseph River, from the Indiana line to its mouth, flows entirely within Berrien County, Michigan. It is interrupted by three dams, the last creating a large, long lake. The river itself is winding with many islands. This stretch was entirely navigable in its predam era.

The Lower St. Joseph
Berrien County, Michigan

50. Enter Niles Township, on the east bank, Bertrand township on the west bank, Berrien County, Michigan

49.7 Kimball Creek enters the river from the west.

49.5 **Pokagon's Village** Leopold Pokagon established a village on the west bank of the St. Joseph River just north of Kimball Creek in the 1820s. His third son, Simon, attended the University of Notre Dame and became something of a scholar. He is credited with writing several articles and one book, a largely autobiographical Indian romance. Simon was a staunch advocate of temperance and felt that "firewater" had been very detrimental to the life of the Native Americans. He was a popular speaker, his best-known engagement being an appearance during "Chicago Day" at the 1893 Columbian Exposition in Chicago.

49.4 **Madeline Bertrand County Park** A large county park, named for the wife of fur trader Joseph Bertrand, is located on the east bank between Adams Road and the river, reached via Ontario Road, west from Third Street (U.S. 31). Facilities at the park include hiking and bicycling trails groomed and lighted for cross country skiing in the winter, picnic areas, toilets, children's play equipment and an 18-hole disc golf course. There is a fee for entrance. The area was called *Parc aux Vaches* (or "cow pasture") by the early French, named for the herds of buffalo which grazed there. Two major Indian trails crossed near here: the Sauk Trail which connected Detroit and Chicago, and the Miami Trail which

went between the Wabash and Grand rivers.

49.1 Bridge. Bertrand Road crosses the river east-west and goes into Bertrand.

49.1 **Bertrand** was the early home of Joseph Bertrand, a French-Canadian settler who opened a trading post on the river in 1812. After the Potawatomi ceded their lands to the government in 1833 his part Indian wife became a large land owner in the area. Daniel G. Garnsey secured permission and Mrs. Bertrand's consent, to locate a village at the site and Alonzo Bennett platted it in 1833 and became its first postmaster in 1834. the post office operating until April 15, 1901. A brick church built near the riverbank and dedicated to St. Joseph was the scene in September 1844 of the investiture of three new members of the Sisters of the Holy Cross, said to be the first Roman Catholic nuns created in America. They opened a school

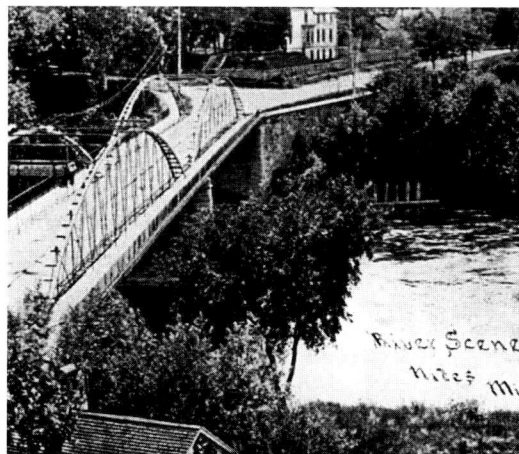

Bridge south of Niles crosses the river high above the water. The photo is from an old postcard.

The memorial stone erected on the hill on Fort Street in Niles in 1913 to mark the existence of Fort St. Joseph. Eroding letters in the face of the stone read, "Fort St. Joseph 1697 – 1781."

the same year which, in 1855, was moved to Indiana, and later became St. Mary's College. The brick church in Bertrand was torn down in 1911.

48.9 – 48.3 An ox-bow with high banks and swift current begins just past the bridge.

46. Bridge. Pulaski Highway, U. S. 12, crosses east-west on a four-lane bridge, constructed in 1954 by the L. W. Lamb Company of Jackson. It is actually two large plate girder bridges side by side.

45.3 Brandywine Creek enters from the east.

45. Two important and old memorials are located on the east bank of the river a short distance up Fort Road, not easily visible from the river.

Allouez Cross. A stone cross sits on the north side of the road about half way up the hill. There is a small turnout on the road and a handrail along a series of concrete steps. The cross at the top was erected in 1918 by the Womens Progressive League of Niles, to mark more permanently than an old wooden cross, the grave of Jesuit missionary Father Jean Claude Allouez who died at the Niles mission August 27, 1689. (See chapter 3)

Fort St. Joseph State Park. A small wooden fort was built by the French in 1691 near the Sauk Trail, a noted cross-peninsula route, and the St. Joseph River which was a portage route to the south and the Mississippi River. The fort controlled Michigan's principal Indian trade routes. It was taken over by the British in 1761. Two years later it was seized by Indians during the uprising of

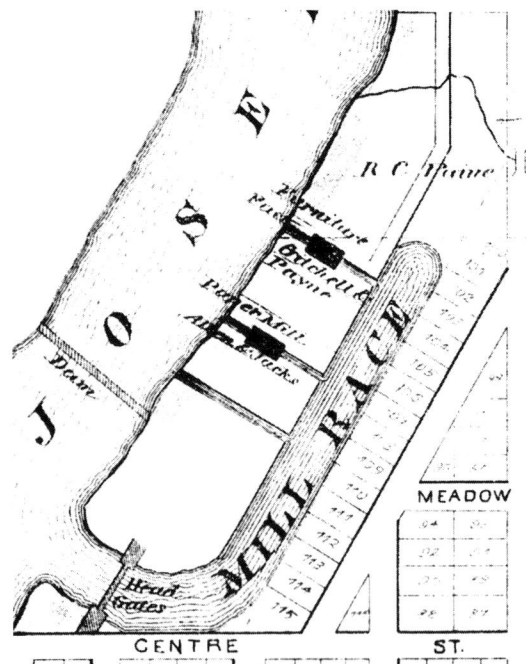

This 1873 map shows a furniture factory and a paper company on the mill race north of the Niles dam.

138

A 2010 photograph of the Niles dam showing the French Paper Company across the river and the remains of the old factories and mill race on the east side.

Chief Pontiac, and in 1781 Spanish raiders ran up the flag of Spain at the fort for a few hours. To commemorate the existence of the fort a large boulder was erected on a platform in 1913 at the top of the Fort Street hill in Niles where the original fort was thought to have stood. The memorial includes two stone benches, and four corner posts bearing the names of the countries whose flags had flown over the fort. (See chapter 4.)

45. **St. Joseph River Park Project.** Beginning at Fort Street on the east side of the river and continuing to the bridge in downtown Niles there is a series of parks operated by the City of Niles, and constructed by the French Paper Company. The park project begins with a small canoe launch area at the foot of Fort Street, then French Field with picnic facilities, a ball field, toilets and a view of the dam. Also visible from this point are the remains of an old wooden bridge, still standing on each side of the river.

44.5 **Niles Dam**. The dam at Niles was begun in 1866 by the Niles Hydraulic Company, but work moved slowly. In 1867 parts of the project were taken over by the Niles Manufacturing Company. French & Millard bought into the project in 1872, and the French Paper Company was still operating the power plant, located on the west bank of the river, in 2010. A fish ladder was built below the dam in 1991, a vertical slot ladder which is very deep. Fish pass through the ladder and exit directly into the river channel. A viewing window is used to make a continuing fish census.

44.3 Park. On the east riverbank there are several brick and stone remains from old factory buildings, sluices and a race. The small park has a picnic shelter, fishing, access to the river and a portage route for small boats around the dam.

44.3 – 42.7 **Niles** A short distance north of the remains of the old fort Eli P. Bunnell and Abram Tietsort of Ohio built cabins, but later sold out to Samuel

NILES BOARD AND PAPER CO., NILES, MICH.

The Niles Board and Paper Company along the St. Joseph River from an old postcard.

B. Walling and Obed P. Lacey. The settlement was first called **Pogwatigue** ("running water"), but when the village was platted and recorded in 1829 it was named for Hezekiah Niles, publisher of the *Niles Register*, a Whig newspaper in Baltimore, Maryland. The first post office was called **Carey**, because it was adjacent to the Carey Mission, when it opened in 1828 with Samuel B. Walling as postmaster. It was changed to Pogwatigue in 1829, and to Niles in 1841. The settlement was incorporated as a village in 1835 and as a city in 1859. It is often referred to as the "City of Four Flags" because the area has lived under four flags: the French, British, Spanish (for about a few hours in 1781) and American. In 2000 the population was 12,204 with an area of 5.9 square miles.

44. Ring Lardner Birthplace. A house at 519 Bond Street, atop the bluff on the east side of the river, was the birthplace

of writer Ring Lardner on March 6, 1885. He began his reporter career covering sports for the *Niles Sun* and moved upriver to the *South Bend Tribune* and later the *South Bend Times.* His only novel, *You Know Me, Al*, was a success and he wrote many short stories and magazine articles. Lardner died in 1933 at the age of 41. The house is now a private residence, but there is a Michigan historical marker on the bluff across the street from it.

43.9 – 43.7 **Island Park** in the river has a playground and picnic shelter. It is accessible from the west bank off Parkway at Elm Street.

43.6 **City Park** There is a small city park just south of the bridge with a boat launch, picnic facilities and a toilet.

43.5 **Clifford D. Eden Memorial Bridge** Niles-Buchanan Road, called Broadway Street in town, crosses the

140

river east-west on the Eden Memorial Bridge and goes into downtown Niles. An act to establish a ferry at this site was passed by the Michigan Territorial Legislative Council on March 2, 1831. The ferry, large enough to carry two teams, was launched in the spring, and run by Benoni and Moses Finch as a toll ferry for three years. Ferry users then launched a subscription drive and raised enough to make it a free ferry, run by Thomas Huston. The ferry continued until the completion of the first Broadway bridge in December of 1836. An earlier charter had been granted to build a toll bridge at that point, but the opposition of the people to charging for passage held up construction until the project was rechartered as a free bridge March 21, 1836.

43.3 Bridge. Main Street which carries business U.S. 12 across the river east-west was erected in 1919. In 1834, only three days after a similar meeting had been held to secure a free bridge at Broadway, businessmen of the town met to advocate a free bridge at Main Street, but it was not until May 24, 1845, that the contract for construction, to cost about $2,000, was let. It opened in December, 1845, but was partially carried away by a flood in 1850. It was replaced in 1854, a few feet above the old one, and in turn replaced by an iron bridge which opened in January of 1869. The present bridge is of yellow colored concrete with black coachlights..

42.65 – 43.3 A city park which includes a veterans' memorial, pavilion, playground, volleyball court, and a track for skate boarders stretches along the river from the Main Street bridge to the railroad bridge. On East Main Street stands a steel sculpture entitled *High-*

Bred Form #2 by Chicago sculptor Richard Hunt. The sculpture was dedicated in 1974 to Albert and Freda Aronson, early settlers of Niles.

42.65 **F.O.P Park** on the west bank, just before the railroad bridge is mainly a team sports park.

42.6 Railroad bridge crosses the river southwest to northeast. The structure is a high and large metal-pinned Baltimore deck truss bridge.

42. Dowagiac River enters from the east having already picked up Dowagiac Drain, Dowagiac Creek, Osborn Drain, Mc Kinzie Creek, Peavine Creek and Pokagon Creek.

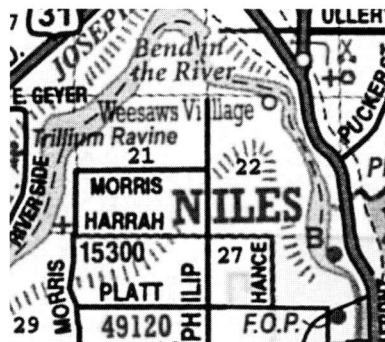

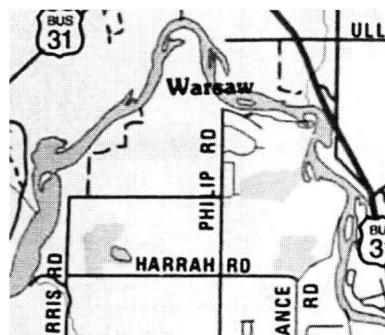

39.2 **Warsaw** and **Weesaw** The place name Warsaw shows on many modern maps and a few old ones, sometimes on the north bank of the river, sometimes on the south bank within the hairpin bend in

A 1902 Trip Down the River in a $3 Boat

Excerpts from the July 31, 1975 *Niles Daily Star*

As I remember we three boys, Payne Phelps, Bruce Earl and Harry Brelsford got together late in the summer of 1902 to talk about a boat trip down the St. Joe River from Niles. I think it was Payne Phelps' idea to start with, but Bruce Earl was very close behind him and the idea struck me, Harry Brelsford, as a good one, for I had never been camping, so it sounded exciting.

Bruce located an old boat that the owner was willing to sell for $3. It was pretty old, a water-logged flat bottomed, three seater about 10 or 12 feet long, needing paint very badly and leaking some but without oars. We found where we could buy oars for a dollar and a half. . . . After a lot of hustling around, we all had permission to make the trip and the day we finally left Niles, we spent gathering together blankets, pans and cooking utensils and plates to eat from, etc., and getting the boat down to the river just south of the Michigan Central railroad bridge. We had to carry all our things in our arms from our homes to the boat and make many trips as in those days there were no family autos and also family horse drawn vehicles were scarce and not at the service of family youngsters.

Payne had along his .38 caliber Winchester repeater rifle, a lever action gun, and I had my single shot Stevens .22 and Bruce had a 32-caliber pistol but not many cartridges so at that we were pretty well armed and well able to protect ourselves from whatever danger presented. I don't know now just what we were expecting, but it could have been anything from bears to Indians or bandits.

We went down the river and soon had to row as we struck the back water from the Buchanan dam and this got us to thinking about how we were to get our boat and equipment over or around that dam. . . the boat was so heavy we knew we would have to have two or three strong men to help us handle it. In those days there was a large drop forge plant at the west end of the dam and soon after we reached the dam, it shut down for the day. In talking to some men about our problems of getting our boat over the dam, one of them said he knew a man working there who had ridden boats over the dam a number of times so he went and located this man and brought him to us. The man looked at our boat and said, yes, he could ride it over for there was about two feet of water pouring over the top of the dam. He said he would do it for $2 – I guess he figured that was about all we could afford. . . He rowed it out about 100 feet from shore where the water pouring over the dam was forming a smooth stream over the apron over the downstream end of the dam, then he rowed fast and straight at the dam until the bow of the boat was almost over the dam then quickly shipped the oars and sat down on the rear seat and the boat went over nice as could be and he did not ship a bit of water.

The next day we went on down the river, fished some but no luck, caught a very large turtle over a foot in diameter and Bruce thought we could cook him so put him in the boat on his back. In those days there was quite a rapids in the river above Berrien Springs with lots of large boulders to dodge. Just as we were getting into the rapids in the river above Berrien Spring that turtle managed to get right side up and was heading toward Bruce Earl who was in the back end of the boat and his feet bare. The turtle had his mouth open and it was a big mouth and Bruce got scare so grabbed Payne's .38 Winchester and shot the turtle. Payne yelled at him not to shoot for, of course, the bullet went right through the turtle and the bottom of the boat too, so now we had a bad leak also and right while we were in the rapids.

 Well, we got through without hitting a rock or capsizing and then got to shore and bailed the water out and cut a plug to fix the leak, then we went on to Berrien Springs. We camped on the island there just above the bridge and stayed two days as there was a fair on and the usual excitement in town. We caught some fish here – the first on the trip. Most of our meals had been bacon and potatoes and some sweet corn and bread.

The next night we camped at the big bend just before reaching Sodus, and on into St. Joseph the next day, chained our boat to a pile and left it for somebody to claim, went to a restaurant and had something to eat, then got tickets on the Big 4 Railroad and came home, bringing all our equipment and the oars with us. I think we were all flat broke when we got back to Niles. I know I had to carry all my stuff home on my back.

We had a lot of fun on the trip, went swimming every day, did not have any quarrels and got pretty well organized right away at the start. Payne did the cooking. Bruce washed the dishes and I put up the tent and made up the beds and we all packed up each morning and all gathered wood for the fire. We usually camped where there was a spring for water so got along O.K. It is about 48 miles from Niles to St. Joseph by river.

HARRY E. BRELSFORD,

April 29, 1968

Old bridge across the St. Joseph River at Buchanan.

the river. On two maps the name Warsaw is discovered at the tip of a triangle formed by Berrien Center Road, Ferry Street and Ullery Road just north of Niles. Records show there was never a post office or a train station by that name, but a cluster of residences, old and new, are on a northward pointing peninsula formed by the river near the center of Niles Township where a small, unnamed stream, comes into the St. Joseph from the north. Older maps show, also in the same vicinity, a small settlement headed by a Potawatomi chief called Weesaw, who married a relative of Topinabee whose village was near Niles. He was said to be a well dressed Indian, something of a dandy, and a friend of the Americans. He died from a gunshot wound in 1845 suffered when he tried to intercede in a drunken quarrel

between two members of his own tribe. There may be some relationship between Weesaw and Warsaw.

36.5 Bridge. Twin blue bridges carry U. S. 31 over the river north-south.

36. **Site of Riverside Church Camp**. A summer camp was established on the north bank of the St. Joseph River off East Riverside Drive at Camp Road by the Evangelical Churches of Portage Prairie in 1891. After the merger of the Evangelical United Brethren Church with the Methodist Church in 1968, use of the camp declined. The facility closed in 1974 and the buildings have since been demolished.

35.5 Enter Buchanan Township, Berrien County

35.3 McCoy Creek enters from the southwest

35.3 **Benton** A settlement named Benton, after Thomas Hart Benton, was founded by William Broadhurst and Joseph Stephens across the river from the mouth of McCoy Creek on section 25, Buchanan Township. The town was platted by John Woolman and registered on August 18, 1832. There were seven streets laid out on the map, with 106 lots, but it never gained reality outside of the map. Today it is a residential area, with nothing to show where Benton might have been.

35. Bridge. Walton Road, called River Street in town, crosses southwest-northeast and goes into Buchanan

34.8 **Upper Access Park** On the north bank there is a small park west of the river with a trail to the water.

The dam at Buchanan photographed in the spring of 2010.

34.7 **Buchanan Dam**. The Buchanan dam was built in 1908 and still produces hydroelectric power for Indiana Michigan Power affiliated with American Electric Power, in a power plant on the south bank. Inside the fence, not accessible to the public, there is a vertical slot fish ladder. Fish enter the ladder below the dam, move upstream through a system of vertical slots and exit the ladder in the power canal. The fish ladder was completed in 1990 at a cost of about $3 million dollars. There is a small island below the dam.

34.5 **Lower Buchanan Dam Access**
There is a launching area for small boats and canoes, and a fishing platform out over the water below the dam on the north side.

34.7 – 34.4 **Buchanan** The first settler was Charles Cowels who built a shingle mill. Russell McCoy and John Hatfield arrived shortly afterwards and each built a sawmill on McCoy Creek. (Over the years there has been much discussion about whether the creek was named after Russell, or for Isaac McCoy, a Baptist missionary, who was the first white settler in Berrien County and whose mission was established between Niles and Buchanan.) The settlement was first known as **McCoy's Creek**, but in 1842 it was platted and recorded as Buchanan by mill owner John Hamilton. It was named for U. S. Senator James Buchanan of Pennsylvania, who assisted Michigan with its efforts to become a state 1835 to 1837. Buchanan became President of the United States in 1857. John D. Ross became the first postmaster on March 2, 1848. The Michigan Central Railroad was completed from Detroit to Niles on October 7, 1848, and completed through Buchanan to New Buffalo in 1849, and all the way to Chicago by 1852. A mill was built on McCoy Creek near the junction with the St. Joseph River in 1857. Now called Pear's Mill it still grinds flour in the summertime and is

145

open to visitors. Buchanan was incorporated as a village in 1858 and as a city in 1929. Population in 2000 was 4,681 with an area of 2.5 square miles. The community is now known as the Red Bud Tree City. Its northern boundary barely touches the river.

34. Red Bud Riverfront Park on the south bank is accessible from the Redbud Trail. There is a boat launching site.

33.6 – 32.9 Several islands are in the river downstream from the dam. The first and largest is **Batchelors Island**, the only island in the river without a connecting bridge which has year-round residents. It is named for a former owner. A small parking lot and steps to the water's edge have been constructed on the south bank near the island, but users must furnish their own boat. The smaller island downstream is called **Deb Island.**

33.5 Buchanan St. Joseph River Boating Access Site A small parking lot with two concrete launching ramps is located off East Riverside Road, via Mead Road, on the north bank of the river. The ramps are separated from the main channel by a protective barrier.

31.9 – 30.7 Fernwood Botanical Garden and Nature Preserve Located at 13988 Range Line Road, the gardens include 105 acres along the St. Joseph River. Originally the home of Kay and Walter Boydston, the buildings and gardens became a public place in 1964 through the efforts of Niles philanthropists Lawrence and Mary Plym. The Mary Plym Visitors Center opened in 1989, and has a lodge and kitchen when may be rented for weddings and other

events, and a variety of different types of gardens, including one with a miniature railroad and replicas of Berrien County buildings. Fernwood also offers year-round education programs for children and adults. There is a fee for entrance unless you are a member.

31.2 Moccasin Bluff. Site of a village of Potawatomi headed by Moccasin, on the west bank. Some sources call him a "chief," others a "medicine man."

30.5 Bear Cave Resort. Michigan has very few caves of any kind. Bear Cave, which centers this resort on the east bank is probably the only one open commercially in the southern Lower Peninsula. It was formed from tufa, a kind of secondary limestone and is 150 feet long, four to six feet wide, and 10 to 15 feet high, with a handful of stalactites and stalagmites and some interesting colored rock and formations. It was long known to be in the area, but access was limited until a second entrance was opened in 1940. Noted Berrien County historian Robert C. Meyers described the place as "a rather small cave" which "has an extensive and almost entirely fictitious history." He wrote in 2000 that there was no substance to the story that Ohio bank robbers hid booty there in 1875, or that the cave was a stop on the Underground Railroad before and during the Civil War, because there was no supporting activity nearby for that kind of operation. Also the cave did not appear in the 1903 movie, *The Great Train Robbery*. He said that part of a 1908 movie about Jesse James, entitled *James Boys in Missouri* was shot on the Pere Marquette Railroad nearby and in Berrien Springs, which might have started the idea. The cave is part of a camp ground and camper facility, but the

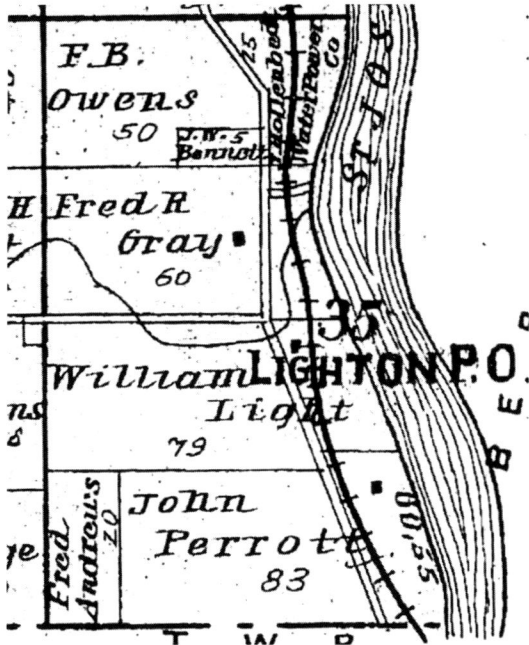

Lighton P.O., in the southeastern corner of Oronoko Township, on a map from an early 1900s Berrien County atlas.

cave may be toured by non-guest individuals and groups for a fee.

29.5 The outlet from Colvin Lake enters the river from the east.

29.6 Enter Oronoko Township, Berrien County. At this point the township boundaries are irregular and run down the middle of the river. The west bank is in Oronoko Township, and the east bank is in Berrien Township.

29.4 **Lighton** The settlement of Lighton shows on a turn of the century map of Oronoko Township, on the west bank just north of the township border and south of Painter Creek. It was a station on the Milwaukee, Benton Harbor & Columbus Railroad. A post office was established April 2, 1900, with William Light, owner of most of the land around including the local saw mill, as the first

postmaster. The postoffice closed in February of 1902.

29.42 **Hemlick (or Helmick) Settlement** was located on Grange Road just east and slightly north of the later settlement of Lighton. It was founded by Jesse Hemlick who arrived in the area in 1835 having traveled by horseback from Ohio.

29.4 Gray Run Drain enters from the west.

27.8 Painter Creek enters from the west

27.9 **Camp Oronoko** was a camp for boys from the Chicago Heart Society. The camp's slogan was "A Camp for All Ages and Creeds." The boys spent their time away from the hot and sticky summertime city, swimming in Lake Chapin, fishing, and some camps had agreements with local farmers to furnish manual labor. The central building was a bungalow built of fieldstone on the east river bank. The camp closed in 1941 after the river became too polluted for swimming. It was named for the township Oronoko, which had been set off in 1837 and named by Governor Stevens T. Mason. Early historians said the name was in honor of Oronoko, an Indian chief. However, apart from this story, there are no other mentions of such a chief. Other suggestions are that it was named for the South American river Orinoco, or for the title character of a popular novel *Oroonoko* published in 1688 concerning an African slave's adventures (and romance) in South America.

27.7 **Camp Frank S. Betz,** almost directly across the river from Camp Oronoko, with a small promontory on

147

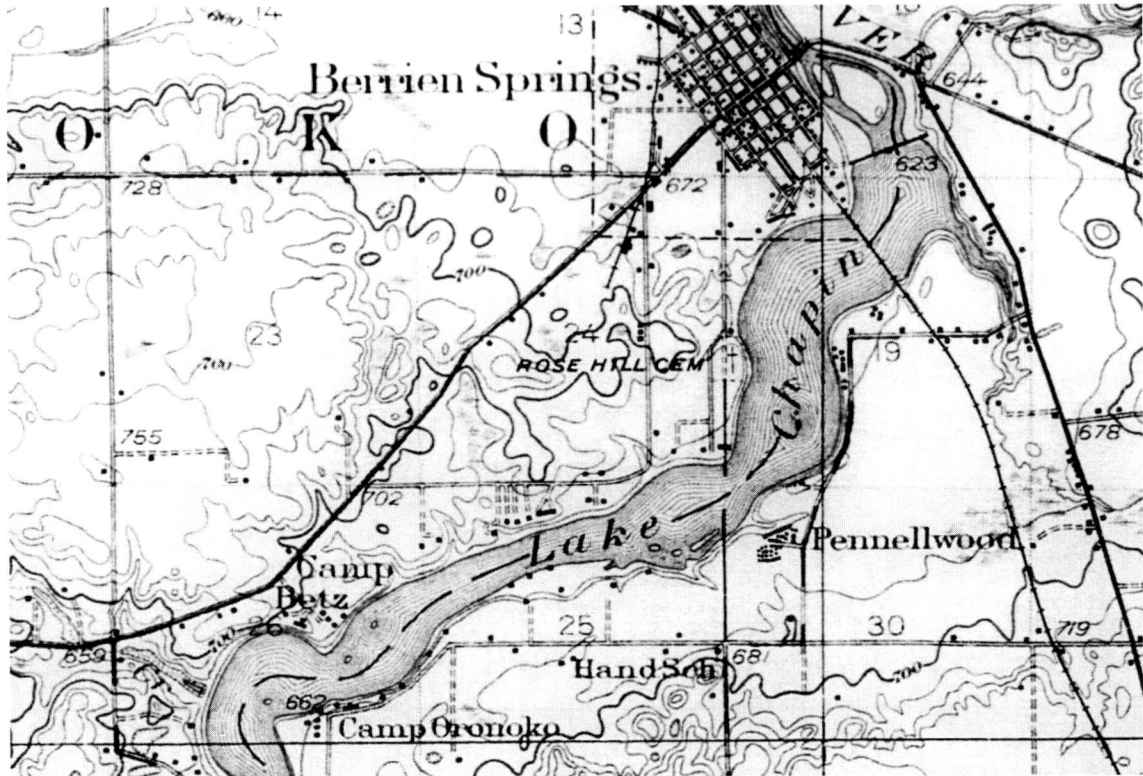

Camp Oronoko, Camp Betz and Pennellwood Resort on the shores of Lake Chapin just south of Berrien Springs on this 1930 U. S. Survey Map.

the northwest bank, has been in continuous service as a camp since 1922. In 2010 the 57-acre preserve was under the auspices of the Calumet Council of the Boy Scouts of America. It caters mainly to group camping by troops within the Calumet Council. Camp Betz is said to be the real camp that was included in the humorous (and probably fictionalized) memories of Jean Shepherd published as *A Fistful of Fig Newtons* in 1981. In the book it was called Camp Nobba-Wa-Wa-Nockee, a jab at summer camps, like Camp Oronoko across the river, taking on Indian, or Indian-sounding names.

27.3 Bridge. Twin bridges carry U.S. 31 across the river northwest-southeast.

26.6 **Pennellwood Resort** was established in 1893 by Edgar S. and

Mary Pennell when they began taking boarders at a farmhouse they had purchased in 1850. Later in addition to paying guests at the farmhouse the Pennells allowed the guests to build their own cabins. The resort was also known for good homegrown and homemade food served at the Red Lodge, a building constructed in 1873. During the growing seasons small groups would sometimes gather for an afternoon of canning and jelly making using locally grown fruit. The old lodge and resort on the southeast bank of the river off Rangeline Road was purchased by the Adventist Frontier Mission, a branch of the Seventh Day Adventist Church and in 2010 new dormitories and meeting space buildings were under construction for planned seminars to train missionaries for work around the world.

25.45 **Old bridge remains** Nine massive concrete pillars are all that is left of the world's longest interurban bridge which carried the Southern Michigan Railway Company's electric railroad across Lake Chapin from the opening of the rail service, New Year's Day, 1906, until 1934 when the interurban discontinued service. The bridge stood unused until September of 1939 when, because of the need for metal during World War II, the Wisconsin Salvage Company removed the eight steel spans between the pillars. The structure was 1,635 feet long and each pillar is approximately 60 feet in height.

25.3 A small bayou or creek enters from the southeast above the dam.

25. **Berrien Springs Dam** was built in 1908, although its construction was slowed by serious flooding in the spring of 1908. The dam has 32 feet of fall, with a pool elevation of 623 ½ feet. In 2010 it was still producing hydroelectric power for Indiana Michigan Power, a division of American Electric Power. The river above the dam is wide and called Lake Chapin to honor Henry Chapin of Niles, a major stockholder in the company which built the dam.

THE $1,000,000. DAM AT BERRIEN SPRINGS, MICH.

The Berrien Springs dam photographed shortly after it was completed in 1908. Flooding and ice damage were problems in the spring of 1908 causing much destruction to the partially built dam and a delay in completion. As the postcard notes, a million dollars was the cost of construction, a particularly extravagant amount at that time to spend on as single dam. The older interurban bridge is in the background above the dam.

24.9 Townsend Creek enters the river just below the dam.

24.8 **Fisherman's Haven Access** run by Berrien Township offers access to the river below the dam on the east bank with a boat launch and a small parking lot.

24.4 **Pardee Island** and several smaller islands are near foot of the dam.

26. – 23.5 **Berrien Springs** The area which would later be Berrien Springs was first known as **Wolf's Prairie** as it had earlier been the home of an Indian named Wolf. In 1831 when a village was surveyed at this site by Samuel Marrs, it was called simply **Berrien**, a name given the post office when it was established in 1832 with tavern keeper Pitt Brown as the first postmaster. Berrien was the name of the county for which it hoped to be the county seat. The county had been named for John B. Berrien, President Andrew Jackson's attorney general. (It is one of several southern Michigan counties named for members of Jackson's cabinet others include Vice-President Martin Van Buren, Secretaries of War John H. Eaton, and, later, Lewis Cass; Postmaster General William Barry, Secretary of Treasury Samuel D. Ingham, and Secretary of State Edward Livingston.) However when R. E. Ward settled there in 1835 he had the name of village and post office changed to Berrien Springs because of "the presence, near there, on the east bank of the river, of sulphur and other medicated springs" according to an early county history. In 1837 the place received the coveted designation as county seat, but in 1894 the courthouse function was moved to St. Joseph in 1894. The old courthouse building is now a museum. Berrien Springs was incorporated as a village by supervisors in 1863 and by the legislature in 1867. Its population in 2000 was 1,862 with a land area of one square mile.

23.8 **Indian Fields Park** offers boat access and fishing in a small park off Mechanic Street at Oak Street, in Berrien Springs.

23.75 **Rotary Island Park** is located on a small narrow island just south of the bridge. This park was established by the Berrien Springs-Eau Claire Rotary Club in 1998.

23.7 Bridge. Ferry Street crosses southwest-northeast and enters directly into downtown Berrien Springs. There is a small parking area and fishermen frequently use the area beneath the bridge. On the town side there is boat access near the southwest corner of the bridge. The first bridge to Berrien Springs was built in 1843 near the present site of the dam. In 1862 a bridge replaced the scow ferry which had been operating since 1831 from the foot of Ferry Street. A new bridge was constructed in 1888, which washed away in a spring flood in 1904. It was replaced by a new camel-back truss bridge which succumbed to a grocery semi-trailer truck on April 23, 1948. The present concrete bridge was dedicated May 1, 1995, and includes reproductions of 1930s-style coachlights.

23.4 **Shamrock Park** on the east bank is a multi-use facility run by the City of Berrien Springs. It offers camping, both full hookup and primitive sites, plus

A view of the river as it runs along old M-58 near Berrien Springs from a postcard published in the 1920s.

small cabins, a launching ramp, and bank fishing for varying fees. It is open year round and the cabins, toilets and showers and fish cleaning shed are all heated for wintertime use. The park is also a clearing house for charter boat rental and fishing.

20.8 Farmers Creek enters from the northeast.

21.7 -- 19.2 **Andrews University** The campus of Andrews University is on the north edge of Berrien Springs. The institution was founded in Battle Creek in 1874 as Battle Creek College, and moved in 1901 to the banks of the St. Joseph River where it was renamed Emmanuel Missionary College. In 1959 the School of Graduate Studies and the Seventh-day Adventist Theological Seminary from Maryland relocated to the area and the combined educational

institutions were renamed Andrews University in honor of John Nevins Andrews (1829-1883), pioneer Adventist theologian, editor, administration and the denomination's first official missionary outside of North America. In the fall of 2009 Andrews University had an enrollment of 3,589 students. The 1,573 acre campus also includes the Horn Archeological Museum.

After it passes behind Andrews University the river winds to the north with many islands and high banks.

19.1 Lemon Creek enters from the south.

17.8 Love Creek enters from the northeast.

16.4 Bridge. U. S. 31 crosses the river north-south.

15.7 Enter Royalton Township, Berrien County, on the west bank, and Sodus Township, Berrien County, on the east bank.

15.7 **Arden**, a small settlement west on Linco Road which had a post office 1896 to 1906, does not actually touch the river. The road next to the store in Arden gives access to the **Berrien County Sportsman's Club**. The club was established in 1934 according to the web site (but the sign and logo says 1947) and owns approximately 95 acres of land on the river. Facilities include archery, muzzle loader, pistol, rifle, and skeet shooting with a voice-activated trap range. Members also raise, in association with the Michigan DNR, salmon and trout for release each spring. Club facilities, launching ramps and camping are for members only.

14.5 **Tabor or Tabor Farm Resort** (6020 River Road) Wallace Tabor began growing fruit on the west bank of the river in 1854. In 1891 his son, Ernest, built the first cottages, the start of a popular summer resort. Many more cottages were added, and, later, a swimming pool and nine hole golf course. It was one of the longest operating resorts in Berrien County, but closed in 1991.

14. There are two large islands in the river at this point.

13.8 **Jasper Dairy Boating Access** is on the west bank off Niles Avenue via Jasper Dairy Road and a small gravel road. There is a concrete launching ramp, parking and toilets.

12.7 **Oxbow** is a small settlement at the end of Oxbow Road near its intersection

with River Road. There a steep road formerly allowed traffic down to the river bank which at this site is level and dry enough for a tent campground which was very popular beginning as early as 1900. The level ground is part of an oxbow in the river, and a 150-foot portage over the narrow peninsula will cut about a mile off a river trip.

10. **Kings Landing**, on the east bank, west of Sodus, was the site of a proposed dam in a 1933 federal assessment, but the dam was never realized. There is still a small community on Naomi Road. Kings Landing was a stop on the interurban from Benton Harbor to Dowagiac.

8.8 Pipestone Creek enters from the northeast.

6.1 Yellow Creek enters from the south.

6.05 Big Meadow Ditch enters from the south just to the east of the U. S. 31 bridge.

6. Bridge. M-139 (old U. S. 31) crosses the river north-south.

5.4 **Somerleyton** was a picnic spot and as late as the 1930s had a small dock which served as a destination for excursion boats from St. Joseph and Benton Harbor.

5.1 Bridge. Twin bridges carry I-94 over the river northwest-southeast.

5. There is a small park, called **Benton Park** on some maps, **Riverside** on other maps, just north of I-94 on Zollar Drive.

4.5 Enter St. Joseph Township, Berrien County.

CAMPING ON THE ST. JOE RIVER, NEAR
ST. JOE AND BENTON HARBOR, MICH.

Entire families spent summer weeks camping on the banks of the St. Joseph River in Berrien County. This is a 1911 scene, probably at the big camp at Oxbow.

STEAMER MILTON D.
LANDING AT SOMERLEYTON ON
ST. JOSEPH RIVER

Somerleyton was a destination for excursion boats from St. Joseph until the 1930s.

Bessie Ray Hoover
Author of Popular Novels

Bessie Ray Hoover was a sometime college teacher born in St. Joseph in 1874. She used St. Joseph, and nearby communities along the river, as the setting for her novels. Some writers have suggested that Berrien Springs is the actual model for "Hollywood," the setting for her 1922 novel *Rolling Acres,* although an 1893 map shows a community named Hollywood south of Benton Harbor, not far from the river. The novel is about Norman Lybrook, related to English aristocracy, whose efforts to live the aristocratic life in southwest Michigan get him into financial trouble. At the same time his 18-year-old daughter is inundated with beaus, each with his own tale to tell. Just in time, when it looks like they will lose the farm, Lybrook's English brother dies and a portion of the inheritance lands in his mailbox.

Some excerpts:

> Hollywood, a pretty inland village, set above the winding St. Joseph river under fine old trees, was the center of a rich farming district. . . The real population was about fifteen hundred, though a bold-faced little real estate folder said, "Upwards to three thousand souls," a commercial compliment that deceived nobody.

> As they drove down the hill to the river bridge, the myrtle runners carpeting the roadside fluttered like small triumphant banners in their progress. And the very planks of the bridge were gilded by the afternoon sun into a golden way. The river muttered and chucked mysteriously below them. . . and Kelpie's shod hoofs beat decorously on the worn planks like hidden music. .

Hoover had begun in 1907 to contribute stories to Eastern periodicals about the fictional Flickenger family of southwest Michigan. In the first story Hoover sets

> "the family's cheerfulness, kindliness and determination to make the best of everything off against the . . . ever pitiless squeeze that attaches to those whose wallets are inconsiderably lean."

The stories were eventually published as *Pa Flickenger's Folks* in 1909. *Opal,* which debuted in 1910, is a novel of the "new woman," a common type of story in the early 1900s. In it Opal Fickenger finds that the primitive conditions of her home, make it difficult for her to "become a lady." She finishes high school, unusual for rural girls at that time and, despite the family's wish that she teach school, she marries a well-to-do young farmer.

Some lists of her works indicate that there was a third book, between *Opal* and *Rolling Acres* entitled *Ivy May.* Bessie Hoover was still living in St. Joseph as late as 1930.

The old iron Napier Bridge from a 1909 postcard view.

4.7 – 3.9 **Riverview Park** is on the south bank. Facilities include a boat ramp, toilets, playground, nature trails, picnic area and the Waldo Tiscornia Boys Field to honor the founder of Auto Specialties, an important local industry. To reach the park on land follow M-63 (Niles Road) and turn north into the park access road located just south of Riverview Cemetery.

4. – 3.7 **Carronde Park** on north bank has a boat ramp, toilets and picnic area.

3.6 – 3.4 **Emery Island** sits in the middle of the river channel even with the end of Jakway Drive on the east bank where **Emery Fruit Farm Resort** welcomed visitors, mostly Greek vacationers from Chicago, from 1906 to 1950. The place featured Greek dancing and singing, late night card games and Greek food. It was one of several resorts in the area catering to ethnic groups. Elsewhere in the area, not always on the river, were establishments favored by Czechs, Germans and Jewish vacationers.

3. Hickory Creek enters from the southwest

2.8 – 0 **St. Joseph**. Before 1700 the site of St. Joseph was visited in the 1600s by French fur traders and Robert La Salle and his company. They built a small fort there and later a mission and called it **Fort Miamis.** The first settlers who arrived in 1827, called their settlement **Saranac** after a boat on the Great Lakes. Calvin Brittain arrived in 1829 and

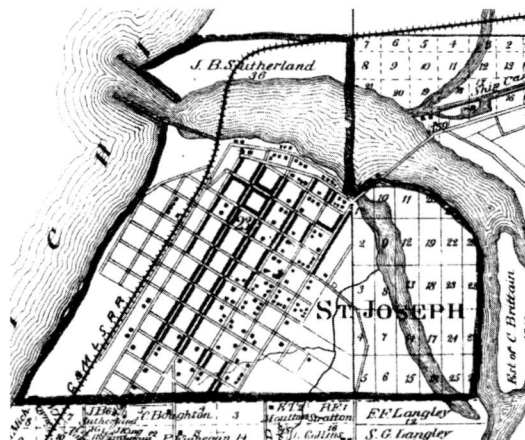

St. Joseph in 1873, note Morrisons Channel is still only a bayou.

155

platted a village in 1831which he called **Newburyport,** probably after Newburyport, Massachusetts. Brittain was the first postmaster in March 1829, of a post office called Saranac. Even the early French settlers often called the place and the river St. Joseph after the patron saint of travelers and missionaries. In 1832 the name of the post office was changed to St. Joseph and the following year the legislature officially changed the name of the village. The settlement was incorporated as a village in 1834, and as a city in 1891. The Berrien County seat was moved from Berrien Springs to St. Joseph in 1894 following a bitter contest between Niles, Benton Harbor and St. Joseph. None of the candidates could win a majority of votes of the county board. Finally Benton Harbor and St. Joseph joined to keep the center of government on their side of the county. The population of St. Joseph was 8,789 on the 2000 census, with an area of six square miles.

2.4 – 2.25. **Triangular Island,**

2.5 **Fair Plain** is an unincorporated area on the north bank of the river, south of the City of Benton Harbor. It is part of St. Joseph Charter Township and has no legal status as a municipality, but is a census designated place with a population of 7,828 in the 2000 census. Fair Plain was a largely agricultural area in the 19th and early 20th centuries and there are still many large stately homes overlooking the St. Joseph River.

2.5 Bridge. A modern bridge which replaced an old iron bridge, carries Napier Avenue across the river southwest-northeast.

2.3 **Site of Burnett's Trading Post** on the west bank off Langley Street. Former New Jersey resident William Burnett established a trading post here on the west bank of the river in 1775. He married Kakima, daughter of Aniquiba and sister of Topinabee who was chief of a village near Niles.In 1785 the British arrested Burnett and charged him with "exciting sedition" among the Indians. He was sent to jail in Canada, but was later released without trial. During the War of 1812 William Burnett disappeared, but the trading post was kept open, operated by his wife and then his son, until 1833. There is an historical marker on Miller Drive off Langeley.

2.1 **Spinks Spring Bluff Resort** was opened about 1860 by Robert Spink, on the bluff at the end of May Street on the east bank of the river. There were accommodations for about 80 people, with a water slide down the bluff into the water, rafts, canoes, and hiking in the woods. The Spinks sold the establishment in 1896.

2. – .9 **Morrison Channel,** suitable for small boats, separates Harbor Island from the St. Joseph on the west side of the main river. The channel is named for Alexander Hamilton Morrison, who had a large woodenware factory nearby. Until at least 1873 it was a long narrow bayou, closed at the bottom end. About 1890 the channel was cut thorough and dredged to assist in keeping small boats and fishermen out of the busy main channel and creating a new island.

2. – .9 The large island created by Morrison Channel is variously called **Harbor Isle**, **Radio Island** or **Marina Island.** It contains the Benton Harbor–

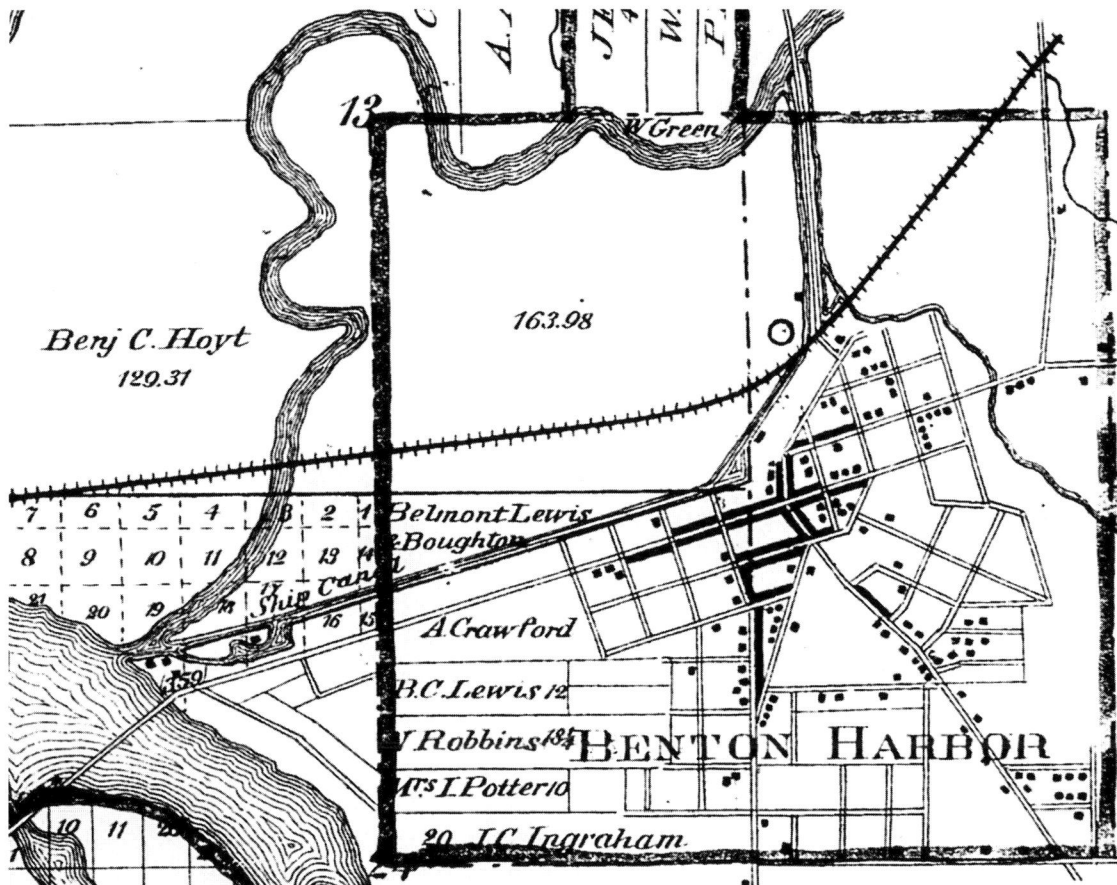

Benton Harbor from an 1873 map showing the Ship Canal which runs from the St. Joseph River, lower left, into downtown Benton Harbor, with a triangular turning basin. Water for the canal is augmented with a connection to the Paw Paw River, upper center.

St. Joseph Wastewater Treatment plant, numerous marinas and yacht clubs and a four-lane launching ramp with a large parking lot, run by the City of St. Joseph near the northeast end of the island. A similar boat ramp is located at Benton Harbor on the north bank of the river.

2 – 1.7 **Benton Harbor** Although there had been Europeans at St. Joseph as early as the 17th Century, the northwest side of the river was developed much more slowly. It remained scattered households until 1860 when a handful of local businessmen financed a canal from the St. Joseph River into what would become downtown. They platted a village in 1863 and named it **Brunson Harbor** for Sterne Brunson. It was later renamed for Thomas Hart Benton, a Missouri senator who had helped Michigan become a state. Henry C. Morton was the first postmaster when the office opened in 1865. Benton Harbor was incorporated as a village by the supervisors in 1866 and by the legislature in 1869. It was incorporated as a city in 1891. The city is known for the Benton Harbor Fruit Market established in 1860 and open each growing season on Territorial Road. It is billed as "the world's largest 'cash-to-grower' wholesale market." The population of the city was 11,182 in

Blossomtime

In 1906 Blossom Sunday was suggested by Rev. W. J. Cady of the First Congregational Church in Benton Harbor who urged parishioners to drive through the orchards and view the blossoms. Cady called them "the symbol of life renewed." Observance of Blossom Sunday continued with time out for two World Wars. Both towns were always included, the big parade began in St Joseph and ended in Benton Harbor. Today it draws from a larger area and is held the first Saturday in May. It bills itself the "oldest and largest multi-cultural festival in Michigan."

2000, with a land area of 4.5 square miles. Only a small portion of Benton Harbor, near the southwest corner, actually touches the river. Most of that river footage forms Riverfront Park.

2 – 1.6 **Riverfront Park** is located on the east side of the river and includes a fishing area, children's play area, picnic facilities and a boat launch to access fishing up and down the river. It is located on Riverview Drive, on the Benton Harbor side, and is actually three facilities, along the river from Empire Street to the end of Riverview. Moving downriver the first section is **Charles L. Yarborough Park** with a playground, picnic pavilion and portable toilet, the second section is a three lane paved launching ramp, with parking available for a fee, and the closest-to-town section is a series of fishing piers including some facilities for wheelchair-bound fishermen.

1.2 **Bicentennial Bridge**. A bridge from Wayne Street, on the St. Joseph side near the Berrien County Courthouse crosses Morrison Channel, touches down on Harbor Isle, then crosses the main channel of the St. Joseph River and comes into downtown Benton Harbor on Main Street.

1. **Benton Harbor Ship Canal**. In 1860 Sterne Brunson, Henry Morton and Charles Hull commissioned civil engineers J. E. Miller and Martin Green of Chicago to design and dredge a shipping canal to run about a mile from the St. Joseph River into downtown Benton Harbor. It would contain a basin approximately 150 feet wide to allow the largest commercial steamers to turn around. It was later enlarged several times and was the home dock for some active boat lines including the Graham & Morton Transportation Company. By 1937 transportation by boat was little utilized and the City of Benton Harbor began filling in the canal to create space for a parking lot and better roads in the area. By 1970 the old canal was little more than a drainage ditch. However in the 1980s the city began to consider renewing the canal for use, primarily, for fishing and recreational boats. As a candidate for a Cities of Promise designation, a program begun in 2006 to revitalize struggling urban areas, Benton Harbor might be able to receive Economic Stimulus Funds to make it a reality.

.9 Paw Paw River enters from the north having already picked up Brush Creek, Mill Creek, Blue Creek, Ox Creek and the east, south and north branches (the north also known as Campbell Creek). The Paw Paw River serves as an outlet

The Blossomland Bridge is an unusual Scherzer rolling-lift bascule bridge. It opens on a regular schedule in the boating season to allow large boats, and those with high masts, to get upriver.

for Paw Paw Lake in the northeastern corner of Berrien County near the villages of Watervliet, Coloma and the old summer resort community of Paw Paw Lake. For three-quarters of its length it flows crookedly south, parallel to Lake Michigan, it furnished some of the water for the Benton Harbor Ship Canal.

.7 Blossomland Bridge A concrete highway bridge carries the Harry Gast Parkway (M-63, Main Street in downtown St. Joseph) over the river southwest-northeast. It is a Scherzer rolling-lift bascule bridge and counterbalanced to lower one end while the other is raised. During the navigation season the bridge is manned to allow it to open as needed. The first bridge at this site was built in 1948 to relocate what was then U. S. 31and relieve traffic congestion between St. Joseph and Benton Harbor.

Bluff Lighthouse The first lighthouse at St. Joseph was built in 1832 on the bluff on the south side of the river mouth overlooking the harbor. It was a 30-foot conical rubble-stone tower with a one story detached keeper's house. It was replaced in 1859 with a combined tower and keeper's home on an even higher vantage point. A short, square tower rose from the front roof peak of a two-story clapboard house. When lights were installed on the pier in 1907 the government wanted to discontinue the bluff light, but an active campaign in Congress by residents and Lakes captains kept it operating until 1924. The second bluff lighthouse stood until September of 1955 when the City of St. Joseph had it razed to make way for a parking lot.

.6 Lighthouse Depot A brick lighthouse depot was opened in 1893 on the north side of the river, just inside the piers

The Life-Saving Station crew practicing their drill from a 1908 postcard. The large dark building in the center of the picture is the Lighthouse Depot.

where it was easily accessible to supply ships and lighthouse tenders. It was to service all of Lake Michigan, but proved to be too small to winter the boats, so in 1904 a new depot was constructed in Milwaukee. The St. Joseph River installation continued in service to supply the east shore of the lake and grew to be a four-building complex before it was discontinued in 1917. In 1918 the depot was transferred to the Navy, and when government funding was discontinued it was used by the Army Reserve, and then the Michigan National Guard until 1993. In 1993 the depot was placed on the National Register of Historic Places. Three years later it was bought by private parties and opened as a brewpub and restaurant. In 2003, again available, it was purchased by the **St. Joseph River Yacht Club** which traded its old headquarters just upriver for the old depot and a new swimming pool. The complex includes the old keeper's dwelling to the east of the depot which was renovated by the yacht club in 2007.

.5 – . 2 **Margaret Upton Arboretum and Howard Family Recreational Trail** on the south bank of the river extending roughly from the railroad bridge to the Blossomland Bridge is the Upton Arboretum with unusual plantings, benches, drinking fountains (for people and animals) and old fashioned "porch" swings. Above the gardens, but clearly visible from the river, is the modernistic **John E. N. Howard Bandshell** where free concerts are offered weekly in the summertime by the St. Joseph Municipal Band, the only tax-supported band in Michigan. Above the bandshell on the bluff is a sculpture of a fireman carrying a small child, which tops a monument dedicated to five firemen from St. Joseph who died September 6, 1896, while fighting a fire in Yore's Opera House in Benton Harbor. The sculpture was created by W. L. Cottrel. The paved trail which runs along the top of the park includes a series of historical information boards on area maritime and art history. Near the small parking lot off Water Street there

160

is a bronze sculpture of a man and two children playing in the sand entitled *Sand Castles – What Dreams are Made of . . .* The sculpture is the work of Charles Park and was dedicated in 1989 in memory of Frederick S. Upton.

.5 **Pioneer's Watch** Near the Fireman's Monument there is a concrete platform with an iron railing which was erected in 1939 to offer a place to view the mouth of the river. This spot has been used as a lookout point since the days of Fort Miamis.

.5 Railroad Bridge. The railroad swing bridge is actually the third constructed at this site. The first one, built in 1870 by the Chicago & Michigan Lake Shore Railroad, was replaced in 1887 by the Chicago and West Michigan Railroad because the bridge was too light for the new train engines. In 1904 the third and present bridge was constructed by the Pere Marquette Railroad. The 231-foot, 300-ton bridge is so well balanced that it can be turned with one ten horsepower motor, and can be opened in less than a minute. It is now owned and maintained by CSX Transportation and is still in use. During the boating season an attendant is on duty 24 hours. In winter it is locked closed to accommodate trains, including daily Amtrak passenger trains, which stop at the old depot south of the river between Silver Beach and the bluff.

.4 **Coast Guard Station** In 1855 the U. S. government began a volunteer Life-Saving Station St. Joseph by furnishing a Francis Life Car. By May of 1877 Joseph A. Napier had been named the first chief of the station, although the crew was still volunteer. It was not until 1879 that U. S. government formed the

Life-Saving Service, and stationed a full complement of trained life savers at the station near the north pier in Lake Michigan. The present station dates from that time. In 1881 a story and a half addition was made to the original building. It contained a mess room, crew quarters, kitchen, pantry and keeper's room. The upper story was used for light storage. The old building remained for boat and equipment storage. The men of the station were responsible for many daring rescues including one at Saugatuck in 1880, when a grounded tug was in danger of breaking up in high seas. The crew of the life-saving station with their equipment hurried to the scene by train, being met at the nearest station

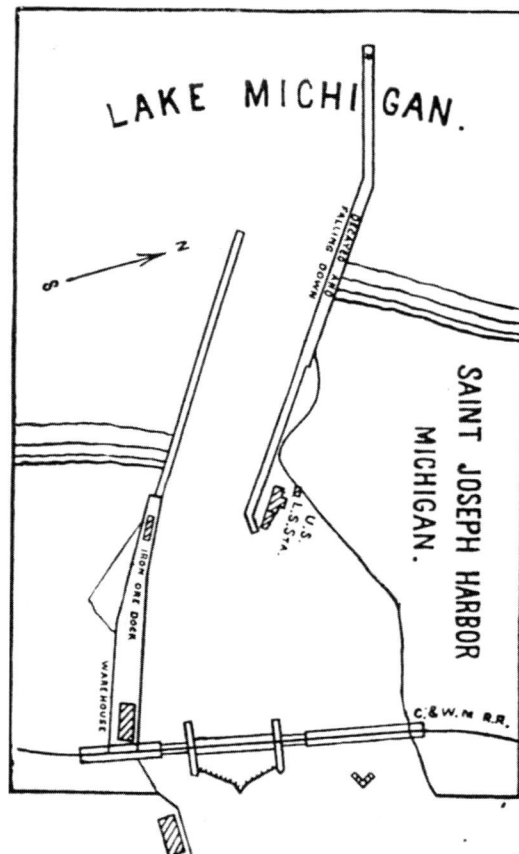

An 1896 chart of St. Joseph Harbor showing the railroad bridge and the Life-Saving Station just inside the north pier.

Silver Beach Amusement Park with the roller coaster "Chase through the Clouds." The carousel is in the center foreground, and Shadowland Ballroom at lower left.

to Saugatuck, New Richmond, by a small tug which took them down the river. Unable to get near the distressed tug, the men set up their Lisle gun on the beach and were able to bring 16 stranded sailors ashored on a breeches buoy. One man washed overboard before the life-savers arrived. In 1915 the Life-Saving Service and the Revenue-Cutter Service were combined to establish the U.S. Coast Guard. The St. Joseph Coast Guard station was renovated in 1920, and the boathouse was replaced in 1933. It is one of the oldest continuous stations on the Great Lakes and is still active.

.6 – .4 Silver Beach, on the south side of the river under the bluff at St. Joseph, is one of the largest and finest swimming beaches in West Michigan. In the 1890s two St. Joseph men began a "resort" with a series of rental cottages. Wooden concession stands, a water slide, and a boardwalk were added to make the resort

a destination. A moving wooden staircase made the climb from the bluff less arduous, and an indoor swimming pool, using heated lake water, was built in 1902. Many new amusements became part of the park: a dog cart ride for children, an indoor skating rink, a carousel imported from Germany, bowling alley, aeroplane ride, and a roller coaster called "Chase through the Clouds." In 1927 the Shadowland Ballroom opened. The park was still owned by the same family which had begun it, when it finally closed in 1970. The rides and some buildings were removed in a controlled fire in 1975. The site was purchased by the City of St. Joseph which leased the beach area to the Berrien County Park system, and began a revival of summertime activities. A brand new carousel, open year round, debuted in the summer of 2009, and the Whirlpool Compass fountain, a summer splash park,

*The **City of Chicago** enters St. Joseph harbor in this 1920 postcard. The boat may be waiting for the railroad bridge to be opened.*

*The **City of Chicago** passing the St. Joseph pier, at left, and the Life-Saving Station boathouse at right.*

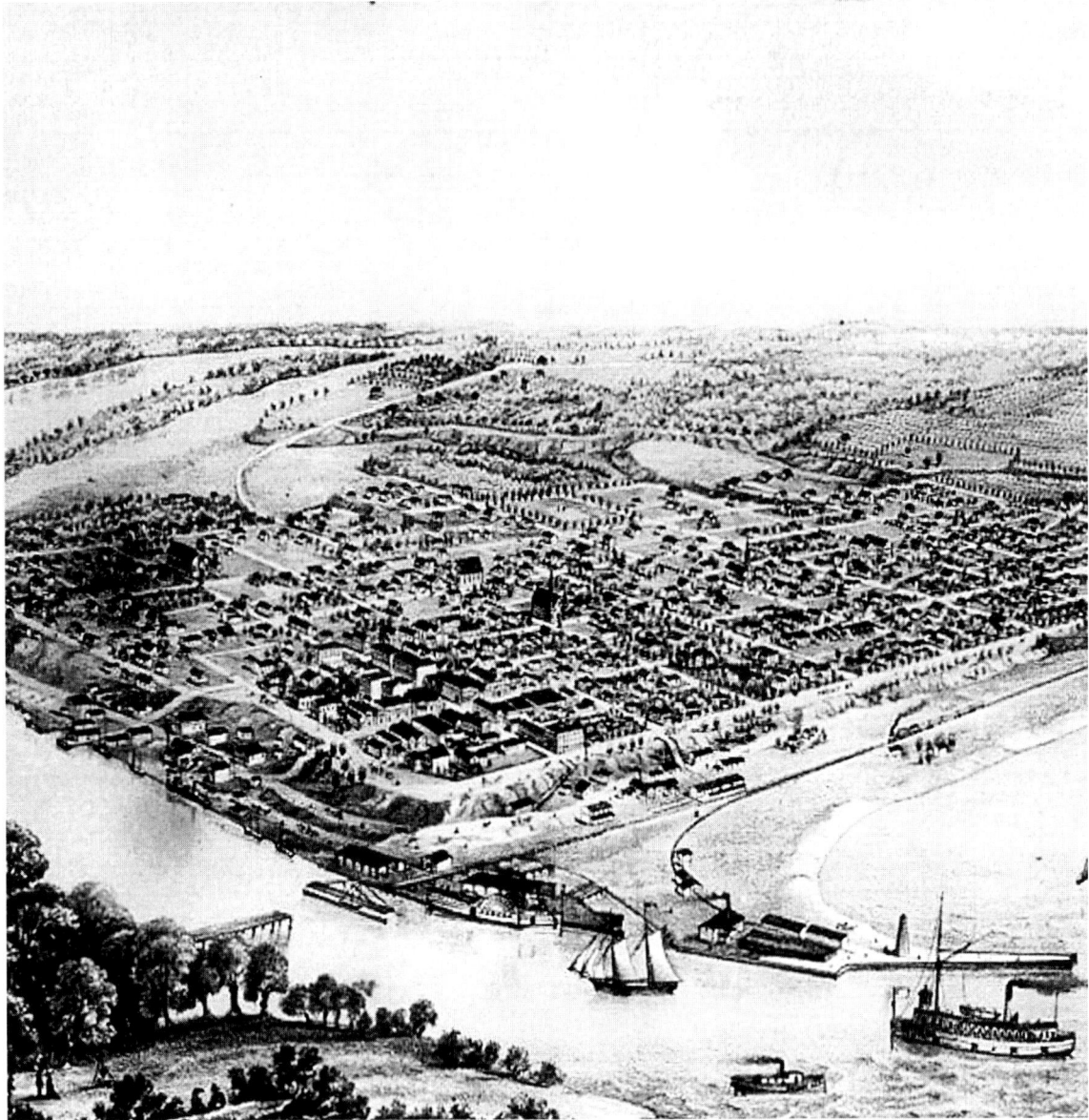

A birdeye view of St. Joseph Harbor drawn in 1870 showing a bustling harbor, and several boats, both steam and sail entering the piers. The railroad tracks run along the beach, with a swing bridge which opens to let the boats go upriver.

First Powered Flight at Silver Beach

It was on the beach at right that the first powered flight took place on October 11, 1898, when. Augustus Moore Herring took one of his gliders fitted with a motor to Silver Beach. Herring's machine lifted ever so slightlyoff the ground and actually flew for seven seconds. Eleven days later he made another flight of ten seconds. While Herring had a powered, heavier-than-air craft, he has not been credited with the first powered flight because he did not have a way to control it. It was left to the Wright brothers to make the first motor-powered controlled flight five years later at Kitty Hawk, North Carolina.

combined with computerized light shows, opened in September of 2009. Other activities include Michigan's tallest kaleidoscope and a new Shadowland pavilion, with a large dance floor and a seating capacity of more than 300 for concerts and which is available for rent. A Silver Beach Amusement Park Museum is planned.

.4 – .3 **Tiscornia Park** A small park on the beach at the land end of the north pier. There is a swimming beach on Lake Michigan, access to the north pier for fishing, rest rooms, and a picnic pavilion. There is a fee for non-residents sometimes in the summer. Take Klock Road off M-63, turn right on Marina Drive, right on Ridgeway Street, and right on Tiscornia Park Drive.

.05 – .01 **Pier Lights** It is not certain when the first light was built on the north pier. When the pier was lengthened in 1907 another light was placed on the new end of the pier. The pierhead light, the front range light, is a 35 foot slightly conical cast iron tower. The rear light on the north pier about 900 feet behind the front light, is a bigger structure which houses the diaphone fog signal, but also had a light tower. It is 57 feet tall. Boat pilots align the two range lights to enter the harbor correctly. A catwalk connects the range lights to shore. The fog horn was taken out of commission in 1970 and replaced with an electric signal. In May of 2008 the pierhead lights were deemed excess and the Federal government offered them at no cost to any municipality with a plan for their upkeep. In 2009 the City of St. Joseph had made an application which was approved pending restoration work on the light. In 1995 the North Pier lighthouse was featured by the U. S. Postal Service as part of a series of commemorative Great Lakes lighthouse stamps. Both piers are accessible to the general public, the North Pier from Tiscornia Park, and the South Pier from Silver Beach.

0. Enter Lake Michigan.

Fishing from the St. Joseph harbor south pier some time after the 1907 extension.

Bibliography

Alvord, Clarence Walworth *The Conquest of St Joseph Michigan by the Spaniards in 1781* (Reprinted from the Missouri Historical Review, April, 1908).

Andrews, Clarence A. *Michigan in Literature* (Wayne State University Press: Detroit) 1992.

Bachman, Patricia Benson *Carey Mission: Home of the Brave!* (Graphic Press: Flint) 1972.

Baker, George A. *The St. Joseph-Kankakee Portage* (North Indiana Historical Society: South Bend) 1899.

Baker, Ronald L. and Marvin Carmony *Indiana Place Names* (Indiana University Press: Bloomington) 1975.

Ballard, Ralph *Old Fort St. Joseph* (Niles Printing Co.) 1949.

Ballard, Ralph *Tales of Early Niles* (Niles Printing Co.) 1948.

Bartlett, Charles H. and Richard H. Lyon *La Salle in the Valley of the St. Joseph* (Tribune Printing Co.: South Bend, Indiana) 1899.

Blois, John T. *Gazetteer of the State of Michigan* (Sydney L. Rood & Co.: Detroit) 1838.

Bradford, Ken "Owner sells grounded riverboat to give it new chance at life in Georgia," *South Bend Tribune,* May 5, 2003.

Brelsford, Harry E. "A 1902 Trip Down the River in a $3 Boat" *Niles Daily Star,* July 31, 1975.

Buchanan Centennial Commemorating 100 Years of Progress (Buchanan Centennial Association) 1958.

Bugbee, W. A. "Early Navigation on St. Joseph River," *Niles Daily Star-Sun,* March 18, 1922.

Callary, Edward ed. *Place Names in the Midwestern United States* (The Edward Mellen Press: Lewiston, New York) 2000.

Carleton, Will *Songs of the Centuries* (Harper & Brothers: New York) 1902.

Detzler, Jack J. *South Bend 1910-1921; A Decade Dedicated to Reform* (Northern Indiana Historical Society: South Bend) 1960.

"Diggin' Fort St. Joseph" *Michigan History* Sept/Oct 2001, p. 39-43.

Dixon, David *Never Come to Peace Again: Pontiac's Uprising and the Fate of the British Empire in North America* (University of Oklahoma Press: Norman) 2005.

Dowd, Gregory Evans *War Under Heaven: Pontiac, the Indian Nations, & the British Empire* (The Johns Hopkins University Press: Baltimore) 2002.

Dowling, Edward J. "The Dustless Road to Happyland," *Michigan History,* June, 1947, p.162-173.

Drake, Samuel Adams *The Making of the Ohio Valley States* (Charles Scribner's Sons: New York) 1894.

Echoes of Summertime Pleasures; St Joseph and Benton Harbor The Twin Cities of the East Shore and Their Multitude of Attractions (Graham & Morton co: Benton Harbor) 1893.

Emery, B. Frank *The Passing of the Mission and Fort St. Joseph 1686 – 1781* (The Old Forts and Historic Memorial Association: Detroit) 1931.

From a Meek Beginning: Village of Constantine, Reflections of 150 years, 1828-1978 (n. p.) 1978.

Gilbert, Arlan K. *Historic Hillsdale College; Pioneer in Higher Education, 1844-1900* (Hillsdale College Press) 1991.

Harburn, Dr. Todd *British Folly on the St. Joseph* (Michilimackinac Society Press) 2002.

Hawes, Daniel *The Story of Buchanan* (Berrien County Historical Association: Berrien Springs) 2004.

Hillsdale Area Centennial, 1869-1969 n. p. n.d.

Hinsdale, Wilbert B. *Archeological Atlas of Michigan* (University of Michigan Press: Ann Arbor) 1931.

History of Berrien and Van Buren Counties, Michigan (D. W. Ensign & Co.: Philadelphia) 1880.

Hoover, Bessie Ray *Rolling Acres* (Small, Maynard & Company: Boston) 1922..

Howard, Timothy Edward *A History of St. Joseph County, Indiana Vol. I* (The Lewis Publishing Company: Chicago) 1907

Huggler, Tom *Fish Michigan: 50 Rivers* (Friede Publications: Davison, Michigan) 1995.

Hyde, Charles K. *Historic Highway Bridges of Michigan* (Wayne State University: Detroit) 1993.

Illustrated Historical Atlas of the State of Indiana (Baker, Forster & Company: Chicago) 1876.

Kelley, R. W. and W. R. Farrand *The Glacial Lakes Around Michigan* (Michigan Geological Survey, Department of Natural Resource: Lansing) 1967.

Knoblock, Otto M. *Early Navigation on the St. Joseph River* (Indiana Historical Society Publication: Indianapolis) 1925.

Lake Bluff Park Monuments, Memorials & Historic Sites (St. Joseph Today) n.d.

MacLean, Harrison John *The Fate of the Griffon* (The Swallow Press Inc: Chicago) 1974.

Myers, Robert C. *Historical Sketches of Berrien County Vol. 3* (Berrien County Historical Society) 1994

Myers, Robert C. *Historical Sketches of Berrien County Vol. 4* (Berrien County Historical Society) 2001.

Odekirk, Veronique decq *Bertrand, Michigan, It's Origins, Development and Decline, 1833-1855* Thesis in partial fulfillment for a Masters of Arts Degree in American Studies (Notre Dame, April 1983).

One Hundredth Anniversary of Constantine 1828-1928 (The Constantine Advertiser Record)

Paddling Through History in St. Joseph County, Michigan (River Country Heritage Water Trails) 2006.

Parkman, Francis *The Conspiracy of Pontiac* (Collier Books: New York) 1962. C. 1851.

Parkman, Francis *La Salle and the Discovery of the Great West* (The Modern Library: New York) 1999 (Boston: Little, Brown and Company) 1913. C. 1897

Plym, J. B. ed. *Charlevoix, 1682-1761: Fort St. Joseph Historical Association Leaflet No. 1* (Niles, Michigan) May, 1942.

Plym, J. B. ed. *Hennepin: Fort St. Joseph Historical Association Leaflet No, 2 (Niles, Michigan) April, 1948.*

Reber, L. Benj. *History of St. Joseph* (St.Joseph Chamber of Commerce) n.d.

Rice, Bernard, ed. *J. Harold Kiracofe's History of Osceola; A Biographical and Historical Record of Osceola, Indiana* (Osceola Historical Society) 1988.

Riebs, George E. *Elkhart: A Pictorial History* (G. Bradley Publishing Inc: St. Louis, MO) 1990.

Rieder, Marcia L. and John L. Manuszak *The Course of a River: A St. Joseph River Experience, River and Shore Connections* n.p., n.d.

Riley, H. H., *Puddleford and Its People* (Samuel Hueston: New York) 1854.

Ringwelski, Brother Romanus *Early History of Bertrand, Michigan* (Thesis in partial fulfillment for a Bachelor of Arts degree, University of Notre Dame) 1933.

Scott, George *Scott's New Coast Pilot for the Lakes* (The Free Press Printing Co.: Detroit) 1896.

Shepherd, Jean *A Fistful of Fig Newtons* (Doubleday: New York) 1981.

Smith, Timothy S. *Missionary Abominations Unmasked or a View of Carey Mission containing an Unmasking of the Missionary Abominations Practiced among the Indians of St. Joseph County at the Celebrated Missionary Establishment known as Carey Mission under the Superintendence of the Rev. Isaac McCoy* (Beacon Office: South Bend) 1833.

Souers, James L. *A Paddling Guide for the St. Joseph River* (Published by author) 2000.

St. Joseph River *Michigan and Indiana, map to accompany report to the Corps of Engineers* dated Mar 5, 1932 (U. S. Engineer Office: Milwaukee Wisconsin).

Terrell, John Upton *La Salle: The Life and Times of an Explorer* (Weybright and Talley: New York) 1968.

Thomopoulos, Elaine Cotsiriles *Resorts of Berrien County* (Arcadia: Chicago) 2005.

Thurtell, Joel "He got forecast right, but. . ." *South Bend Tribune,* July 8, 1979.

Thwaites, Reuben Gold *Father Marquette* (D. Appleton & Company: New York) 1902.

Turner, T. G. *Gazetteer of St. Joseph Valley of Michigan and Indiana for 1867 with a View of its Hydraulic and Business Capacities* (Hazlitt & Reed, Printers: Chicago) 1867.

Waterman, Nixon, ed. *Ben King's Verse* (The Press Club of Chicago) 1894

Webster, Mildred E. *French Saint Joseph: Le Poste de la Riviere St. Joseph: 1690 – 1780* (Published by the author) 1986.

Weissert, Charles A. *Southwest Michigan and St. Joseph County* (National Historical Association) n.d.

Wesley, Jay K. and Joan E. Duffy *St. Joseph River Assessment, Fisheries Special Report 24 and Appendix* (Michigan Department of Natural Resources, Fisheries Division) September 1999.

Woodruff, James C. *LaSalle and Michigan's History: About the Adventures of Rene Robert Cavelier, Sieur De LaSalle In and around Michigan 1679-1683* (Published by the author) 1999.

Woodruff, James C. *Locating Michigan's Old Canoe Portages* 2 vols. (Published by the author) 2006.

Wright, Jerome *Three Rivers Historical Scrapbook, Vol. 1* (World of Publishing: Three Rivers) 2006.

Zerler, Glenn and Kathryn *Blossomtime Festival Southwest Michigan: A Pictorial History, 1906-1996* (Blossomtime Incorporated: Benton Harbor) 1995.

Index

Blois, John T. 5
Blossom Lake 89
Blossom Sunday 158
Blossomland Bridge 159,*159,*
    160
Blossomtime 158
Blue Creek 158
Bodine, Richard Clay 120
Bodner, Pierce 97
Boot Lake 71
Bowman, John H. 100
Boydston, Kay and Walter
    146
Branch County 4,5,11,58,80,
    81,87-89
Brandywine Creek *136,*138
Brelsford, Harry 142-143
Brewer, J. W. 35
Bridgeman 54
Bristol 32,*110,111,*111-112
Bristol Conservation Club
    111
Brittain, Calvin 155
Broadhurst, William 144
Broadway bridge 51
Brooklyn *99,*100
Brown Creek 101
Brown, Pitt 150
Brown, Samuel R. 7
Brownsfield Park 132
Brunson Harbor 157
Brunson, Sterne 157,158
Brush Creek 158
Buchanan 19,36,53,54,58,63,
    *136,*145-146
Buchanan dam 36,48,52,
    55,142-143,145,*145*
Buchanan fish ladder 56
Buchanan St. Joseph River
    Boating Access Site 146
Buchanan Township 22,144
Buchanan, James 145
Buck Creek 109
Buck, George 98,100
Bucks 100
Buell Drain 88
Bunnell, Eli P. 139
Burgee, John 129
Burlington (gunboat) 85
Burlington *80,85,*85
Burlington dam 85

Burlington Station *85,*85
Burlington Township 85,87
Burnett Creek 86
Burnett, William 31,156
Butler Township 81
Buzzard, Jim 104

Cady, W. J. 158
Cahokia 26,27,*27*
Calhoun County 5,11,80,81,
    83,85,90
Calumet Council of Boy
    Scouts of America 148
Calumet River 38
Cambria Township 70,72
Camp Frank S. Betz 147-
    148,*148*
Camp Nabba-Wa-Wa-
    Nockee 148
Camp Oronoko 147, *148,*148,
Campbell Creek 158
Canada *99,*100
Canoeing 59
Carey 140
Carey Mission 19,21-23,
    31,140
Carey, William 22
Carleton, Will 75
Carolina Parakeet 6
Carp Rodeo 58
Carronde Park 155
*Carte du Canada ou de la
    Nouvelle France* 4
Cass County 5,11,109, 111
Cass Lake 111
Cass, Lewis 9,22,150
Cassopolis 53
Castacrow, Mr. 26
Castle Manor 122
Cathcart Cemetery 112
Cavelier, Jean 13
Cavelier, Rene-Robert 13
Cayuga Creek 14
Cedar Island 37
Central Park (Mishawaka)
    122-123
Century Center 52,54,129-
    130
Charles L. Yarborough Park
    158
Champion 34

Champlin, Elisha P. 77
Chapin Company 54
Chapin, Henry 149
Chardon, Francis 21
Charles III of Spain 28
Charleston Township,
    Kalamazoo Co. 101
Charlevoix, Francois Xavier
    12,24,25,31
Chattahoochee River 40
Chevalier, Louis 28,29
Chevalier, Louison 26
Chicago 10,28,32,33,34,37,
    41,77,94,108,137,145
Chicago 33-34
Chicago & Michigan Lake
    Shore Railroad 161
Chicago and West Michigan
    Railroad 161
Chicago Heart Society 147
Chicago River *14*
Chicago Road 108
Chicago, South Bend and
    Northern Indiana Railway
    126
Chicangoni 8
Chim, Mr. 26
Chippewa 21
Christiana Creek *110,*112,114
Christiana Lake 114
Church Drain 76
Cities of Promise 158
"City Beautiful Movement"
    129
City of Chicago *163*
City of Elkhart 40
City of Four Flags 140
City Park (Niles) 140
Civil War 36
Clarendon *80, 82,*82,83
Clarendon and Eckford Drain
    83
Clarendon Centre 82
Clarendon Station 83
Clarendon Township 81
Clarendon, New York 82
Clark, George Rogers 26
Clark, Lloyd 17
Clay Township 133
Clay Township Park 135
Clean Water Act 64

Boat names are in **bold.**   *Italic* page numbers indicate an illustration.

Kit Lane is a Michigan native who has been researching and studying the state's history for more than 40 years as a newspaper reporter, a publisher of weekly newspapers on the western side of the state, and, finally, an author of more than 20 books on various aspects of Michigan history. Topics range from *John Allen: Michigan's Pioneer Promoter* published in 1988, through *Ohio vs Michigan; Guns Across the Maumee*, a study of Michigan's struggle for statehood 1835 to 1837, and the present volume, the fourth in the *Rivers of Michigan* series (although this river dips also into Indiana). Other works include a four volume Saugatuck Maritime series on boatbuilding in the area, shipwrecks on Lake Michigan, South Haven to Grand Haven; passenger boats, and the drama surrounding the disappearance of the steamship **Chicora** in 1895. The Lanes live in Douglas, Michigan, and have four grown sons and five grandchildren. Future volumes of the *Rivers of Michigan* series are planned.

Photo Credits and Acknowledgments

p. 1, 11 Watershed map and gradient diagram from *St. Joseph River Assessment, Fisheries Special Report 24 and Appendix,* by Jay K Wesley and Joan E. Duffy, published by the Michigan Department of Natural Resources, Fisheries Division, 1999.

p. 12 Diagram of the portage from *The St. Joseph – Kankakee Portage* by George A. Baker, published by the North Indiana Historical Society, 1899.

p. 13, 17 Portraits of La Salle from *La Salle in the Valley of the St. Joseph* by Charles H. Bartlett and Richard H. Lyon, publishing by the South Bend Tribune Company, 1899.

p. 18, 24 Drawings from written descriptions and on-site visits by artist Ann G. Gray, of Ganges Township, Allegan County, Michigan.

p. 27 Detail from a map "showing positions of French and English forts, towns, etc." in 1775, from *The Making of the Ohio Valley States, 1660-1837* by Samuel Adams Drake, published by Charles Scribner's Sons, 1894.

p. 48 Map "Dams of the St. Joseph River" created by the Friends of the St. Joseph River Association.

p. 50 Advertisment from *Gazetteer of St. Joseph Valley of Michigan and Indiana for 1867 with a View of its Hydraulic and Business Capacities,* by T. G. Turner, 1867.

p. 60, 61 Poem and illustrations from *Ben King's Verse*, edited by Nixon Waterman and published by the Press Club of Chicago, 1894.

p.62 Line drawing of Simon Pokagon from an 1895 circular advertising *Red Man's Greeting.*

p. 69 Map of watershed from map which accompanied a U. S. Corps of Engineers report on the St. Joseph River to Congress dated March 5, 1932.

p.81, 82 From a Clarendon Township map in a Berrien County atlas published by George A. Ogle in 1916.

p. 85, 89, 103 from *Tackbury's Atlas of the State of Michigan including statistics and descriptions of its topography, hydrography, climate, natural and civil history, railways, educational institutions, material resources, etc.* by Henry F. Walling, 1873.

p. 99 Three Rivers map based on one prepared by William and Robert McDonough with computer-aided drafting by Gove Associates, courtesy Three Rivers Area Chamber of Commerce.

p. 102 Map showing Eschol from a Michigan map by T. G. Bradford, published in 1838.

p. 104 Excerpt from book and illustration from an 1854 edition of *Puddleford and Its People* by H. H. Riley.

p. 125 Map from *A History of St. Joseph County, Indiana, Vol. I* by Timothy Howard, published in 1907.

p. 142, 143 From an account found in the clippings file of the Niles District Library.

p. 147 Map showing Lighton from an early 1900s atlas of Oronoko Township, Berrien County, Michigan.

p. 154 Excerpts from a 1922 edition of *Rolling Acres* by Bessie Ray Hoover.

p. 161 Chart of St. Joseph Harbor from *Scott's New Coast Pilot for the Lakes* by George Scott, published by the Detroit Free Press Printing Co., 1896.

All other maps, old postcards, and photographs are from the collection of the author.

The author would like to recognize the assistance of many people along the course of the St. Joseph River including the museum staff and researchers at the Elkhart County Historical Museum in the Rush Memorial Center, Bristol, Indiana; guide and staff at Ruthmere, Elkhart; Gerard and Cheryl Clarke, innkeepers at the Mendon Country Inn; staff of the Three Rivers Area Chamber of Commerce; John Cleveland of the Elkhart River Queen; guides at the Fort St. Joseph Museum, Niles; maintenance department of the University of Notre Dame; employees of Twin Branch dam, Mishawaka; Nelson Shedd and family of Tekonsha; and director Kenneth Pott and staff of the Heritage Museum and Cultural Center, St. Joseph, Michigan.

Also the ever-patient librarians and other staff at the Maude Preston Palenske Memorial Library, St. Joseph; the Benton Harbor Public Library, Hillsdale Community Library, Tekonsha Township Public Library, Union City library, Colon Township Library, Niles District Library, and especially Susan Lowery of the Heritage Center at the Mishawaka-Penn-Harris Public Library and Connie Johnston of the reference staff.

And Jack Sheridan of the Saugatuck-Douglas Historical Society for technical assistance.

Rivers of Michigan Series

The Kalamazoo

The Kalamazoo River of southern Michigan rises in the Irish Hills south of Jackson in Hillsdale County and flows gently westward for about 200 miles before it exits into Lake Michigan at Saugatuck. On the way it passes through two of Michigan's middle-sized cities, Battle Creek and Kalamazoo, and many smaller towns with big histories, Homer, Albion, Marshall, Concord, Ceresco, Galesburg, Allegan, Otsego and Plainwell. A few places which were once important stops on the river, Singapore, Sheridan, Bath Mills and Harmonia, no longer exist.

In this volume there are chapters on the meaning of the name "Kalamazoo" and how it has been used in songs and poetry, information on the almost-annual flooding and the steps taken to protect cities from health concerns caused by water which invades homes. Environmental problems that once caused the Kalamazoo to be known as the "sewer of West Michigan" are described along with some steps undertaken to remove contaminants left by earlier industries.

A mile by mile trip down the river tells the history and present-day status of settlements along the banks with many maps, old and new, and vintage postcard views.

978-1-877703-40-9   128 p., illustrated, index, bibliography, 2006.

The Grand

The Grand River was the superhighway of early Michigan. It connected with the Saginaw River or the Huron River to help travelers cross the peninsula. Dams on the rapids at Eaton Rapids, Grand Rapids, Lansing and elsewhere furnished power for grinding wheat, turning the saws in lumbermills and manufacturing furniture. Steamboats carried a steady traffic into the 20th Century, especially on the lower river, but today the smoke-belching giants have been replaced by excursion boats taking tourists on scenic trips. Canoes, kayaks and motorized pleasure boats share the ripples.

Also featured in this volume are plans to create a cross-peninsula canal, difficulties caused by floods, ice buildup and log jams, including the famous incident in the spring of 1883 when a log jam from Lowell to Grand Haven threatened every bridge along the way. Read how fishing has actually improved, bringing steelhead trout as far inland as Lansing.

978-1-877703-39-3   160 p., illustrated index, bibliography, 2007.

Rivers of Michigan Series

The Raisin

About 1780 the residents of Detroit began to look for new areas to settle. One of the first places they moved to was a river south of the city which was Michigan Territory's only port on Lake Erie. Here the mostly French newcomers began to lay out ribbon farms on both sides of the river they called *Riviere aux Raisin,* after the wild grapes that grew along its banks. Even into the 21st Century the river passes through a mainly rural landscape touching, also, the small cities of Tecumseh, Petersburg, and Monroe and the villages of Brooklyn, Manchester, Dundee, Blissfield, Deerfield and Clinton.

The book covers the battle on the banks of the River Raisin against the invading British and their Indian allies in 1813, floods and other disasters along the river beginning in 1836, and power creation, including five of the Ford Company's "village industries," where old mill sites were put to new use manufacturing parts for automobiles. Today the focus is on river clean-up and rehabilitation. With continuing application of government funds and local efforts the lotus plants are once more blooming on the River Raisin.

978-1-877703-04-1 112 p., illustrated, indexed, bibliography, 2009.

The St. Joseph

The valley of the St. Joseph River was one of the first places in the Lower Peninsula, after Mackinac Island and Detroit, to be inhabited by Europeans, mainly French explorers, fur traders and missionaries. When the French flag was lowered the British banner was raised, followed by the American flag after the Revolution. Unique among the rivers of Michigan the St. Joseph also saw the unfurling of the Spanish flag – for a few hours in 1781. The St. Joseph River starts in Hillsdale County, not far from the Grand, Raisin and Kalamazoo, but spends one-quarter of its length in Northern Indiana, passing through Elkhart, Mishawaka and South Bend, before re-entering its native state and exiting into Lake Michigan at St. Joseph.

The mile-by-mile survey goes through the "magic" town of Colon, Three Rivers where the St. Joseph meets the Rocky and Portage Rivers, Niles, the site of a 17th Century fort; and northern Indiana where the mills and factories which formerly lined the banks have been razed in favor of parkland and walking trails, and a white water canoeing course.

978-1-877703-05-8 184 p., illustrated, indexed, bibliography, literary excerpts, 2010.